D1038448

Renaissance
Of The
Film

RENAISSANCE

Of The

FILM

Edited and with an Introduction
and Headnotes by

Julius Bellone

PN
1993
.5
.A1
B45
1970

COLLIER BOOKS
COLLIER-MACMILLAN LTD., LONDON

Copyright © 1970 by Julius Bellone

All rights reserved. No part of this book may be reproduced or transmitted in any form or by any means, electronic or mechanical, including photocopying, recording or by any information storage and retrieval system, without permission in writing from the Publisher.

The Macmillan Company
866 Third Avenue, New York, N.Y. 10022
Collier-Macmillan Canada Ltd., Toronto, Ontario

Library of Congress Catalog Card Number: 79-109447

First Printing

Printed in the United States of America

Grateful acknowledgment is due to Mr. Emery Wimbish, Librarian, Vail Memorial Library, Lincoln University, for his kind assistance and to the following authors, editors, and publishers for granting permission to reprint these essays by:

James Agee: *"Farrebique,"* reprinted from *The Nation*, March 13, 1948, by permission of James J. Storrow, Jr., publisher; and *"Monsieur Verdoux"* reprinted from *Agee on Film: Volume I* by permission of Grosset and Dunlap, Inc.

Joseph Bennett: "The Essences of Being," reprinted from *The Hudson Review*, Vol. XIV, No. 3 (Autumn, 1961), by permission of The Hudson Review, Inc. Copyright 1961

J. Blumenthal: *"Throne of Blood,"* reprinted from *Sight and Sound*, Vol. XXXIV, No. 4 (Autumn, 1965), by permission of Penelope Houston, editor

Jacques Brunius: "Every Year in Marienbad: or The Discipline of Uncertainty," reprinted from *Sight and Sound*, Vol. XXXI, No. 2 (Spring, 1962), by permission of Penelope Houston, editor

Robert Brustein: "Out of This World," reprinted from *The New York Review of Books*, February 6, 1964, by permission of the author

Carolyn Geduld: *"Bonnie and Clyde*: Society vs. the Clan," reprinted from *Film Heritage*, Vol. III, No. 2 (Winter, 1967–68), by permission of the author

Dennis Giles: "The Tao in *Woman in the Dunes,"* reprinted from *Film Heritage*, Vol. I, No. 3 (Spring, 1966), by permission of F. Anthony Macklin, editor

Roger Greenspun: "Through the Looking Glass," reprinted from *Moviegoer*, No. 1 (Winter, 1964), by permission of the author

Norman N. Holland: "The Follies Fellini," reprinted from *The Hudson Review*, Vol. XIV, No. 3 (Autumn, 1961), by permission of the Sterling Lord Agency; and "*The Seventh Seal*: The film as Iconography," reprinted from *The Hudson Review*, Vol. XII, No. 2 (Summer, 1959), by permission of the Sterling Lord Agency

William Johnson: "*Balthazar*," reprinted from *Film Quarterly*, Vol. XX, No. 3, pp. 24–28, by permission of The Regents of the University of California. Copyright © 1967 by The Regents; and "*Marnie*," reprinted from *Film Quarterly*, Vol. XVIII, No. 1, pp. 38–42, by permission of The Regents of the University of California. Copyright © 1964 by The Regents

Pauline Kael: "*Masculine Feminine*," reprinted from *Kiss Kiss Bang Bang* by Pauline Kael, by permission of Little, Brown and Company. Copyright © 1966 by Pauline Kael

Stanley Kauffmann: "*Red Desert*" from *A World of Film* by Stanley Kauffmann. Originally appeared in *The New Republic*, February 20, 1965, and reprinted by permission of Harper and Row, Publishers. Copyright © 1965 by Stanley Kauffmann

Edouard de Laurot: "*La Strada*: A Poem on Saintly Folly," reprinted from *Film Culture*, Vol. II, No. 1, 1956, by permission of Jonas Mekas, editor and publisher

Wolfgang A. Luchting: "*Hiroshima, Mon Amour*, Time, and Proust," excerpts reprinted from *The Journal of Aesthetics and Art Criticism*, Vol. XXI, No. 3 (Spring, 1963), pp. 299–313, by permission of *The Journal of Aesthetics and Art Criticism* and by the author

F. Anthony Macklin: "Dark Pilgrim: The Vision of Ingmar Bergman in *The Silence*," reprinted from *Midwestern University Quarterly*, Vol. II, No. 1, pp. 93–101, by permission of the author

Hubert Meeker: "*Blow-Up*," reprinted from *Film Heritage*, Vol. II, No. 3 (Spring, 1967), by permission of the author

Jonas Mekas: "*Ordet*," reprinted from *Film Culture*, Vol. IV, No. 1 (1958), by permission of the author

William S. Pechter: "The Ballad and the Source," reprinted from *Kenyon Review*, XXIII (Spring, 161), by permission of the author

Eric Rhode: "Satyajit Ray: A Study," reprinted from *Sight and Sound*, Vol. XXX, No. 3 (Summer, 1961), by permission of Penelope Houston; and "*Ugetsu Monogatari*," reprinted from *Sight and Sound*, Vol. XXXI, No. 1 (Winter, 1961–62), by permission of Penelope Houston

T. J. Ross: "*The Servant* as Sex Thriller," reprinted from *December*, Vol. VII, No. 1 (1965), by permission of Curt Johnson, publisher

Richard Rowland: "*Miss Julie*," reprinted from the *Quarterly of Film, Radio and Television* (now *Film Quarterly*), Vol. VI, No. 4, pp. 414–420, copyright © 1952 by The Regents of the University of California, by permission of The Regents

Andrew Sarris: "*Citizen Kane:* The American Baroque," reprinted from *Film Culture*, Vol. II, No. 3 (1956), by permission of the author; and "The Devil and the Nun: *Viridiana*," reprinted from *Movie*, No. 1, June, 1962, by permission of the author

Joel Siegel: "I Found It at the Nudies: Jacques Demy's *Lola*, At Last," reprinted from *Film Heritage*, Vol. I, No. 4 (Summer, 1966), by permission of the author

Parker Tyler: "*Rashomon* as Modern Art," reprinted from *The Three Faces of the Film* by Parker Tyler, and appearing in *Cinema 16* by Parker Tyler, by permission of the author

Robert Vas: "Arrival and Departure: *This Sporting Life*," reprinted from *Sight and Sound*, Vol. XXXII, No. 2 (Spring, 1963), by permission of Penelope Houston, editor

Elsa Gress Wright: "*Gertrud*," reprinted from *Film Quarterly*, Vol. XIX, No. 3, pp. 36–40, by permission of The Regents of the University of California. Copyright © 1966 by The Regents

Vernon Young: "*Umberto D.*: Vittorio De Sica's 'Super'-naturalism," reprinted from *The Hudson Review*, Vol. VIII, No. 4 (Winter, 1956), by permission of The Hudson Review, Inc. Copyright © 1956

To *Adrienne, Chris and Amy*

Contents

Introduction

ROGER MANVELL of the British Film Academy looks upon the post-World War II period as the liveliest and most interesting in the history of cinema:

> To find any parallel in the growth of invention and imagination we would have to return to the period between *Birth of a Nation* (1915) and the close of the silent period (1928–9), a mere fourteen years later, the period that saw the film leave its swaddling clothes and develop the mature art of such directors as Griffith, von Stroheim, Mack Sennett, Chaplin, Keaton, Clair, Pabst, Flaherty, Eisenstein, Pudovkin and Dovzhenko, as well as the experimentation of the French avant-garde. [*New Cinema in Europe*, Dutton, 1966]

This anthology is intended to give discerning moviegoers a collection of *some* of the best criticism about *some* of the best films in the post-World War II, or contemporary, period, a period which merits the label "renaissance of the film."

These essays re-create with heightened perceptivity and sensitivity the immediate confrontation between art and audience. They are an attempt to approach critically the art of a medium that, because of physical unwieldiness and lack of easy access, frustrates possibilities of appreciation as no other art does— architecture, music, poetry, etc. Jean Cocteau felt keenly this handicap:

> Whenever people see a film for the first time, they complain about some passages being too long or too slow. But quite apart from the fact that this is often due to the weakness of their own perception and to their missing the deep underlying design of the work, they forget that the classics,

too, are full of passages that are longwinded and slow, but are accepted because they are classics. The classics must have faced the same reproaches in their lifetime. The tragedy of the cinematograph lies in its having to be successful immediately. [*Cocteau on the Film*, Roy Publishers, 1954]

The rise of film criticism in the post-World War II period is a response to the challenge presented by the medium itself, a verbal effort to resist the pull to oblivion that is the fate of the celluloid product.

For most films, which are usually seen and forgotten, the journalistic review is their commentary. While not necessarily ephemeral (witness the fruits of Pauline Kael, Stanley Kauffmann, and others), newspaper and weekly magazine reviews are usually unenduring moments of information not intended to outlast the utility of their immediate service; at best vivid and analytical description and at worst heavy and superficial judgmental rendering of a "yes" or "no," a "for" or "against." In addition we expect reviews, particularly in pictorial magazines, to be entertaining in themselves as witty, sometimes sardonic pieces of prose—delightful bagatelles—rather than being principally about the specific film; or to be springboards for reviewers to jump onto ideological hobby horses—socio-economic, political, religious, or aesthetic.

This is not so with the authors in this anthology. The crucial difference between them and the reviewer is that they do not possess the enormous readership that most reviewers have felt is out there listening to them. Ironically, their unrestricted freedom and independence is the result of having only a limited, homogeneous readership, a group devoted to the proposition that the movies are a vital art form, yet a group whose numbers and tastes do not affect the fortunes—the commercial success or failure—of a film. Since most of the criticisms in this anthology were written for film periodicals such as *Sight and Sound*, *Film Culture*, and *Film Quarterly* and for periodical journals such as *The Kenyon Review* and *The Hudson Review*, these critics have been spared editorial control. These essays cannot be regarded as mere consumer information.

Most often these essays were written after multiple view-
ings which allow for a yeasty contemplation of the film and a
secure knowledge of its actual content. In some instances the
critic's assumption is that the reader enjoys a comparable familiarity with the film. Owing to this and to the tacit agreement
between critic and reader that the film under discussion is
equal to the greater achievements of other art media in its
poetic expression of important meaning and emotion, these
critics focus on the intrinsic rather than extrinsic values of a
film, offering discernment rather than panegyric, insight rather
than hyperbole. The critical intelligence and energy of each
of these critics is directed toward the attempt to explicate
the imaginative rationale and coherence of a film, treating the
particular film as an organic entity—film as film; bringing to
bear critical perception that uncovers the purpose and execution of a film, scrutinizing and illuminating the imaginative
logic of its pattern, its function, its form.

The various essays indicate a wide range for approaching
the film, while at once maintaining a steady and nearly exclusive aesthetic preoccupation with the film in question. Carolyn
Geduld identifies the genre traditions brought together in
Bonnie and Clyde; Norman Holland explores medieval culture
and traditional Christian imagery to illuminate setting and
symbolic meaning in *The Seventh Seal;* Roger Greenspun
analyzes the way in which technique is expressive of meaning
in *Shoot the Piano Player;* Hubert Meeker interprets *Blow-
Up* in the perspective of the theme of gratuitous discovery;
W. A. Luchting discusses the literary analogues for the techniques applied to express the complexities of time in *Hiroshima,
Mon Amour;* and Robert Brustein interprets *Dr. Strangelove*
as massive social purgation. Often in approaching the particular film, the critics in this anthology open vistas of appreciation into other films of a director by virtue of developing
ideas that apply to other films as well, such as Vernon Young's
"*Umberto D.:* Vittorio De Sica's 'Super'-naturalism"; and other
critics render insights into the mind and art of a director that
relate to the totality of his film-making, such as William Johnson's piece on Alfred Hitchcock's *Marnie.*

In many essays one recognizes the ascendency of the French tradition of close analysis *(explication de texte)*, which has been a substantial influence on the development of both literary and film criticism since World War II.

To any recognizable degree, except for *Close-Up* in the silent film days, the attempt to approach films with the seriousness of critical purpose represented by these authors is a phenomenon of the contemporary period. Although independent critical activity within the country of any given national cinema exists, nonetheless the critics in this anthology have been influenced—not always consciously—by the international reverberations of the situation in French film criticism in the late forties and early fifties.

It was a time of much excitement and ferment. The national film school, Institut des Hautes Études Cinématographiques, quite young at the time, enrolled a number of potential film-makers and critics eager to attain new achievement in the already rich tradition of French films. A central force in creating esprit and a sense of community is the figure of André Bazin, who loomed large because of his personality as well as his writing. He was connected to the school, wrote for *Le Parisien Libéré*, and became co-editor of *Cahiers du Cinéma*.

As a savant he philosophically demonstrated the aesthetic importance of cinema through rigorously developed answers to his own basic question "What is Cinema?" which generated an atmosphere for thinking about cinema as serious art. He probed divers ramifications of this question in the pages of *Cahiers du Cinéma*, the publication he shared with spirited followers such as François Truffaut, Jean-Luc Godard, and Claude Chabrol. Essentially a realist who did not perceive the prospect of cinema flourishing in a symbolistic direction, in the direction of the film-maker shaping the raw photographic image according to his vision of the human condition through the use of montage, Bazin stressed the development of cinema in the perspective of the American tradition of realism. The impact of his argument that photographic reality is the reality of cinema encouraged these followers to go beyond their already substantial enthusiasm for Hollywood comedies, gangster movies, and Westerns. In so doing they arrived at an aesthetic and intellectual discovery of the genius of certain American directors, particularly John Ford, Howard Hawks, and Alfred Hitchcock.

Their commitment as critics, however, is not revealed in Bazin-like speculative discourse but in the intensive searching for relationships between a director's personality and his films, the study of a director's development from film to film, and the analysis of individual films by employing a combination of these points of reference. Ironically, what surfaced when the follower-critics became feature-length film-makers in the late fifties was that their deepest artistic impulses ran counter to the teaching of their master-theorist. With Chabrol's *The Cousins* in 1958, Truffaut's *The 400 Blows* in 1959, and Godard's *Breathless* in 1959, the arranging and juxtaposing in sequence of many camera shots, the strong presence of the art of montage modifying and sometimes transforming photographic art dominates. Yet the residual influence of Bazin is seen in the awareness they show for the value of the pictorial composition, the relationships between people and between objects, the so-called *mise en scène*.

A critical postulation of the French critics of some influence is the *auteur* theory of direction. In the famous *Politique des Auteurs* manifesto of 1951, Truffaut, speaking for his *Cahiers du Cinéma* colleagues, made the analogy between the director and the literary author as a strategy for critical analysis. While the idea has been vehemently contested on the basis of the complexity of human and mechanical involvement in making a film and by the fact that a work of art need not reveal the personality of its creator, nevertheless the *auteur* theory has enjoyed acceptance in varying degrees. Even when critics overtly disassociate themselves from the notion, implicitly they often reveal its presence as a part of their thinking. The approach has been most effective whenever a director has exerted consistently an individual style, forging upon the eclectic components of the medium—the energies of scriptwriter, cameraman, technicians, etc.—the strong imprint of his artistic signature. One indication of the currency of the theory

is the fact that book-length studies (see bibliography), emphasizing the maturating process in the director's artistic career,
have been written about most of the directors whose films are
represented in this anthology.

This surge in France for the establishment of the cinema as
an important art form and the heightening of aesthetic expectations concretely evident in the pages of *Cahiers du Cinéma*
and *Positif*, which was launched in 1952, is seen in England
and America as well. But whereas French critics, rebelliously
oblivious to the merits of their own tradition, showed a
priority interest in American film-making, the British and
American critics looked toward Europe with much greater
circumspection.

In England a group of young critics, later to become film-
makers, wrote criticism that preponderantly involves questions
of directorial style. In *Sequence* (1948–52) and in the distinguished publication of the British Film Institute, *Sight and
Sound*, Karel Reisz, Gavin Lambert, Lindsay Anderson, Tony
Richardson, and others who were to spearhead the movement
in British film-making known as the "New Realism" approv-
ingly evaluated the works of directors such as Max Ophuls,
Jean Cocteau, and John Ford; and liberally condemned amor-
phous Hollywood products. Ian Cameron and others have
exhibited an *auteur* approach of sorts in *Oxford Opinion* in
the late fifties and in *Movie* in the sixties. Beginning in 1954
Films and Filming, though actor-oriented, has shown sustained
and perceptive critical concern for what is artistically worthy
but not necessarily popular, particularly in the writing of
Raymond Durgnat.

In America, as in France and England, the new critical interest in the post-World War II period was due, to some
extent, to a common enemy—a general dissatisfaction with the
national product. Although the movement in criticism in
America came a few years later than in England, it appeared
as a more fundamental kind of probe. Jonas Mekas' *Film
Culture*, begun in 1955 and published irregularly thereafter,
has abounded with fresh speculation about the nature of
cinema. Many contributors have theorized about the possibili-

ties of a poetic cinema that, through radical experiment, departs from conventional or "narrative" uses of the medium. Toward this goal the independent film-makers have aspired. The "underground films" of Mekas and his followers, though intentionally not made for general audiences, enjoy a range of audience that is much too large to be considered merely an avant-garde coterie. Although primarily devoted to furthering the cause of this movement, "The New American Cinema," *Film Culture* has also steadily put out criticism of feature films that reveals a keen sense of how a film makes meaning and an uncompromising readiness to denounce the spurious. Equally notable as a distinctive and established publication is *Film Quarterly*, known before 1958 as *The Quarterly of Radio, Television, and Film*. Under the editorship of Ernest Callenbach it has been international in scope and has also exhibited a lively concern and open-mindedness toward the Hollywood industry, offering reasoned judgments and critically articulate evaluations.

In the decade of the sixties an extensive literature on the film has developed. Film books of various kinds have appeared, introductory manuals or "grammars," histories, aesthetic and theoretical books, biographies, interviews, etc. Perhaps more significant is the radical increase in the number of academic programs, both classroom and workshop. Along with the frequent advent and demise of numerous small film magazines, these facts suggest that films have become a part of the intellectual life of America. And indeed the best films of the sixties demonstrate the confidence of directors that, in significant numbers, a knowing, critically alert audience expects not a sentimental diversion or an escape but an intensified and illuminating depiction of the human condition.

Although this book reflects a general correlation between great films and heightened critical response, there are many exceptional films not dealt with. Holding to the pattern of selecting explicatory essays that focus on a particular film is in itself an exclusionary factor. In some instances films have been excluded not because of the absence of such criticism but because of a lack of space. Furthermore, in the case of numerous directors whose films are represented, I have selected films where perhaps there was good reason to select others instead. It is with regret that I have excluded such films as *Bicycle Thief, The Treasure of Sierra Madre, Beauty and the Beast, Open City, The Lady With a Dog, Ashes and Diamonds, The Elusive Corporal, The Sound of Trumpets, Black Orpheus,* and others.

JULIUS BELLONE

Lincoln University
Lincoln University, Pennsylvania

The Apu Trilogy

Eric Rhode, "Satyajit Ray: A Study"

ooooooooooooooooooooooooooooooooooooooooooooooo

From the status of an employee in a Calcutta advertising agency in the early fifties to a position of international fame as an important director by the end of the decade, Satyajit Ray's career has been spectacular. The diversity of creative approaches to film-making is seen in his unique and wholly private directorial apprenticeship. In their book, *Indian Film* (Columbia U. Press, 1963), Barnouw and Krishnaswamy give the following account of Ray's preparations for making his first film, *Pather Panchali (On the Road)*: 1) When a film adapted from a novel was to appear, he would study the book and make his own script from it. Then in watching the movie he would note mentally similarities and differences, observing what were strengths and weaknesses in his own version; 2) he sketched out completely the screenplay, including a series of sketches specifying the composition of key shots in the film; and 3) he made detailed washed sketches of dramatic highlights. *Pather Panchali* was two years in the making and then remained two years in obscurity before it was shown at the Cannes Festival in 1956. It deals with the young boy Apu, who in *Aparajito (The Unvanquished)*, 1957, grows older and who reaches manhood in the third film, *Apur Sansar (The World of Apu)*, 1959.

Because of his affinities with the directors of the Italian neorealist movement (low budget, nonprofessional actors, outdoor and shabby surroundings), Ray has been judged by some

Pather Panchali, directed by Satyajit Ray, 1955 *(Edward Harrison)*

critics as possessing rather limited talent which yields only a kind of flat realism and not the universalization of subjects. In his analysis of Apu's evolution in the trilogy, Eric Rhode finds that in *Apur Sansar* Ray raises "his subject to a mytho-poeic level without at any point destroying its realism." Mr. Rhode's statement concerning the conclusion, when the wandering Apu returns to his son in his own native village, is as follows: ". . . the two characters, without losing their definition as human beings, take on the firm lines of allegory. The feeling of eternal recurrence in this scene—Apu in a symbolical sense returns to the village where he was born and confronts his childhood self—gives the whole trilogy the cyclic form proper to myth."

————◆————

IN GENERAL, SATYAJIT RAY's films embarrass the critics. Admirers go impressionistic, talk airily of Human Values, and look offended when asked to be more precise. Detractors are no less vague. Some of them call his work charming, in a tone which could hardly carry more weight of suspicion and distrust, or say they are not interested in the problems of the Indian peasantry. Only M. Truffaut, in describing *Pather Panchali* as Europeanised and insipid, has firmly placed himself in the opposition. This mustn't have taken him much trouble, since he apparently walked out of the film after the first two reels. Those who stayed on to the end, however, had every reason to be more hesitant; for the supposed simplicity of this work—and indeed of all Ray's films—disarms the critic. Only after close scrutiny do most of them turn out to be artefacts of the most subtle sort. It is a case of art concealing art, brought about by Ray's precise construction of plot—so that craftsmanship seldom shows—and by his ability while shooting to improvise against this structure in a way which gives his work a continual spontaneity.

I have heard some of Ray's admirers say that analysis of any kind can only destroy this spontaneity, and therefore distort one of the most important qualities of these films. But to believe this surely is to fall into an old trap. The myth of the

Natural Genius, piping his native wood-notes wild, dies hard in certain quarters; and Ray it seems is to be the latest victim sacrificed upon its altars. He can only be made to play this part, however, if one ignores his robust plots and the density of his symbolism. Not that his best work is mannered, as this might suggest. His symbolism is not like that of Bergman and Pabst (say), who are usually considered symbolist directors. All art in a sense is symbolic, and the success of symbolism lies in its being unobtrusive. This is not so with Bergman and Pabst, who, in trying to conceal the thinness of their material, let symbols sprout out of their feeble plots like straw out of a scarecrow. They fail because they are unable to construct suitable plots, which in turn is a failure properly to explore their material. In the best of Ray's films, on the other hand, the integration of symbol and action is so assured that we are hardly aware of the technical problems involved in such a feat. Yet Ray's continuing success has not been bought cheaply. After shooting *Pather Panchali* he went through a period—at about the time he was filming *Aparajito* and *Parash Pathar* (*The Philosopher's Stone*)—when he had great difficulty in making plots. It is part of his talent's strength that he managed to break through this sterile passage into the lucid and rich world of *Apur Sansar*.

What is so interesting about this talent is the limited means by which it has reached such richness. Ray's vision so far has been a narrow one. In his films there is no portrayal of evil (in the Christian sense), nor is there any sign of violence. The staple ingredients of the Occidental film—lust, murder and rape—play no part in his work. Most of his central characters are sensitive, often idealised people, usually scholars or rich men who have been dispossessed and therefore made vulnerable to poverty and suffering. (The trilogy could as well have been called *The Unprotected* as *The Unvanquished*.) Though this range is highly limited, I don't think it counts against him; for within it Ray has managed to deploy the old tragic conflicts with remarkable ease. What he has in fact done is to describe the relationship between art and life, duty and the emotions, free will and destiny, in very personal terms. And this he has brought off, I believe, by showing us how, in a most vivid way, these conflicts tie up to his major, almost obsessive, theme.

2

"In what way," asks Ray, "can man control the world, and what is the price he must pay for trying to do so . . . ?" This, as I would see it, is the Promethean theme behind all his films. Why it should be this one rather than any other is a debatable point; but I would surmise that Ray is haunted in this case by the most traumatic event in recent Indian history: the granting of independence in 1947. With this event India was born into responsibility. Besides her foreign problems she had to handle the problem of industrialisation; of modernising the agricultural techniques of backward settlements; and of coping with the underfed and the under-privileged. Though the scope of such a task may have been invigorating, there was always a heavy price to be paid. Independence brought with it the most terrible of border massacres, and mechanisation involved the destruction of ancient pieties. Inevitably, the India of Science was against the India of Myths.

Though Ray is clearly troubled by this situation, and is indeed involved in it, his feelings remain ambivalent; and from this ambivalence arises a tension which gives his work its force. In *Jalsaghar*, the protagonist is an ageing nobleman who, finding himself out of place in the modern world, tries to escape from it into the world of music. He fails. The sound of trucks passing to a factory owned by his *nouveau riche* neighbour echoes through his hollow palace and shatters the necessary silence. Unable to continue his traditions into the modern world, he destroys himself. Though this nobleman is little more than an old panjandrum, he becomes for us an oddly moving figure; for he is shown as the last representative of a civilisation Ray admires, a civilisation in which the mandarin virtues of ceremony and folly are prized and in which love of the arts take a central place.

Ray's feelings may be divided about this nobleman, but they

aren't half as complex as are his feelings about the characters of the trilogy. Though Ray's sympathies are primarily with the new men (like Apu) as they break away from superstition and ignorance, he is at the same time aware of the price they must pay for this liberation. The power involved in trying to control the world requires ruthlessness. It may also imply an evasion of life. So Apu betrays his mother's affection by leaving her to die alone in a remote village; and later, as a man of learning, begins to lose touch with life—with Mother Earth, as he puts it—to his natural detriment.

3

One would never call Ray a reactionary—too obviously is he one of the new men himself. This doesn't stop him feeling great tenderness for those who have lost out, for those who have been unable to control the world, at least in part. Most of *Pather Panchali*, for instance, is taken up with describing the hopelessness of such people—a hopelessness which, as Ray makes clear, is in no way a matter of despair. He shows us that they are fatalists who yet manage to enjoy the world. This mood is established from the opening moments of the film, as a child ineffectually sweeps a sun-baked courtyard while kittens frolic in the shade. This is life lived at its most primitive, biological level. Food is the primary pre-occupation: the mother continually crushes harsh roots; the children steal fruit or yearn for sweets they can't afford; the grandmother quietly gobbles in a corner. At no point does the family stop eating its scraps of rice, its rotting guavas, or its pieces of raw sugar-cane.

At first these biological processes seem to be the only defence against a destructive universe, in which the impending jungle creeps through a broken wall, and the monsoon beats down the house. Even amongst the villagers there seems to be no defence. Neighbours are rapacious, and education at the hands of the local grocer seems as futile a preparation for life as is primitive medicine a guard against death. (Death with

Ray, though regular, is always unexpected. Not surprisingly he wishes to film *A Passage to India*). The world is uncontrollable and the family—each in his own way—is its victim. The father, a gentle, distracted egoist, dreams about his ancestors' greatness but is unable to make a living. His neighbours cheat him and he writes plays no one wants. The mother, as the inarticulate conscience of the family, is the only one close to achieving some control over her life; but her failure is evident in her continual scrubbing and scraping, and in the nagging which alienates those about her. Above all there is the grandmother, who never despairs though she has the least hope. It is not in gloom but with wry joy that she says, "I am old and I have nowhere to go." Unlike Gorki's grandmother, who is an earth-goddess embodying (as one of the revolutionaries says) the best of Old Russia, she is never more than irresponsible and childlike. All she can offer is love.

From the difference between these two women one can deduce a significant difference between the Gorki and the Ray trilogy. Gorki is concerned with the drama of revolution and with showing how his characters, even at second-hand, react to this. Ray is not interested primarily in such a drama. In developing his characters he is more concerned with understanding the world than with changing it—though to understand *is* to change it. His comment on social progress remains, often aggravatingly, ambiguous. The difference between these two trilogies is not necessarily antagonistic: it is the difference one might say between the zestful Russia of the late Twenties and present-day neutralist India.

Anyway, even if they wanted to be, the characters of *Pather Panchali* could never be revolutionaries. Unable to control their lives in any way, they are never more than childlike. Though it may be a brilliant touch to have all the characters like children in a film which purports to be about a child, and therefore to relate a primitive agricultural society to the limitations of this age group, it does induce a certain ambiguity of vision. Are we or are we not looking at the world through the eyes of a child? Ray never makes this clear. But he does deal effectively with another problem arising from this situation. Though similar, the characters never become monotonous; for the scenes in which they are involved are always epic, and therefore embody the differing strands of the various themes.

There is the pivotal moment, for instance, when Apu sees a train for the first time and begins to understand the nature of man's power. (Trains are a recurring motif in the trilogy, and this scene takes on a particular force when we realise how later in Calcutta Apu is to try to commit suicide by throwing himself beneath one.) Though the sequence is a short one, it does —by its build-up—dominate the film. We see Apu and his sister move through the wilderness of a cotton field. As they listen to the eery humming of telegraph wires, seeds drift from white plumes. Then the train chatters past. Its smoke, like a feather, obliterates the sky. For us, all quite unimportant perhaps: but for Apu a mechanical Messiah has been born. Just as typical of Ray's art is an earlier, more complex sequence which in its unstressed interplay of moods reminds us of Chekov. It is evening, and the house is in darkness. The grandmother tries to thread a needle but is too proud to admit failure. Near her the mother fusses alone. The father stops trying to write a play and, holding up a moth-eaten bundle of manuscript, says gently, "Things have come to a pretty pass." Beside him Apu is learning to write. The father smiles at the success of his work. A passing train whistles. "Now," says the father, "write the word for wealth."

Through such a mosaic of action Ray establishes his major themes. In an uncontrolled world the comic travelling theatre, the father's escapism, and the folklore of the grandmother appear incongruous. The mother, in trying to control a dwindling budget, goes out and sells the family silver; and the price she pays is to rob Apu of his patrimony and to destroy the lingering remains of a family tradition. This theme of control and its cost is, as I have written, the central one of Ray's work; but it does have an almost mystical extension which is to play a large part later in *Apur Sansar*. It is to be found even in such a simple scene as the grandmother rocking the newborn Apu in his cradle. Though she fears for his future she yet looks at him with hope. This mingled regard reveals her knowledge and her strength; for the old woman knows that ultimately the power of life itself transcends the suffering of people caught in an uncontrolled universe.

In the last resort, the destructive force is negated by the force of continuing life. Though the fetid lake may swallow the last trace of the sister's existence, and the jungle obliterate the house, it is the images of the passing bands and kickshaws, of children running through sunlit glades, and of trains, especially trains, with their hope of work in Benares and their promise of a new and better society, which remain burnt into the mind. Aptly does the English for *Pather Panchali* mean *On the Road;* for it is above all the activity of life that counts. As one of the villagers sagely remarks, "it's staying in one place that makes you mean."

4

And now the growing Apu begins to control the world. Premonitions of this in the pivotal scene of *Pather Panchali,* when he first saw the train, are confirmed by the pivotal moment in *Aparajito* when a shot of the boy triumphantly holding a small globe is followed by a shot of his home-made sundial. Time and space have begun to be conquered.

Aparajito is an uncertain film. There is no plot to it, only a series of episodes related to each other by the most tenuous of connections. Symptomatic of this is the restless shifting of location: Benares and the father's death, Dejaphur, a village, Calcutta, and another village—it is all very fragmentary, and Ray tries to obscure this by over-playing the train motif, by sensationalist cutting, and by a symbolism which is too often of the Bergman and Pabst sort. Even the pathetic fallacy, of all things, is dragged in at one moment. As the father dies, pigeons scatter over the city.

The problem in making a sequel to a well-plotted film is that of finding another plot for the same characters in which they can, without strain, be put to a different use. In *Aparajito* Apu has become the protagonist, but has neither the personality

of a child nor the character of an adult to sustain the role.
The kind of adolescent problems which could interest us are
beyond the range of Ray's fastidious talent, and the character is
seen in middle distance. The mother, too, doesn't fulfil the
new demands made on her as a central character. In *Pather
Panchali* she was never more than a form of conscience,
nagging away like an aching tooth. There was no need for
her to be more than this. Naturally such a character can
never develop into a major role. The consequence of this is
that her part in *Aparajito* becomes an increasing embarrassment to Ray, until finally—she is so much at cross-purposes
with the action—he forces disastrously the pathos of her death.
To enact this scene expressionistic technique runs riot. The
camera veers over the walls and lingers on ominous flames. It
is all very embarrassing. Unfortunately it is not the only
confusion here: we never learn if we are looking at the world
through her hallucinatory vision or not; nor is it explained
why this sick woman, chatelaine of a large house, is allowed to
die alone.

These failures are a matter of more than one film. They
relate to an overt self-consciousness in Ray himself, which
manifests itself in the mannered facetiousness of his next film
(*Parash Pathar*, 1958–59) and in the obtrusive symbolism of
Jalsaghar. The latter is a curious piece (imagine *Rosmersholm*
rewritten by W. B. Yeats), but through being consistent it
does work: and because of this such symbolism as the chandelier, representing the Tree of Life, is made plausible. But in
Aparajito no such convention is sustained. The film is neither
realistic nor symbolic: it is merely awkward. There is a sense
of hiatus about it which only just manages not to be a sense
of void. It is saved, in fact, by a number of typical Ray
vignettes, such as the school inspector who admires Apu's
work and so bestows on him a benign smile, or the bed-sitter
bachelor who lends the boy a box of matches and then makes a
pass at the mother. On the lesser level it is helped by a
magnificent evocation of Benares with its lively ghats. It would
be wrong therefore to describe *Aparajito* as a failure. It
manages (just) to hold our interest between the earlier master-

piece of *Pather Panchali* and the later, probably finer, master-piece of *Apur Sansar*.

5

At this point, Ray conquered his self-consciousness by find-ing a way in which he could develop the themes of *Pather Panchali* into a new unity. By making Apu give up his study of science in order to become a writer, Ray puts him into a position which also tells us much about his own preoccupa-tions with art at that time. Apu's failure as a novelist reflects on Ray's most serious problem: that of transforming the dialetic of his themes into a direct sensation of life. "He doesn't make it," says Apu to his friend Pulu, speaking of a character in his novel but referring unknowingly to himself. "He doesn't make it, but he doesn't turn away from life. He faces up to reality." Ray wants to do better than this. He wants both to face up to reality *and* to make a work of art that conveys such an apprehension. In showing why Apu fails as a novelist, and how he comes to terms with life, Ray has, I believe, succeeded in doing this.

Apu fails because his art is wilful. In trying to control the world he has gone too far, and so cut himself off from the sources of life. Ray brings this out vividly. From a shot of Pulu inviting Apu to a wedding and telling him in an affec-tionately mocking tone of the Olde World village where it is to take place, Ray cuts immediately to a panning shot of Apu walking along an embankment, chanting a poem which iron-ically reflects on his own predicament. "Let me return to thy lap, O Earth! . . . Free me from the prison of my mind. . . ." This is in fact what has happened to Apu: he is caught in the prison of his mind. Inevitably divorced from the industrial with his onanistic flute-playing and with his (of all things) society around him. Apu is locked away in his garret room autobiographical novel. People enter his room as if they had come from some foreign land.

But this deadening sense of control is jolted by his unex-pected marriage—by quite extraordinary circumstances he is

forced into this, and so initiated into the happiest period of
his life—before being finally destroyed by his wife's death.
What the universe giveth it taketh away . . . or so at first it
seems to Apu. Reality becomes incomprehensible to him, uncontrollable in a way he had never envisaged. He thought he
had achieved some sort of order—in one of his books he kept
a dead fern leaf—and that he had somehow categorised the
world. But now, as he moves grief-stricken through a forest,
he comes across a bunch of ferns growing by a tree and is
shocked by their mysterious otherness. His novel, he sees, is
inadequate: he has misunderstood everything. Unable to carry
on as a creative being, he withdraws from life. It is only
later, in his first encounter with his five-year-old son, that he
realises how wrong he has been. The boy, by his very presence,
acts as a criticism of Apu and makes him aware of how he
has failed to face up to life. (Life here is understood to relate
inextricably to a sense of duty and obligation.) It is through
the boy, in his uniqueness and his unselfconscious vitality, that
Apu begins to return to sanity.

It is not difficult to see behind this final scene the kind of
criticism Ray must have been making of his own past work:
how art without life leads to a kind of death, and how the
artist should neither have a total control over his material nor
be entirely controlled by it, but must in some way transcend
this situation. One of the reasons why I think *Apur Sansar* is
the best film of the trilogy is that in it Ray has managed to
see how this can be done. He has brought it off, I believe, by
raising his subject to a mythopoeic level without at any point
destroying its realism.

As he sails with Pulu down a river to the Olde World
village, Apu sings: "Where are you taking us, O Fair One?"
The boatman, thinking he is being referred to, smiles. But this
humour masks a profound irony, for Apu is unaware that the
fair river is leading him directly to his yet unknown wife. The
river in fact is the central symbol, linking together both the
realistic and the mythopoeic levels of the work. It represents
both the arbitrariness of nature and the regenerating power of
water. It is by a river that Apu theatrically decides to marry;

it is by a river—now shrunken to a stream—that Pulu tries to pull him back to life after four years of mourning; and it is by a river finally that he and his son are reconciled.

On a mythopoeic level the film tells of a god's death and resurrection. The point is stressed that Apu is an avatar of Krishna, the flute-playing god. Krishna, you will remember, was allowed for a brief time to love a milkmaid named Radha; and so for a brief time is Apu allowed to love Aparna, his wife. But only for a brief time. After Aparna's death Apu descends into the underworld, where he is imprisoned with his own echo in a landscape of salt. (Though he is like some holy man, going with mat and shawl into the wilderness, his sacredness is sick. Ray—and this is an unexpected belief for an Indian—shows little sympathy for those who seek spiritual contemplation at the expense of duty.) Apu's resurrection into the world through his son is a clearer, more enacted statement of the theme of regeneration which we found in *Pather Panchali* (see the grandmother rocking Apu in his cradle). Ray's touch, however, is here more sure; and the two characters, without losing their definition as human beings, take on the firm lines of allegory. The feeling of eternal recurrence in this scene—Apu in a symbolical sense returns to the village where he was born and confronts his childhood self—gives the whole trilogy the cyclic form proper to myth.

Quite a number of people have criticised the way Ray idealises his characters; and certainly to see Apu as an avatar of Krishna may be thought presumptuous. Ray reassures us, however, through his use of Pulu, Apu's friend, who laughs at Apu for his self-regard and yet admires him to the point of idealisation. On this point the myth works for us, because we are conditioned by Pulu's critical approach. Where it does falter perhaps is during the wedding scene. As one of the guests says that the curse has become a blessing, the music on the sound track implies that Ray takes such a magical suggestion seriously. This is never made clear. Again, symbolism is forced when Apu throws his novel away and the sheets fall gently over the forest. But these are minor points. In general the myth works beautifully. It ties together themes, illuminates details, and brings an immediate sense of life to the machinery of plot.

6

This account of Ray's films has so far neglected his originality as a director: his ability to apprehend experience in cinematic terms. There is his sense of cutting, for instance, which has developed from the clumsy opening sequences of *Pather Panchali*, where the figures often appear to be caught in the frame, into an unusual, implicatory style. This style falls somewhere between Eisenstein's anti-narrative montage and Hollywood's story-telling techniques. The success of Ray's symbolism, his ability to compress densely, is in part brought about by this style (see, for instance, Apu's attempted suicide, or his search for a job). Too often, though, Ray's diffidence in committing himself is helped by this implicatory—and therefore illogical—technique. We never learn, for example, if the nobleman in *Jalsaghar* has lost his fortune because of an obsessive interest in music, or because he has abandoned himself to mourning after the death of his family.

Ray's handling of actors is also exceptional. Like De Sica he knows how to winkle performances out of children, and how to create relationships in a quick though not a glib way through the use of the striking glance or the precisely right gesture. Unlike De Sica though, whose characters must always be up and doing something, he has (and I think this is an unique achievement) a sense of the inner poise of his characters, of a stillness which is never static. His frequently sustained shots of the *Jalsaghar* nobleman, as he sits meditating, do not bore us.

These accomplishments are technical, and as much the work of Ray's excellent and permanent team of collaborators (Mitra, the cameraman, Ravi Shankar, the composer) as of Ray himself. What first concerns us is the single-minded way in which he has grown as an artist. His achievement, for me anyway, has been that he has managed to find a rich connection between his own personal problems and the problems of a society. In coming to terms with his own creative powers, in other words, he has found it easier to understand the world about him. The duel between life and death, between manic control and hopeless abandonment, relates closely—if one can use Melanie Klein's psychological terms—to the artist's need to pass through the depressive (or mourning) phase in order to re-create his destroyed inner world. In discovering this in his own terms. Ray has temporarily managed to resolve the conflicts within himself and the conflicts between his various themes.

Under Western eyes Ray's diffidence—his unnecessary ambiguities of vision and statement—is often infuriating. Yet in the last resort his achievement is so positive that we forget this. In his hands the most unusual of occurrences, like the *ad hoc* wedding or the first encounter of a father and his five-year-old son, become representative of our deepest feelings, of our most normative of day to day experiences. This golden touch should be more than respected. Indeed, for my own part, I believe that what a Bengali doctor once said to Yeats about Tagore could as well apply to Ray: "He has spoken out of life itself, and that is why we give him our love."

L'Avventura

Joseph Bennett, "The Essences of Being"

○○○

Joseph Bennett's "The Essences of Being" is an analysis of
how Michelangelo Antonioni has poetically expressed meaning by creating rhythms for the eye and ear in *L'Avventura*.
He examines the ways in which Antonioni illuminates the
reality of human isolation and connection: "Isolation. Reconciliation. Separation. Recurrent waves of the cycle." Antonioni, referring to *L'Avventura* (1960), *La Notte* (1961),
and *The Eclipse* (1962), has said that his films are "about
nothing, with precision." That *L'Avventura* is about nothing
is not to say that it is about nothingness (nonexistence or
the absence of consciousness) but that it is a contemplation
of being as opposed to an Aristotelean action about something, a drama of becoming. Movements, images, and sounds,
therefore, must communicate directly. Antonioni's empa-
thetic observation of the physical world—his deep evocation
of place, his penetrating use of land, sea, and sky scapes, and
his deft framing of architectural forms—conveys the subtlest
feelings. Mr. Bennett stresses this aspect of the film as well
as the significance of sound, about which Antonioni has said:

> I attribute enormous importance to the sound track,
> and I always try to take the greatest care with it. And
> when I say the sound track, I am talking about the natural
> sounds, the background noises rather than the music.
> For *L'Avventura*, I had an enormous number of sound
> effects recorded: every possible quality of the sea, more

and less stormy, the breakers, the rumble of the waves in the grottoes. I had a hundred reels of tape filled with nothing but sound effects. Then I selected those that you hear on the film's sound track; for me, this is the true music, the music that can be adapted to images.

———————◆———————

THIS FILM IS ABOUT THE IMPOSSIBILITY of communication between human beings. At its intensest moment, Monica Vitti turns to Gabriele Ferzetti, her handsome, good-natured, weak-willed lover, and finds that he, after consummating his desire, is lost in meditation. The beauty of the great honey-colored baroque squares of Noto outside their hotel balcony has accused him with the failure of his youthful dreams as an architect, for he has fallen into a squalid success in commercial contracting. Her ecstasy, rhythmed by the blare of a popular song in the square below, is stopped by his detachment. He is gnawing his defeat.

He goes out to the cathedral square and is confronted by his failure in the form of an ink sketch being made of a superb shell-concave niche. He spills the ink, to scourge himself, and ruins the work of the artist. He tells us that he too, at twenty-three, had fought many fistfights; a solemn queue of black-robed ecclesiastical students marshaled by their priestly instructors, emerging from the huge Chiesa Madre, tells him that life goes on; that at forty, defeated, he is of the process.

He returns abruptly. He is accused anew by the façade of the Immacolata Church, visible from their balcony, sought and sharply held by the marvelously intuitive camera. He slams the shutters, seizes her, in the manner of rape. She does not know him. Then it will be a new adventure, he tells her as she weeps. They break apart, leave the hotel. Surely one of the great sequences in cinema.

There is a nominal narrative thread, vaguely stringing together the episodes. Gabriele Ferzetti has not been able to strike through to communication with his self-abstracted fiancée, played by Lea Massari. She prefers absence, a month, a year; she prefers separation to being together; resists their

L'Avventura, directed by Michelangelo Antonioni, 1960 (*Janus*)

meetings. They cruise, with her friend, played by Monica Vitti, to the Liparian islands. There are also with them two couples, connected with his business.

On the harshly beautiful rock of Liscabianca, they still fail of communication. His fiancée disappears. He, her friend, the couples, search the rock; the police, a helicopter, a hydro-foil arrive. To no avail. He and her friend continue the search on land.

At the florid *municipio* of Bagheria, the Villa Gravina Palagonia transformed by Antonioni to a customs station at Milazzo, the friend, Monica Vitti, leaves him to return to Monreale. They are in love. He pursues her. On the train[1] a charming folklore interchange between rural Sicilian boy and girl underlines the theme of impossibility of communica-tion; at the villa of Princess Lampedusa near Monreale the couples from the cruise are as far apart as ever. One woman (perfectly rendered by Esmeralda Ruspoli) has exchanged her lover for her husband, with equal ennui.

The gaiety and vivacity shown by Antonioni in the folklore interchange returns again in the publicity stunt of the *poule de luxe* (again: no communication between the sexes; between human beings); it is shown further in the serenely abstract joyousness of the wig-changing scene between the two women at the villa; in the adolescent amorousness of the Princess' seventeen-year old grandson (again no communication: he is attempting to seduce a married woman twenty years older). By a newspaper ruse Gabriele Ferzetti tricks Monica Vitti into meeting him at a pharmacist's shop "at Troina." This scene (shot on the plain, not at Troina) is again richly folkloristic; the pharmacist and his wife underline the impossibility of communication anywhere.

The lovers go on alone. The search for the lost girl has become the excuse for their amour. They pass through one of the new Cassa del Mezzogiorno towns near Caltanisetta; the

[1]The train pulls in to the station at Castroreale. When Ferzetti gets off, and the train pulls out, the locale has changed to a station near the great rock of Cefalù, so that the camera can take in its grandiloquent desolation.

cinema "desertion" of the new village underlines the soul-isolation of modern life. A hazy view of Etna from the immense distance of the Augusta plain, smoky, abstract, incredibly distant, rendered with miraculous camera vision, provides the locale for their union. The train sweeps past, close to them.

Finally they arrive at the great *platersque* architectural ensemble of Noto. This triumph of the late Spanish-Sicilian baroque provides the background for the episode described earlier; furnishing the proper challenge for the architect to recognize his career defeat. Architecture too had been the camera theme in the customs station at the Villa Palagonia. But now it provides the offset to love, and there is no communication.

Nearly two hours have gone by before these moments arrive. Quickly the scene changes from the simple inn at Noto to the San Domenico Palace hotel at Taormina. They arrive by no route at all that leads from Noto to Taormina, but rather Antonioni shoots their automobile passing out of one of the rock-hewn galleries near the north coast. In their room in the luxurious San Domenico, Ferzetti is about to go down to dinner with the contractor. The woman remains in bed. She speaks first:

> "Tell me that you love me."
> "I love you."
> "Tell it to me again."
> "I don't love you."
> "I deserved that."

She means that she deserves his reproach for asking him to repeat that he loves her. He closes the door, reopens it:

> "It isn't true. I love you." (He leaves.)

There is an exquisitely delicate fluctuation here between poignancy and barrenness; the threat of isolation is implied. In this scene and the one cited at Noto Antonioni has projected shapes and emotions out of his own mind directly into ours, in faithful variability and intangibleness. The medium has been cinematic; the veil has broken; two minds have come into contact, that of the audience and that of the director, without a medium, without a stream of flickering light and shadows between the two intelligences.

The demonstration of the theme is then made in a few sharp strokes. She surprises him (the following dawn) in flagrant infidelity on a public couch with the *poule de luxe* of the earlier comic sequence. He is weak. Handsome, good-natured, accommodating; not the master of himself. She discovers her own fidelity to his weakness in a reconciliation scene that emphasizes the absolute, the unchanging: the bombed-out tower of the San Domenico church; the snow-mantled Etna; the shrill urgency of the train whistles coming up from Giardini seven hundred feet below. The sound track has exaggerated the three crescendoing train whistles; and it has greatly amplified the rolling of the waves, to bring into the conclusion all the work done by the film on the Liparian island of Liscabianca. The same dry and clean, abstract flute solo (the Liparian theme) comes into the sound track, with the sea waves, to complete the film. Isolation. Reconciliation. Separation. Recurrent waves of the cycle.

What has gone on in the preceding two hours? It seems to me that this film is the first important step forward since Fellini's extraordinary *I Vitelloni* (1953). But in this film Antonioni exhibits an incomparably greater range, depth and subtlety. Starting with *Il Bidone* (1955), much more so in *Cabiria* and exhaustingly and disappointingly so in his current and by far poorest film, *La Dolce Vita*, Fellini has become the moralist, the Puritan, the maker of parables and allegory. But Antonioni has seized after the thing which Fellini did in *I Vitelloni*, and carried it further, with greater delicacy, greater syncopation, and less charm. The form demands great length.

This film is *about* the impossibility of communication between human beings, but it is much more than that: it is the creation of a reality, a world which can be entered, therapeutic and more relaxing than the one in which we live, and yet more interesting, more unconventional, more vital. It shares with *I Vitelloni* the ability to create a world, alternate to our own world, and more inviting; it offers us a vision of reality, at least as authentic as our own, and invites us to live within it. Both films, if successfully seen, have this therapeutic, relaxing quality. A discharge of the present, a liberation into a world of greater clarity and range, greater breadth and more subtle texture, and finally, greater innocence, despite the sophistication of (at least) Antonioni's worldlings.

In essence what I am saying is that what Antonioni is creating is not a film, not a theme, but a world, a vision of reality which is gentle and embracing and seductive and extraordinarily satisfying, despite some surface harshnesses in plot progressions. The test of the effect is whether, after the two hours and twenty odd minutes of the film, you are tempted *not* to go back to the street; but to stay there with the film, not to find out what is happening, or what is being done, but simply because you do not want to leave a world deeper in texture, in form, and alternate to your own.

This was, I think, in essence the undefinable charm of Fellini's *I Vitelloni*, its fantastic depth and durability. It was *about* adolescents adjusting to the progress of time, their resistance to maturity, just as this film is *about* something. But really, was *I Vitelloni about* anything? I think not; I think it was an earlier version of a strikingly similar reality of which Antonioni's film is the full, and full-length, development. People are looking at landscapes: Fellini's old actor gazes at the sea at night; his young men gaze at the sea from the pier. What are they gazing at? Is Antonioni's architect *really* gazing at the square and his lost genius, when his attention drifts far from his love?

Fellini did not continue with *I Vitelloni*, and turned away to more tangible themes, essentially to parable. Perhaps both it and Antonioni's film represent a cinema ultimate—pure contemplation, the spiritual life, aesthetic monasticism. Certainly there is purity in both films such as Mallarmé aimed at; they too are working toward the blank page. There is just enough left to catch a visible world, a tangible reality.

Whether or not we like the *poésie pure*, I think we can make the point that here we have the *cinéma pur*. Fellini stopped, some would say had the good sense to stop, and turned to more simple and more justifiable work. He is now busily engaged in giving us a *Pilgrim's Progress*. Perhaps beyond *L'Avventura* lies the *Un coup de dès jamais n'abolira le hasard* [poem by Mallarmé] or the *Finnegans Wake* that Fellini had the good sense to turn away from, knowing they would be failures. The inescapable failure of the absolute, the attack on the absolute.

Sound track. Music. The richest, most devious sound track, the subtlest musical score since *I Vitelloni*. The lack of music—not the haunting, torturing emotionality of the *Vitelloni* score, but the waiting, waiting for the superb dry abstract jazz of the wig-changing scene (one of the many "pure" frivolities, "pure" untouched life-scenes, not adding up, not meaningful in themselves). And again we wait, and wait, in silence, for the arrival at the San Domenico hotel: the mandolins sweep out as the door opens but they are not the lax and uninspired mandolins of convention but pure rhythm, working counter to melody; they are the beat of the south, of *south-ness*, abstracted to a philosophic principle. There is silence. More music: the dialect of the people. The smugglers at the customs station: "C'è mi sora ch'è malatt' d'un annu"; the pharmacist; the men-wolves in the square, the landlady, the taxi diver, all at Noto: "No saccio. No saccio. Francesa? Furastiera?" The Liparian shepherd: "Che fu? Che fu?" [dialect expressive of "*south-ness*"]

And then there is all the variability, the silkiness, the vague *sfumato* [hazy] quality of Scavarda's camera work under Antonioni's direction. A camera dry and yet romantic, obsessed with architecture, both natural (rocks, cliffs, seas, shores, islands) and man-made. Long shots from the villa near Monreale to the distant heights of Sferracavallo and Monte Gallo, mist-shrouded, as the comedy of the pubescent painter's seduction of a giddy married woman is played out.

There is much comedy, much variability, and no justification in this film. This film *exists* because it *is*. It does not think. It does not plan ahead. There is no drive, no line. Every movement is a succession of asides. Antonioni is dealing with essences here, with what is pragmatic, with that which succeeds itself. *On, onta* [Gk. the present, reality]. He is dealing with "being," with "what is."

Balthazar

William Johnson, "Balthazar"

○○

The release of a new film by Robert Bresson, an event
that has occurred only nine times in the past twenty-five
years, has usually resulted in critics proclaiming a new film
masterpiece. As with *Les Anges du Péché* (1943), *Les Dames
du Bois de Boulogne* (1944), *Diary of a Country Priest*
(1950), *A Man Escaped* (1956), *Pickpocket* (1959), *The Trial
of Joan of Arc* (1962), *Mouchette* (1967) and *Une Femme
Douce* (1969), the release of *Balthazar*, or *Au Hasard Balthazar*, in 1966 brought forth positive critical responses. *Balthazar*
is formally structured by the cycle of the birth, life, and
death of a donkey, Balthazar; the interaction between him
and a variety of humans is the content of the film. William
Johnson contrasts it with Bresson's earlier films which are
shaped for intensive concentration upon the figure of a
central protagonist. His discussion then narrows to *Balthazar*,
and concludes: "Within a brief period of time (the film runs
little longer than ninety minutes), Bresson condenses the
diverse struggles for life of his five humans and a donkey.
The complex experience is honed to a sharpness that touches
one deeply and haunts one's memory for a long time."

In an interview with Jean-Luc Godard and Michel Delahaye published in *Cahiers du Cinéma in English*, No. 8,
Bresson speaks of the many lines of story in *Balthazar*: ". . .
the film started from two ideas, from two *schemata*, if you
will. First schema: the donkey has in his life the same stages

as does a man, that is to say, childhood, caresses; maturity, work; talent, genius in the middle of life; and the analytical period that precedes death. Well. Second schema, which crosses the first or which starts from it: the passage of this donkey, who passes through different human groups representing the vices of humanity, from which he suffers, and from which he dies. . . . He must suffer from what makes us, ourselves, suffer." And when asked about the problem of forging an artistic unity out of materials that could be the subjects of several films, Bresson said that ". . . I tried my utmost to let it [the film] have one [a unity] all the same, thinking that, thanks to the donkey, in spite of everything, in the end the unity would find itself again. . . . The film has perhaps also a unity in the way in which I cut up the sequences into shots. . . . Including the way of speaking. That is, moreover, what I always seek: that the people almost all speak in the same way. To sum up: it is through form that one finds unity again."

———————◆———————

THE FILM BEGINS WITH the birth of Balthazar, the donkey, and ends with his death. In between his life intertwines with those of the inhabitants of a small French town. Marie, a silent, withdrawn girl, first adopts Balthazar as a pet. They are parted when her father takes over the management of an estate belonging to a friend. The friend's son, Jacques, loves Marie, but she falls under the spell of Gérard, an amoral, sadistic youth. Balthazar meanwhile is bought by the village baker for making deliveries. Gérard becomes the baker's delivery boy and torments Balthazar. The donkey falls ill and the baker is about to kill him when a strange tramp named Arnold bursts in and takes Balthazar away. After a while Balthazar runs free, is taken in by a circus and taught a computing act. Meanwhile Marie's father has become estranged from his friend because he refuses, out of pride, to deny false rumors that he is embezzling from the estate.

And so the film goes on, until in the end Marie is raped by a gang of Gérard's friends and dies; her father dies;

Balthazar, directed by Robert Bresson, 1966 *(French Film Office)*

Arnold dies; and Balthazar, "borrowed" by Gérard and his gang for a smuggling expedition, is shot by a border guard.

In any verbal summary the plot is bound to seem like a morass of disconnected and sometimes far-fetched incidents. As in *Diary of a Country Priest*, Bresson builds up an unusual density of experience by pressing rapidly from episode to episode. But unlike *Diary*—or any of Bresson's other films, for that matter—*Balthazar* does not have a central character that binds this varied experience together. The principal characters, including Balthazar himself, alternate between foreground and background, or disappear from the scene to reappear much later. Bresson's laconic style, his unapologetic use of coincidence, and his insistence on deadpan acting (the donkey that plays Balthazar is more expressive than most of the cast) make the surface events of his film seem even more arbitrary and inscrutable.

It's tempting to look to symbolism for an answer. Marie ritually dedicates herself to Balthazar, as if he were a stand-in for God. Arnold, who might easily be a Christ figure on the lines of the bearded halfwit in Dreyer's *Ordet*, suggests that the donkey represents a passive observer of human frailties. But how does this jibe with Bresson's remark (quoted by Richard Roud in *Sight and Sound*) that the donkey is a symbol of virility?

All of these symbols—and others just as "obvious"—may have a brief validity at different times during the film, but clearly there is no one symbol that will reveal the meaning of the film as a whole. There's always the possibility, of course, that the film *doesn't* make sense as a whole, that Bresson himself was confused. Many of the elements in the film are unexpectedly modern, outside Bresson's usual ambit. Marie and Gérard, for example, might need only a touch of flip humor to be at home in a Godard film. Could Bresson be trying, and failing, to enter the world of alienated youth, like Carné in *The Cheaters* and Antonioni in *Blow-Up*? But in these films one can easily peel away the style—the romantic melancholy that Carné imposes on his young Parisians, the brilliant surface that overlays Antonioni's near-

Victorian moralizing about young Londoners—and reveal the banal content just below the surface. *Balthazar* has no such weak seams between style and content. If one strips away the trappings of contemporary youth—Gérard's transistor radio, his rock-and-roll, his gun, his destructiveness—the film remains as richly textured as before.

Though *Balthazar* represents something of a new departure for Bresson, it does not depart so far from his previous films as to be influenced by film-making fashions. Right from the start Bresson has gone his own way. All his films are religious in the deepest sense of the word, which sets him far apart from directors like George Stevens and John Huston who observe only the conventional pieties. But he also differs fundamentally from the few other serious religious directors, and this difference has emerged more and more clearly with each of the seven films that he has made in the past twenty-four years.

Bresson's first two films, *Les Anges du Péché* (1943) and *Les Dames du Bois de Boulogne* (1944) had a fairly conventional dramatic form which partly obscured the distinctiveness of their themes. The transformation of pride into humility through the fire of humiliation recurs in most of Bresson's films. An even more important theme is launched: the idea that one attains freedom not by trying to smash one's way out of one's circumstances but by struggling patiently within them. Thus the over-confident nun in *Les Anges du Péché* finally comes to grips with a crisis for which she is at first totally unprepared; and the man trapped into marrying a *danseuse* in *Les Dames du Bois de Boulogne* accepts her gladly.

Beginning with *Diary of a Country Priest* (1950) Bresson's style becomes as idiosyncratic as his content. *Diary* does still have a dark, brooding intensity about it which might call to mind the atmosphere of Ingmar Bergman's films; but the resemblance is only superficial, and it disappears entirely from Bresson's subsequent films. For Bergman, God and the after-life are matters of doubt and mystery. For Bresson—as for his country priest—they are matters of certainty: it's only in this world that doubts and mysteries arise.

Holding this view, Bresson has no need for the symbolism that Bergman wields, ax-like, against the wall of mystery between this world and whatever lies beyond. Bresson is concerned with clarifying the situation of man here and now, dipped in flesh for a brief moment in eternity; and to do this he uses not symbolism but synecdoche—choosing the particular section of a particular character's life that best reveals the human condition. The method may overlap symbolism; the country priest's hereditary disease may perhaps be taken as a symbol for original sin. But nothing is lost if one rejects this symbol: the disease in itself is a powerful enough handicap to establish the intensity of the priest's struggle.

In Bresson's next three films—*A Man Escaped* (1956), *Pickpocket* (1959), and *The Trial of Joan of Arc* (1962)—he strives to drill closer and closer to the heart of the human condition as he sees it. Emotionalism is out; so is any suggestion of divine intervention. All that counts is the individual soul struggling against the difficulties of this world. The condemned man in *A Man Escaped* struggles against imprisonment, scraping away at his cell day after day with a spoon. Just when he is ready to escape, a cellmate is thrust on him, and he must take the risk of trusting the newcomer—the struggle must be crowned with charity. The young hero of *Pickpocket* lacks this charity; he knows he must struggle but he does not know what he should struggle for, and he directs his energies into acquiring the skill and grace of an expert pickpocket.

Here Bresson's central character has become little more than a single driving force. And this spareness is carried even further for *The Trial of Joan of Arc*. It's easy to compare this Joan to Dreyer's, the *Trial* with the *Passion*, to Bresson's disadvantage. But even though I do not like the *Trial*, I can see why Bresson wanted to make it the way he did. Dreyer's film can be appreciated entirely as a humanitarian drama in which a defenseless woman stands up to a tyrannical establishment. As in all his films, Dreyer lingers lovingly on objects, faces, textures, light in its myriad qualities; frequently he pans or dollies from one point of interest to another as if he cannot bear the brutal parting of a cut. In Dreyer's view, since the world is God's creation, it is marvelous in itself. One result is that his *Passion* makes not merely the circumstances of Joan's death but the fact of death itself seem terrible.

To Bresson this is all wrong. Life in itself is not wonderful, and death in itself not terrible. Since Joan was a soldier, Bresson sees her as tough and level-headed, with a matter-of-fact assurance of life after death. In his film she is temperamentally a match for her accusers and judges, and—during the trial at least—she arouses little pity. Only when it comes to the manner of Joan's execution does Bresson seek to engage our emotions, beginning with the close-up of her bare feet treading the cobblestones on her way to the stake.

That close-up is crucial. Although Bresson does not linger as Dreyer does on objects and faces, there is nothing abstract about his use of the camera. He does not rely on noble postures, reverent tableaux or grandiose compositions in the style of *The Bible* or *The Greatest Story Ever Told.* Many of his shots arouse strong physical sensations, like the close-up of Joan's feet or the similar shot in *Balthazar* where the donkey's hooves are seen stepping hesitantly over rocky ground; or indeed like the opening scene of *Balthazar,* where young Marie's smooth white arm stretches into the frame to caress the dark and fluffy baby donkey, making one almost literally feel the simultaneous closeness and separateness of the two creatures. Bresson may take a detached view of the world, but he sees it sharply. Just as his most saintly characters are not passive souls but activists working through the flesh, he himself works through the cinematic flesh of familiar sights and sounds.

This is what makes Bresson's films so fascinating to a non-believer like myself. He does not reject or distort the world as we know it but places it as is in the light of eternity. The transformation is done without flourishes; yet it is fully as startling as the altered modes of reality in *Marienbad* or in science fiction films like *La Jetée* or *The Damned.*

The comparison is not far-fetched. Like the woman in *Marienbad* and the man in *La Jetée,* all of Bresson's central characters from *Dairy of a Country Priest* onward have been adrift in a disconcerting continuum of time and space. What science fiction presents as allegory Bresson presents as fact: his priest, his pickpocket, and even his Joan are space travelers trying to preserve their identity in an alien world.

The pickpocket is the first of Bresson's central characters to come close to failure. He is in much the same predicament as Losey's mutant children: his defense mechanisms against the threats of the modern world have hypertrophied, blocking him from normal contact with other people. *Pickpocket*, of course, has none of the rhetoric of *The Damned;* it errs in the opposite direction, in excessive terseness and understatement.

This is a pivotal film, combining as it does an unprecedented rigor of style with the unprecedented (for Bresson) theme of alienation. With *The Trial of Joan of Arc* Bresson carries the rigor still further; and although Joan is not alienated in the modern sense of the word, she deliberately blanks herself out in dealing with her judges and advisers for fear of being tempted to recant. The country priest and the condemned man, single-minded and self-contained though they are, allow certain countercurrents of feeling to reach the surface. The priest shows an unexpected delight in being taken for a ride on a motorbike; the condemned man, after his escape, is suddenly jaunty. The pickpocket and Joan lack this richness of character. With the *Trial*, indeed, the lines along which Bresson was developing seemed to lead directly to a vanishing point.

But then came *Balthazar*.

Seen in the light of Bresson's other films, *Balthazar* ceases to be an enigma. Not that the film becomes simple to explain; but one can decide with confidence what questions need *not* be asked about it, what subtle meanings are *not* hidden away in its intricate plot.

The novelty of *Balthazar* rests in the fact that Bresson has fused the rigor of *Pickpocket* and the *Trial* with the richness of his earlier films. He has done this quite simply, by presenting several protagonists instead of one. Each of his four previous films revolves around the protagonist named in the title: even when the other characters are as memorable as Chantal and the Curé de Tourcy in *Dairy*, they and their problems remain tributary to the central figure. In *Balthazar,* five characters present different facets of a condition which, in *Pickpocket,* is revealed through the central character alone. Marie, Gérard, Arnold, Marie's father and the miserly corn merchant all lack grace; or in less theological terms, are blocked from finding satisfaction in life. In Marie's father and the merchant the block is a simple obsession: pride in the former, avarice in the latter. Arnold is impelled by gluttony and sloth. Gérard and Marie, like the pickpocket, are more creative, each trying to impose a pattern on what seems to them to be the meaninglessness of life. Gérard's method is sadism: since life is absurd, he will beat it to the punch by himself creating accidents (spilling oil on the road for cars to slither on), himself inflicting pain (tying a burning newspaper to Balthazar's tail) and himself forcing other people to act against their will (gaining sexual ascendancy over Marie). As for Marie, yearning for God in what seems to be a God-forsaken universe, she makes a divinity out of Balthazar.

But the donkey's importance in the film, and his place of honor in the title, do not depend on symbolism. Bresson is still as direct as ever. It is Marie, dreaming of an omnipotent love, who deifies Balthazar and at the same time sees him as an erotic symbol; it is Arnold who projects on Balthazar his own role as a wandering observer. Balthazar's real importance is the fact that he is an animal, and as such denied both salvation and damnation; all he need struggle for is survival. He serves as a touchstone for the human beings he encounters, whose characters are revealed both in the way they treat him and in the way their lives compare in dignity with his. But there can be no real contact between animal and humans. Smooth skin may touch rough hide, and Marie may crown Balthazar with flowers, but any signs of humanity or divinity in the donkey are as illusory as the arthmetical ability he displays at the circus. When Marie throws herself at the mercy of the corn merchant, whose lust is tempered only by greed, Balthazar is standing nearby; but of course he does not spring to the rescue like an asinine Lassie. If Balthazar were able to attack the merchant he would have done so long before to save his own skin; and in any case it is not her body that Marie wants rescued but her mind.

Balthazar is the pivotal though passive character in all the important relationships in the film. Just as Bresson conveys the separateness of Marie and Balthazar through the close-up of fur and skin, he translates the spiritual gulf between Marie and the merchant into sharp physical terms, contrasting the squat body, mean gestures, and crabbed voice of the merchant with the slim, smooth body and direct speech and gestures of Marie. This contrast is reminiscent of the curious scene where Balthazar confronts the caged animals at the circus, impassively staring at and being stared at by a tiger, a polar bear, and a chimpanzee. There is nothing metaphorical about the resemblance between these two scenes—it is not an ornamental way of saying that men are like wild animals. On the contrary, Bresson is once again making a statement of what is for him simple fact: that just as there can be no real contact or understanding between animals and humans, so there can be none between humans who lack grace.

Balthazar may sound like a gloomy film, but it is not, thanks largely to the diversity of its human and animal protagonists. Taken individually they may be drab or unpleasant: Marie, the most important of the humans, is almost as monotonous as Bresson's Joan. But interlinked as they are, with all their desires and sufferings, they form a glowing tapestry of life that exhilarates rather than depresses.

That isn't the only paradox about *Balthazar*. Bresson, as usual, admits no easy appeals to the emotions—and certainly none of the sentimentality that most films about animals smuggle in. And yet, largely because of his rigorous treatment, the film is moving. Within a brief period of time (the film runs little longer than ninety minutes), Bresson condenses the diverse struggles for life of his five humans and a donkey. The complex experience is honed to a sharpness that touches one deeply and haunts one's memory for a long time.

Blow-Up

Hubert Meeker, "Blow-Up"

ooooooooooooooooooooooooooooooooooooooooooooooooo

Based on a short story by Julio Cortázar, Michelangelo Antonioni's *Blow-Up* came as a surprise to many former admirers. Some found it a pity that so much artistic talent, such exquisite technique, had been dissipated on such meager substance. While many thought well of the previous Antonioni films which show no interest in "morality," they unhesitatingly put *Blow-Up* to the moral test and pronounced it amoral. They found it an attempt to make a huge commercial success by aping the fashionable world of the mod scene. Still others, perceiving the swinging ambience of the hero, anticipated a work of permissive morality but were alienated in finding the film Victorian in its moralistic putdown of the Youth Generation. Few, if any, were not surprised.

Coming after *L'Avventura* (1960), *La Notte* (1961), *The Eclipse* (1962), and *Red Desert* (1964) as it did, *Blow-Up* does not fit into the pattern of films Antonioni has taught us to expect. Numerous critics have seized upon the fruitful thesis that *Blow-Up* is a portrait of the artist's modes of perception and his relationship to other men. Hubert Meeker implicitly incorporates this idea into his analysis of the film which develops a theme of gratuitous discovery. "Where selfishness was a general standard in earlier films, a refreshing pattern of giving is established in *Blow-Up*." In evoking various scenes with perceptive appreciation, Mr. Meeker pinpoints a progression of epiphanies that functionally precede and culminate in the final scene. Hence his interpretation is an endorsement of the concluding sequence which some critics have felt is an expedient for ending a film that would otherwise be too long to suit the demands of the producers. "Antonioni needed a very clear and unambiguous statement to close the film, and he found it in the rag party that opened the film. . . . Hemmings returns the imaginary ball, and the game goes on. His new-found faith in that invisible ground for men's sharing is reinforced by the sound track; the pock-pock of a tennis ball, like the sound of one hand clapping. The mystery is complete; not a mystery to be solved, but a mystery to be realized."

———◆———

THE IMPRESSION LEFT on me by previous Antonioni films is one of eloquently composed emptiness, and a mood of sadness too diffuse to produce the sharpness of despair, in which human contact is mostly tentative and anti-climactic.

Blow-Up comes, then, with the distinct shock of departure. The bold use of color, the sharp contrasts of milieu, and the vital rhythmic shifts of cinematic pace are but the obvious surface signs of Antonioni's deeper shift of ground.

Human relationships are depicted as even more ambiguous than before and communication more elliptical. But through these extremes, the pervasive ennui has been sharpened into divergent points of view, forming a pattern and a sense of an external, spiritual presence I don't recall feeling before.

Where selfishness was a general standard in earlier films, a refreshing pattern of giving is established in *Blow-Up*. In the opening sequence the photographer, emerging from a doss house, makes a money contribution to the boisterous rag party. In the last sequence at the tennis court, the revelers return the favor with a gift manyfold in its importance. In a sense he has earned, and must show he has earned, what they have to give. Yet the essential quality of what is bestowed on him is that it must be both earned and given.

Another important gift at the center of the film might be

Blow-Up, directed by Michelangelo Antonioni, 1966 (*M-G-M*)

described as the photographer's gift to himself, except there is also an aspect of outside intervention, the operation of an external wisdom definitely beyond him at this point. It is the delivery to his studio of the propeller he had purchased at the pawn shop. It arrives in time to break up the photographer's seduction of the strange woman, a gratuitous little moment of grace protecting the innocent and delivering justice unawares. (A great deal of trouble was taken with the involved and guilty Miss Redgrave to show her essential innocence in the studio surroundings, and conversely, to point up the guilt of the uninvolved and innocent Hemmings.) The propeller stops the photographer from knowing her in the cliché physical way that has become habit with him, and forces him to aim for a better understanding of her and her situation. Of course the arrival of the propeller, that fragment of the airborne, can be described as chance, but its arrival does work on them in a beneficial way, and whether one describes this chain of events as blind or omniscient, "higher" than their present consciousness or "lower," coming from the "outside" or "inside," hardly matters. The fact that a chance event can alter men's directions for the better can still be called grace, and the propeller noted as a symbol of grace.

The other gifts in the film can be described as sacrificial. The two little girls, who so badly want to become models, return in the wake of Miss Redgrave's departure to find themselves suddenly needed, but in a way they didn't expect. In this chain of events as unwitting as the propeller sequence, the girls are sacrificed to Hemmings' fever, and following that debauch in the torn and crumpled purple backdrop paper, the photographer is able to return to his blow-ups with greater clarity. Where previously he thought his intervention had saved the man's life in the park, he now reads the evidence more closely and sees the shadow of murder. This is the other sacrifice. A man's life has been taken—an older man, by the way—as the culmination of some "trouble" Miss Redgrave speaks of, and in the course of events this "trouble" is passed on to a younger man whose swinging surface existence had apparently never felt the jar of such a real encounter. The "trouble" germinates in him the possibility of new life, which the film celebrates in that ritual tennis court scene. The irony, of course, is that Hemmings doesn't make the sacrifices that lead to his progress, but takes advantage of others in his quest. This doesn't seem fair, but, then, life isn't fair, and it seems part of the film's "message" that the cost of one inch of progress in a man's becoming is inordinately high, and not necessarily meted out in deserving fashion. Yet, in another sense, the cost was nothing, the sacrifices were gratuitous in that the murder and the seduction would have occurred anyway, and the photographer earns his way to the degree he is able to make something of them.

Antonioni uses some of the elements of mystery, as we find them in popular literature, to introduce Mystery, much in the same way Graham Greene has. The capsule of this technique is recorded in the artist's studio the photographer visits. Out of the profligate amount of paint and energy the artist has expended on his canvas, it is all a waste except for one little passage that still intrigues him, like a clue in a mystery story as he puts it, that is worth hanging onto and makes his life and work worth pursuing.

But it is not the mystery that captivates us in *Blow-Up;* it is its reality, the brilliance with which Antonioni has composed fascinating surfaces into lasting meaning. He limits himself to what is available to the artist, what meets the eye, the intriguing and telltale surface of life, a surface which psychologists coming out of the depths of the unconscious are finding far more significant than they previously thought possible. Antonioni studies what washes up to the surface of the swinging London milieu with that combination of scientific scrutiny and a lover's sensuous care that comes naturally to the artist. The super-authenticity of the photographer's huge warehouse studio engulfs us in its wealth of lovely equipment and gorgeous high-fashion colors. It also engulfs us in its make-believe free association of planes and spaces, as illusory screens and backdrops, scenery and props, flow into the "real" places of darkrooms and living quarters with such easy transition.

I was absorbed in David Hemmings' work as a fashion

photographer in this make-believe lair. The first sequence in which he stalks, dominates and ravishes a lithe tigress of a model with his camera is a wonderful evocation of trade technique. That the scene is doubly enriched with its overtones of sexuality, and on a purely animal basis, the hunt and the kill (the hunt for the right picture?) is just as important as a musical instrument's timbre is to the notes it plays. The overtones, rather than detracting from the tone itself, add to its richness and importance and accuracy. What impresses us most in this atmosphere of sexuality is Hemmings' "cool." It is merely work and money, the only formula he knows for achieving the "freedom" he later expresses a desire for.

Antonioni lingers in the studio to elaborate his theme with a second group of models, which Hemmings treats like so many animals in a pen. We have watched him work with one model; now we watch him with four, and Antonioni's variations provide some wonderful color-play before Hemmings leaves his harried models in medias res to rush off on some other tangent of his many-faceted, wheeling-dealing life, held together by radiophone from his Rolls convertible.

There are two other important studio sequences, however. The later one involves the two teen-age girls who have been hanging about looking for a chance to do a little modelling. At their first appearance his approach to them is "cool"; he sees them only in professional terms and dismisses them. But when they come back later, after Miss Redgrave has left, it is significant that he sees them as human beings and takes them in. The action that follows is natural for him in that particular situation. He tears off their clothes, and in a wildly funny scene of childish innocence and exuberance, he ravishes them in a heap of torn purple backdrop paper. Technically it was probably the most difficult scene to photograph and put together, and the mood of innocent playfulness that comes across, in spite of our preconceptions about the deflowering of girls, is a triumph of Antonioni artistry. It is a very warm and human scene, and the mark of the photographer's "humanization" for want of a better word. But the crowning irony of the scene, and the proof that Hemmings' progress is gratuitous, is that these two debauched little girls, numb as statues, seem to harbor one disappointment: they still haven't had their pictures taken!

The pivotal studio scene concerns Hemmings' confrontation with the woman whose picture he has taken in the park embracing an older man. Although Hemmings later makes plain his interest in making pictures from life, when he discusses his book of candid photographs in the restaurant with his writer friend, his trip to the park is the one important instance of his working from life, and is sharply contrasted with his commercial studio. From the intense, op-art studio scenes with the bevy of models, Antonioni makes a careful and deliberate transition to the suburban park. The pace begins to wind down as Hemmings wheels his convertible past a long row of old buildings painted solid red, punctuated at the end by a solitary blue building, and followed by the spaciously sited new apartment buildings in a calm tan brick. Hemmings' rummaging around in the antique shop, from which he later buys the propeller, reinforces the image of Hemmings as a man living a fragmentary existence, a collector of unusual photographic glimpses and odd isolated experiences. Isn't it significant that he never uses a movie camera, but sees life in neatly framed stills? The antique shop is also the last step in Antonioni's winding down of the pace of the film and introducing the lyrical passage in the park. The moist air glistens with pearly light, and the green of the trees and grass is exquisitely pure and fragile. Yet in contrast to the complex and sophisticated studio scenes before it, where a kind of professional security reigned, there is a subtle insecurity and sense of mounting danger in the simple purity of the park, underscored by the ominous sighing of the wind in the trees. The idyll of the strolling lovers as Hemmings stalks them also has a note of strangeness about it. We notice the woman leading the man, not to the seclusion one would suspect her to desire, but into the open light and positioning him as if according to a plan. Whatever is going on is interrupted by Hemmings' presence, and Miss Redgrave follows him back to his studio to bargain for the photos he took of her. Her plain but strong and elegant features establish her immediately as a person of more than cosmetic interest, and her anxious pacing in the studio contrasts sharply with the artificial animal movements of the model earlier on. "My private life is already in a mess," she says. "It would be a disaster if—" "So what!" answers Hemmings. "Nothing like a little disaster to sort things out." His flip tone of voice underscores the authenticity of her predicament by contrast. He talks about disaster while she so obviously is in its grips, and the intensity of her involvement provides the first instance in the film in which Hemmings loses his cool. His rambling conversation about the ill-defined wife who is not a wife, the children who don't exist, and their mother's easy-to-live-with qualities that make it impossible for him to live with her—all reveal that the "mess" of Hemmings' life is far different from the disaster of Miss Redgrave's. Hers comes across as something sharply defined and authentic, while his seems a vague muddle—the product of his own mindlessness. And to carefully visualize this mindlessness Antonioni purposely never sorts out the identity of the woman on the phone, or the exact role of Sarah Miles, or whether or not they are one and the same.

Nevertheless Hemmings tries to dominate Miss Redgrave by turning her into another of his models. "Not many women can stand like that," he observes. "Show me how you sit!" But she is more than a match for him. In removing her blouse and offering him sex in return for the film, she shows herself one step ahead of him and in command of the situation. But the fact that she is a real person, a vulnerable and involvable person, works against her. She suddenly finds herself involved with Hemmings, while he takes advantage of her vulnerability to give her a substitute roll of film. Only the propeller, in its timely arrival, saves her from being further seduced, and saves Hemmings from turning a real encounter into a cliché one.

The careful and exacting sequences of Hemmings developing and enlarging the pictures is exciting in its verisimilitude. I can't recall another film in which the technical aspects of a trade have been used to such powerful effect. Very little use is made of standard suspense techniques to sustain this passage. The process itself is far more interesting for the moment than

the end result. Hemmings tried to make contact with Miss
Redgrave by turning her into something familiar to him, another model; but now he tries to reach the truth she contains
by more honest means, the only thing he really knows, the art
of photography. The photographs he took in the park he keeps
blowing up, larger and larger, almost "larger than life" in
order to discover a clue to the mystery. At one point he sees
that Miss Redgrave was setting up her friend for murder, but
thinks his intrusion saved the man's life. After the intrusion of
the two girls, however, he returns to the photographs, and to
get even larger blow-ups takes pictures of the pictures. In this
second removal from reality, the picture is so enlarged as to
have lost all its quality as photography, has become a kind of
coarse screen through which Hemmings sees the truth he is
looking for: a ghostly image in the shrubbery pointing a gun.

Hemmings returns to the park to look for evidence of murder, and Antonioni treats his repeated climb up the long steps
into the park with the feeling of a pilgrimage, the labor of a
quest, his progress through the night lighted by the neon
gleam of a large sign, which seems to say nothing but simply
registers its presence as a true sign, a primitive emblem casting
its light on this natural preserve and the vulgar cadaver it contains. The brittle skin and eyes of the corpse against the
greensward that is almost black in this night scene, is terribly
striking. Yet in spite of the darkness, the film preserves the
essential greenness of the park, a fitting backdrop for the scene
in which Hemmings has the reality of life brought home to
him by the reality of death. For the swinger whose life has
been one empty happening after another, at last something
has happened.

From here on, images of breakdown, emptiness and death
fill the screen: the shambles of Hemmings' studio as he returns
to it; the soulless hysteria at the soul-rock music performance
with its canned music, the breakdown of the electronic equipment, and the discarding of the broken phallus, the bridge
from the ineffectual musician's guitar; and the empty bliss at
the marihuana party, an urban reflection of the earlier rural
scene, as it were, everyone smoking "grass" and the same per-

fect tranquility with the same overtones of dangerous emptiness. Even the presence of death is carried forward by the
bust of that strangely incongruous 18th century gentleman,
standing solid and cadaverous amid the gently floating marihuana spirits. The help Hemmings is looking for is not to be
found, but apparently the consequences of his detached life
are not too hard to bear. Since his friends are too far gone to
help him, he takes the other alternative and joins them in their
night of escapism. But in the morning the memory of the
corpse must still haunt him, for he returns to confirm its presence and get some proof in the way of a photograph. By the
time he arrives, however, the body is gone. The evidence for
the reality he had encountered has now become invisible,
spiritualized, and the only issue remaining is if Hemmings
understands this and accepts it. The man who was looking for
freedom through money, and had reduced others to ciphers
in this formula, has now been engaged in bondage by—nothing
—by an experience whose tangible counters have vanished into
thin air.

Antonioni needed a very clear and unambiguous statement
to close the film, and he found it in the rag party that opened
the film. These gay celebrants, first seen roaring around the
Economist Plaza in quick-cut contrast with the silent vagrants
leaving the doss house, now come careening through the park
and stop at the tennis courts to play a mimed game of tennis.
Hemmings looks on with his customary detached interest,
compared to the painted and absorbed faces of the students as
they watch the make-believe ball batted back and forth by
two of their companions. It is a fascinating sequence, so well
done that we begin to believe in the invisible ball ourselves,
and when one of the players hits it over the fence and gestures
for Hemmings to return it, we are keenly in touch with this
dilemma whose solution will bring in the last bit of evidence
needed to close the film. Hemmings returns the imaginary
ball, and the game goes on. His new-found faith in that invisible ground for men's sharing is reinforced by the sound
track: the pock-pock of a tennis ball, like the sound of one
hand clapping. The mystery is complete; not a mystery to be
solved, but a mystery to be realized.

Bonnie and Clyde

Carolyn Geduld, "Bonnie and Clyde: Society vs. the Clan"

ooooooooooooooooooooooooooooooooooooooooooooooo

Arthur Penn's *Bonnie and Clyde* has been the most provocative, the most talked about American movie to come around in a long time. Active memories of the hero and heroine from the newspapers of the thirties has tended to escalate the infamy of the movie and also to heighten claims of its quality as a period film. Few have remained neutral, including the critics. While Pauline Kael, Andrew Sarris, and others spoke enthusiastically of the film as a great achievement in American film-making, Charles Samuels, writing in *The Hudson Review*, branded it as "a bunch of decayed cabbage leaves smeared with catsup" and, with intellectual vigor, stoutly condemned it for glamorizing violence. The mixed reaction to the film is epitomized in the complex of hostility and admiration that Joseph Morgenstern candidly revealed by reviewing *Bonnie and Clyde* in *Newsweek* as "a squalid shoot-'em up for the moron trade," then, only a week later, after reconsidering the film, found it thematically substantial and artistically subtle. Carolyn Geduld, being far less judgmental and hence much more dispassionate than the majority of commentators on the film, analyzes *Bonnie and Clyde* in the perspective of its affinities to two established movie genres—the domestic comedy and the "Jesse James" style Western—and also submits revealing insights into Arthur Penn's technique and purpose. Her analysis gives the moviegoer a fresh opportunity for re-evaluating the film.

OF THE MANY RECENT FILMS which have bridged the gap
between art and popular appeal, Arthur Penn's *Bonnie and
Clyde* has probably been the most controversial. The film has
been attacked for the wrong reasons, as, for example, by critics
who object to its association of crime and "fun"; while among
those more concerned with aesthetics than sociology, it has
been interpreted as a Hollywood response to the French "take
over" of American genres. Essentially, to such critics, *Bonnie
and Clyde* seems to be a Truffaut-Godard type parody of the
gangster film. However, a better case might be made for it as
a parody of the Western. But the impact of the film is to be
found not so much in its elements of parody as in its dramatic
shifts of mood between parody and horror. There is a clinical
fascination with shots of flesh being shattered by bullets, which
is heightened by the comic sequences preceding them—a use
of dramatic contrast seen before in *Italiano Bravo Gente.* If
the violent episodes are not a sort of gimmick inserted into
lighter sequences merely to "shake" the audience, they must be
justified in terms of the film's larger interests.

Basically, the ambivalence of the film originates in a narrative which combines domestic comedy with the "Jesse James"
style of Western. In the mood of the former, the emphasis is
on Bonnie and Clyde as "plain folk" who tell bad jokes, have
religious affiliations, sexual problems, and family reunions, and
who are, we are constantly reminded, "just like us." In the
mood of the Western, by contrast, they are "different," a
breed apart from the domestic involvements of society: the
Barrow gang who rob banks, kill, escape in stagecoach-cars,
rest in motel hideouts, and are eventually ambushed and shot
by the "posse." The two genres are, of course, antithetical.
Traditionally, the domestic comedy suggests that no matter
what insanity abounds, the family unit will prevail. In the
Blondie series, for instance, despite the threat of chaos and
anarchy, the structure of the household cannot be destroyed
and domestic values remain intact. In the "Jesse James" type
of Western, on the other hand, domestic values are subverted
or upset, and consequently, anything goes. The nomadic life

Bonnie and Clyde, directed by Arthur Penn, 1967 (*Warner Bros.-Seven Arts*)

itself seems inimical to permanence, and typically, the gang-on-the-run is destroyed by internal dissension: the unfaithful moll, the argument about division of the spoils, the struggle for power, the "squealer." Often the gang begins to dissolve when members are killed by their colleagues, long before the final ambush.

When, in *Bonnie and Clyde*, domestic comedy and the Western meet head on, rather like a mixture of *The Family Way* and *The Dalton Brothers*, the *expectation* of domestic integrity is confounded by the *reality* of the gang members' deaths. The audience is disturbed because—"them's folks what was killed," i.e., a "family," somehow alienated from the grandiose crimes they commit. The sense of foul play over the not very remarkable execution of two murders is, at basis, an expression of indignation at the punishment of the "family," which has, after all, upheld domestic values even if they did break society's larger taboos.

In this context, the opposition between the gang and the "law" can be thought of as the opposition between the clan and society: the primitive, rurally-based tribe and the urban-centered society which evolved out of it. And if sentiments are thrown to the clan in *Bonnie and Clyde*, for reasons which will be discussed later, in the traditional Western, society must kill the clan lest, as every schoolboy knows, the gang destroy the town (or society). Moreover, the bank which every gang aspires to rob is a symbol that gives the "game" away: implicit in the pooled wealth is the individual's agreement to give up his tribal allegiance by storing his valuables with society rather than with the "father" of the clan.

For the Barrow gang, robbing banks is "fun" precisely because they are a clan; they cannot feel guilty about breaking laws which, anthropologically speaking, postdate them. Instead, they are governed by their own domestic "rules" or better yet, by a modification of the primitive taboos of the archetypal clan described by Freud in *Totem and Taboo*: the prohibitions against incest and patricide. In films about Western outlaws, we notice a solidarity the "law" cannot touch until the primitive taboos are violated. Thus, the incest taboo is broken when the leader's moll is unfaithful, often with a lesser member of the gang. Patricide is attempted when a member tries to kill the leader in a bid for power, or to get the moll, or to receive a larger share of the spoils. Often the violation of these prohibitions leads directly to a change in allegiance from the clan to society when the "squealer" informs the "law" of the leader's whereabouts.

These gangland taboos are modified in *Bonnie and Clyde* by the domestic comedy "rules" imposed upon them. The prohibition against incest becomes a prohibition against sexuality —the hero's impotence forces him and his girl to live together like brother and sister. "I'm your family," Clyde tells Bonnie, who adds "I've no Mamma now." The Barrow brothers become a self-sufficient unit who take on the roles—not of lovers—but of the kin their women were forced to leave. Significantly, Blanche calls Buck "Daddy," transferring to her husband the tie she once had with her minister-father. Similarly, patricide is so inconceivable within the domestic setting that it must be turned into its opposite. Unlike the Western gang, whose members are often kept from violence only by the leader's forcefulness, Clyde, Buck, and Clyde's alter ego— C. W. Moss—throw *mock* punches, play checkers, and take each others' photographs. The prohibition against killing the father-leader evolves as filial affection in which brotherly love overcompensates for any remnants of the original hatred. Love and the absence of sexual provocation: these are the elements which keep the family intact in *Blondie* as well as in *Bonnie and Clyde*.

The car, in this context, is used not only to parody the horse and stagecoach of the Western, but also as the *container* which alienates the clan from society. In fact, it is only when the members of the gang leave the car, or open its door in Bonnie's case, that they are killed. Fundamentally, the car divides society into units of five or six people, and when it is in motion, there is no *verbal* means of communicating with the inhabitants—the cars of the Barrow gang have no radios, for instance. Thus they are far more effectively self-contained than in their motel rooms, where grocery boys can knock on the door. Because society's aim is to breach the small unit, the "law" tends to shoot at the car, at times, in preference to the gang itself, and thus, appropriately, one of the last shots in the film is a study of the bullet holes in the "dead" car.

In the end, Bonnie and Clyde die, not because they rob and murder but because they break the archetypal clan taboos and themselves dissolve their domestic solidarity. The agent of their "sin" is, specifically, the newspaper—society's representative. The Barrow gang's fatal mistake is to allow the newspaper into the car, a leverage for society which eventually destroys them. At first, the newspapers are treated as a joke— the Barrow gang laugh when accused of crimes they could not possibly commit. But the joke has soured by the time of Buck's death when an article hints that Clyde left his brother to die. Because the suggestion of fratricide (a nominal form of patricide) has an element of truth in it, Clyde gets angry at the newspaper, an indication that society has at last made its will felt. The taboo against sexuality, furthermore, is broken after Bonnie's poem is published in the newspaper. "You've made something out of me," Clyde says immediately before his first sexual contact with Bonnie. The *fact* of the poem's publication implies that the gang leader has accepted the social recognition which is inimical to domestic prohibitions. The final dissolution of the gang occurs, of course, when the "squealers"—C. W.'s father and Blanche—make personal contact with the "law," changing their allegiance from clan to society. In the attempt of C. W.'s father to get a mild sentence for his son and in Blanche's attempt to justify Buck, the clan's taboos are replaced by society's.

The meaning of Bonnie and Clyde's death is, then, a reaffirmation of society's right to preserve its own structure, *even* at the expense of the primitive (and "innocent") family integrity. The choice is given between the civilized, if brutal, town and the childlike, rustic "paradise," with the advantage always given to the former. In the film, the break-up of the clan is represented by the image of glass shattered. The opening shot of Bonnie's lips seen in a mirror is contrasted by the last shot of the car windows smashed by bullets. Significantly, glass is most often shattered by violence when the "law" confronts the gang—windows are broken, mirrors, windshields, and so forth. But the symbol is used both ways: the farmer whose property is confiscated by the bank (society) shoots the windows of his farmhouse in a largely ineffectual gesture of retribution. Here the puniness of the small man's (and the clan's) destructive intent is heightened in a contrast with the long panning shot of the town's intact glass storefronts, ending at the window of "Eva's Ice Cream Parlor"—the rendezvous of the "squealer" and the "law."

Arthur Penn's obsessive shots of glass are also evident in his playful use of sunglasses. The Greek punishment for the breaker of taboos, blindness, is used in the film in the literal blinding of Blanche (who wears dark glasses) and in the figurative blinding of Clyde, who is wearing *shattered* sunglasses when he dies. In fact, eyes, which are more or less the "windows" separating one human being from another, are especially important in the role of Clyde. Warren Beatty tells a truth with his eyes that is often antithetical to the less honest animation of his hands or to his words. Moreover, Clyde's "sense" of the "law," which often saves the gang, is really his ability to *sight* danger, an ability he forfeits when he wears the broken sunglasses. Blindness becomes the ultimate shattering of the fragile barrier between clan and society, a shattering which virtually means the death of the clan, and which began when their first victim was fatally blinded after being shot through a car window.

Like glass, the camera lens serves as a link between the clan and society. In photographs the Barrow gang assume the pretense of the threat society considers them, rather than the domestic innocents they represent within their own setting. For all the gang's mimicry in front of the camera, the lens records a truth beyond the local occasion: the danger of the small unit when its power is not absorbed by the large.

This danger was particularly felt in the 1930's, when banks failed and society threatened to disintegrate. The film's fascination with the fourth decade of this century is not merely a recreation of a "camp" era; it is fully justified in terms of the film's theme. Because of poverty, the natural barrier between society and the clan threatened to shatter in the Thirties. As the film emphasizes, people were forming tribal allegiances when the "law" failed them. The sequences involving Bonnie's family reunion and the squatters who give the gang water are shot as exteriors with no man-made structure in view—a return to the prenativity of civilization which is quite at odds with the highly developed towns and their huge glass storefronts. The new emergence of the small unit during the Depression has previously been best represented in films by the small man in the role of gangster—Paul Muni, James Cagney, Edward G. Robinson—but Arthur Penn's great achievement in *Bonnie and Clyde* is the use of the domestic comedy–Western as another way of expressing the tension between tribe and town. From this anthropological point of view, the film works beautifully, although its final critical success depends on the extent to which the psychological motivation of the characters coincides with the larger theme. The return of Clyde's potency, for instance, may be explained as the breaking of an archetypal taboo, but it is not quite believable in terms of the character Warren Beatty creates.

Nevertheless, the film's immediate impact suggests its relevance to the present: the 1960's will no doubt be remembered as the decade when urbanization back-fired: when society again threatened to break up into small units that periodically riot and loot and have "fun" doing so. The Barrow gang's closest counterpart today may perhaps be found in Negro ghettos, where local taboos have replaced social law and order.

Citizen Kane

Andrew Sarris, "Citizen Kane:
The American Baroque"

oooooooooooooooooooooooooooooooooooooooooooooooo

Made in 1941, *Citizen Kane* nonetheless belongs in this anthology of post-World War II films because of its inherent
merit and its revolutionary and pervasive influence on film-
making thereafter. Orson Welles violates dramatically the
classical conception of art as imitation, as verisimilitude,
thereby frustrating our sense of order, our expectation for a
story—a beginning, middle, and ending. He begins at the
ending, with the death of Kane; jumps to a newsreel sequence of Kane's historically documented past; establishes the
present tense of the film with a projection room scene;
and then, in discrete sequences that alternate between times
past and the present, relentlessly seeks to get behind the
façade of Kane's public record in order to detect the truth of
his inner reality. *Citizen Kane* is "By Orson Welles," and
indeed the film is very close to being the product of one
man's film art. With Herman J. Mankiewicz writing parts of
the scenario and Gregg Toland directing photography,
Welles produced, directed, wrote, and acted in *Citizen Kane*.

For quite some time there existed a residue of hostility
toward Welles for his anomalous indifference to the "box-office" demands of an industry in which artistic objectives
traditionally yield to financial objectives; and hence recognition of *Citizen Kane* as the work of the brilliant virtuoso
Orson Welles has been a dubious kind of praise. In his essay

"*Citizen Kane:* The American Baroque" Andrew Sarris attempts to critically confront the persistent and overt charges against the film which he reduces to three: "(1) its narrative structure is unduly complicated; (2) its technique calls attention to itself; (3) its intellectual content is superficial." His analysis of the appropriateness of the techniques Welles uses, such as the innovative use of deep-focus photography, runs parallel to the development of his argument that the film "presents an intense vision of American life, distorting and amplifying its materialistic elements at the expense of human potentialities." In conclusion Mr. Sarris states that "Kane emerges as an extension of the nouveau-riche American seeking a living culture in the dead relics of the past. Striving desperately to transcend his material worth, Kane is victimized by the power his wealth possesses to alter the moral quality of his actions. In the end, everything has been bought and paid for, but nothing has been felt."

———— • ————

THE RECENT REVIVAL of *Citizen Kane* has not elicited the kind of reappraisal the occasion demands. It is too easy to dismiss *Kane* as a great film with the smug confidence that everything that is to be said about it has already been said. If nothing else, the fifteen years that have elapsed since its initial release should provide a new perspective. The fact that *Citizen Kane* still seems to be ahead of its time is as much an indictment of contemporary film-making as it is a vindication of the classical quality of its art. Stripped of its personal and topical sensationalism, the film has risen above the capricious attacks leveled against it fifteen years ago.

A great deal of the hostility aroused by *Kane* back in 1941 was directed at its youthful creator, Orson Welles. Many of his enemies have since been appeased by the simple fact that Welles has joined the mortal herd by getting fifteen years older. Others have come to admire his dogged professionalism in the face of disastrously inadequate financing and even personal injury as demonstrated by his recent performance of

Citizen Kane, directed by Orson Welles, 1941 *(Janus)*|

Lear from a wheelchair. Yet, though tempered by adversity and voluntary exile, the spectacular Welles personality still obscures the more substantial aspects of his genius.

On a less personal level, *Citizen Kane* disappointed many who were caught up in the portentous political atmosphere of 1941. Advance publicity had prepared many liberals for a savage political attack on William Randolph Hearst, one of the most prominent enemies of the New Deal. *The Grapes of Wrath* and *The Great Dictator*, both released in 1940, had made their stands at the barricades. Welles himself had recently mounted an anti-fascist interpretation of *Julius Caesar* on the New York stage. The boycott of Welles and *Citizen Kane* by all Hearst publications further heightened the suspense that there would be a collision between the *enfant terrible* of the left and grand old man of the right.

When *Kane* finally appeared, it failed to justify all the ideological anticipation. Charles Foster Kane was not William Randolph Hearst in any "significant" sense. Welles and Herman J. Mankiewicz had merely borrowed biographical details, some virtually libelous, to fashion an intricate screenplay that posed a psychological mystery without advancing any cause.

After subtracting the criticism of the Welles personality and the criticism of the lack of ideology, all that is left and all that is relevant is the criticism of *Citizen Kane* as a work of art. To believe, as some do, that *Citizen Kane* is the great American film, it is necessary to produce an interpretation that answers some of the more serious objections to this film.

Citizen Kane has peculiar claims to greatness in that its distinctive merits are related to its alleged flaws. Adverse criticism of *Kane* is based mainly on three propositions: (1) its narrative structure is unduly complicated; (2) its technique calls attention to itself; (3) its intellectual content is superficial.

If any one of these propositions is fully accepted, *Kane* falls far short of greatness. At first glance, all three points have some validity. The narrative zig-zags and backtracks to its conclusion. The technique dazzles the eye and ear. No profound ideas are explicitly developed. A closer examination of the film, however, reveals an inner consistency of theme, structure, and technique. The implications of this consistency are crucial to any effective analysis of what *Citizen Kane* is really about.

Within the maze of its own aesthetic, *Kane* develops two interesting themes: the debasement of the private personality of the public figure, and the crushing weight of materialism. Taken together, these two themes comprise the bitter irony of an American success story that ends in futile nostalgia, loneliness, and death. The fact that the personal theme is developed verbally while the materialistic theme is developed visually creates a distinctive stylistic counterpoint. Against this counterpoint, the themes unfold within the structure of a mystery story.

Charles Foster Kane dies in a lonely castle. His last word is "*Rosebud.*" Who or what is *Rosebud?* This is the mystery of *Citizen Kane*. The detective is a reporter for a news service which produces *March of Time*-like newsreels. The suspects are all the persons and objects Kane encountered in his cluttered life. The clues are planted in the film on three occasions, but, unlike the conventional mystery key, *Rosebud* is the answer to a man's life rather than his death. And since the intangible meanings of life end in the mystery of death, *Rosebud* is not the final solution but only the symbolic summation.

Rosebud is the means through which the past history of Charles Foster Kane is penetrated by the reporter-detective and the omniscient camera. Time is thrown back and brought forward in the four major movements of the film, the flashback-recollections respectively of Kane's banker-guardian, his business manager, his best friend, and his second wife. Each major flashback begins at a later point in time than its predecessor, but each flashback overlaps with at least one of the others so that the same event or period is seen from two or three points of view.

There is a fifth flashback—a newsreel of Kane's public career—which establishes the identity of Charles Foster Kane for the first time in the film. There is no transition between the opening scene of a man dying in a lonely castle with *Rosebud* on his lips and the startling appearance of the unframed newsreel. This is the first shock effect in *Citizen Kane*, and it has received undeserved abuse as a spectacularly devious method of narration. What has been generally overlooked is the great economy of this device in establishing the biographical premises of the film without resorting to traditional montages of public reactions and telescoped historical events in the major movements of the story.

By isolating the newsreel from the main body of his film, Welles frees his flashbacks from the constricting demands of exposition, enabling his main characters to provide insights on the external outlines of the Kane biography. After the newsreel, the transitions are worked out very carefully through the logical movements of the reporter-detective. This shadowy, though thoroughly professional, character links the present to the past in an interlocking jigsaw puzzle with one elusive piece—*Rosebud*—appearing only at the very end in the reporter's absence since his services are no longer needed.

The newsreel accomplishes more than a skeletal public biography of Charles Foster Kane. On a narrative level, it introduces Mr. Thatcher, Kane's banker-guardian, whose memoirs will provide the first personal flashback of Kane's life and the first significant clue to *Rosebud*. The newsreel also produces a paradox that previsions the non-political quality of the film. While Thatcher is telling a Committee that Kane is a Communist, a speaker in Union Square attacks Kane as a Fascist. The elderly Kane tells newsreel audiences that he is and always has been an American. This is the first indication that Kane is not really committed to any cause but Kane.

The newsreel fades out; a sudden establishing shot picks up a darkened projection room. The first of the many disembodied voices in the film calls out from the darkness, and the shadow plot of *Citizen Kane* begins. A group of cynical newsmen discuss ways of pepping up the newsreel. The reporter is sent out to find the secret of *Rosebud*. The semi-colloquial dialogue is driven forth with relentless persistence from every direction. There is nothing profound or witty about any of it but it moves quickly and economically.

The reporter begins his search and the major movements of

Citizen Kane begin. Through a hard, wide-angle lens, the reporter enters a cavernous museum, a dingy nightclub, a solidly upholstered office, a drab hospital ward, the gloomy mansion of Charles Foster Kane. The reporter's world is functional, institutional; an aging, weathered gateway to the life and time of Charles Foster Kane.

The sixth and last flashback of *Citizen Kane* offers the final clue to *Rosebud* and brings the reporter's quest to its unsuccessful conclusion. Interestingly enough, the three clues to *Rosebud* appear at times when Kane is being treated most remotely—in the cryptic death scene in the beginning, in the unfriendly memoirs of his banker-guardian, and in the final flashback narration of a cynical butler. The narrations of his closest acquaintances yield no clues to the symbolic truth of his life. This is the ultimate confirmation of Kane's spiritual loneliness, and it is upon this loneliness that the mystery structure of the film is based.

The mystery of *Rosebud* is solved in a memorable manner. The reporter and his entourage have departed from the Kane castle. As the cynical butler is directing the disposal of Kane's "junk" into the furnace, a workman picks up a sled in routine haste and dumps it into the flames. The camera closes in on the surface of the sled and the name *Rosebud* as the letters are dissolving in liquid fire. The audience is given the solution with the added knowledge that no one living on the screen will ever know the secret of *Rosebud*.

This solution has been attacked as a trick ending unworthy of its theme. Yet without this particular resolution, the film would remain a jumbled jigsaw puzzle. The burning sled is apt not only as a symbolic summation but as a symbolic revelation. The reporter, the butler, the workman, the friends, the enemies, the acquaintances of Kane never discover *Rosebud* because it is lost amid the "junk" of Kane's materialistic existence.

Kane's tragedy lies in the inability of the props of experience to compensate for the bare emotional stage of his human relationships. Charles Foster collected valuable treasures from all over the world, but his last thoughts were of a sled he used as a boy before great wealth came into his life. At one point in the film, he tells his banker-guardian that he might have been a great man if he had not been so wealthy. *Rosebud* became the focal point of his nostalgia for a different turning point in his life. Kane's view of his own life is deterministic, and Kane's image throughout the film is remarkably consistent with this sense of determinism.

The apparent intellectual superficiality of *Citizen Kane* can be traced to the shallow quality of Kane himself. Even when Kane is seen as a crusading journalist battling for the lower classes, overtones of stiff self-idolatry mar his actions. His clever ironies are more those of the exhibitionist than the crusader. His best friend—a detached observer functioning as a sublimated conscience—remarks to the reporter that Kane never gave anything away: "he left you a tip." His second wife complained that Kane never gave her anything that was part of him, only material possessions that he might give a dog. His business adviser and life-long admirer expressed the other side of Kane's personality when he observed that Kane wanted something more than money.

In each case, Kane's character is described in materialistic terms. What Kane wanted—love, emotional loyalty, the unspoiled world of his boyhood symbolized by *Rosebud*—he was unable to provide to those about him, or buy for himself. It is therefore fitting that the story of Kane should begin with his lonely death and conclude with the immolation of his life symbol.

The technique of Welles and his photographer, Gregg Toland, justifies the narrative structure. Apparently outrageous effects fall into place once the pattern of the film is discernible. *Kane* opens on a solid wire fence with a sign reading "No Trespassing." The camera moves up on a painted castle against a background of dark, brooding clouds. The same shots are repeated in reverse at the very end of the film. This initial and concluding clash of realism and expressionism flanks one of the most stylistically varied of all films.

The opening shots have been attacked as pretentious and the closing shots as anticlimactic. Yet, in a subtle way, the beginning and end of *Citizen Kane* suggests its theme. The intense material reality of the fence dissolves into the fantastic unreality of the castle and, in the end, the mystic pretension of the castle dissolves into the mundane substance of the fence. Matter has come full circle from its original quality to the grotesque baroque of its excess.

As each flashback unfolds, the visual scenario of *Citizen Kane* orchestrates the dialogue. A universe of ceilings dwarfs Kane's personal stature. He becomes the prisoner of his possessions, the ornament of his furnishings, the fiscal instrument of his collections. His booming voice is muffled by walls, carpets, furniture, hallways, stairs, and vast recesses of useless space.

Toland's camera set-ups are designed to frame characters in the oblique angles of light and shadow created by their artificial environment. There are no luminous close-ups in which faces are detached from their backgrounds. When characters move across rooms, the floors and ceilings move with them, altering the points of reference but never transcending them. This technique draws attention to itself both because it is so unusual and because it tends to dehumanize characters by reducing them to fixed ornaments in a shifting architecture.

Sound montage is used intensively within the flashbacks to denote the interval of time within two related scenes. A character will begin a sentence and complete it weeks, months or years later in a different location. On occasion, one character will begin the sentence and another will complete it in the same manner. This device results in a constriction of time and an elimination of transitional periods of rest and calm. Aside from the aesthetic dividends of pacing and highlighting, *Kane's* sound montage reinforces the unnatural tension of the central character's driving, joyless ambition. In all respects, *Kane's* technique is a reflection and projection of the inhuman quality of its protagonist.

One brilliant use of sound montage that has generally been ignored as a piece of aural gargoyle is the piercing scream of a parakeet that precedes the last appearance of Kane in the film. One flashback and several scenes previously, Kane and his second wife are arguing in a tent surrounded by hundreds of Kane's picnic guests. A shrill scream punctuates the argument with a persistent, sensual rhythm. It is clear that some sexual outrage is being committed. When the parakeet screams at the appearance of Kane, the sound linkage in tone but not in time further dehumanizes Kane's environment. In the baroque world that he has created, Kane is isolated from even the most dubious form of humanity.

Kane's lack of humanity is consistently represented in the performance of Orson Welles, who alters the contours of Kane's rigidity from youth to old age. As a young man, Kane is peculiarly joyless. A gala occasion is recalled in which Kane threw a party for his new writers hired away from a competing newspaper. A group of chorus girls come on the scene. Kane is thrown in their midst and begins cutting up. The scene is heavy with Kane's studied posturing as the life of the party.

The acting in *Kane* emerges as an elaborate arabesque of interrupted conversations, harsh dissonances, and awkward physical confrontations. Kane's world, peopled by Mercury Players, is tuned to the egocentric performance of Welles. Joseph Cotten, Everett Sloane, and Dorothy Comingore, as Kane's best friend, business adviser, and second wife, respectively, and the main narrators of the film, achieve a strident rapport with the demanding presence of Welles. The intense pitch of the acting charges each line of dialogue with unexpected meanings. The manner of expression often alters the verbal content toward a new level of self-conscious cynicism. In this, the acting evokes the intentional hypocrisy of the few protestations of principle that appear in the script.

Towards the end of his life, Kane reacts to the desertion of his second wife by wrecking the furniture in her room. Again, his violent actions are rigidly controlled by a chilling self-awareness. As he is completing his unduly methodical havoc, he comes upon a crystal paper-weight in which a minute snow storm beats down on a miniature cottage. He speaks the name of *Rosebud* and walks past an array of guests across the path of endless mirrors and endless reflections of his image—mere repetitions of his ego without magnification. This is the final arithmetic of Kane's life, the last material accounting of his greatness.

Citizen Kane presents an intense vision of American life, distorting and amplifying its materialistic elements at the expense of human potentialities. The implied absence of free will in the development of Kane's character is thematically consistent with the moral climate of his environment. Kane's magnitude, unchecked by limiting principles or rooted traditions, becomes the cause of his spiritual ruin. Kane emerges as an extension of the nouveau-riche American seeking a living culture in the dead relics of the past. Striving desperately to transcend his material worth, Kane is victimized by the power his wealth possesses to alter the moral quality of his actions. In the end, everything has been bought and paid for, but nothing has been felt.

Dr. Strangelove

Robert Brustein, "Out of This World"

○○

Stanley Kubrick's *Dr. Strangelove, or: How I Learned to Stop Worrying and Love the Bomb* (1963) is a rare moment in the history of films because it is a rare moment in the history of the art of satire. It is comedy that is not an end in itself: it mockingly raises the specter of what is most horrible, of what is tragic; like Pope's *Dunciad*, it is a vision of universal chaos. With the exception of Peter Watkins' *War Games*, a thoroughly unpalatable document, *Dr. Strangelove*—as nothing else has, serious or comic—uncompromisingly holds up to the mirror of reality the depth of our idiocy about and fear of the bomb. Robert Brustein in "Out of This World" discusses the film as purgation and analyzes the range, sources, and effects of its satiric elements. He concludes that "*Dr. Strangelove* is a work of comic anarchy, fashioned by a totally disaffected and disaffiliated imagination . . . it also releases, through comic poetry, those feelings of impotence and frustration that are consuming us all; and I can't think of anything more important for an imaginative work to do." Although Mr. Kubrick has said that Mr. Brustein's essay is the one he would like to see get most prominence, he also enjoyed reading a discerning interpretation of the film that appeared in *Film Comment* (Summer, 1965). In "Sex and *Dr. Strangelove*" F. Anthony Macklin points out "how *Dr. Strangelove* is a sex allegory: from foreplay to explosion in the mechanized world."

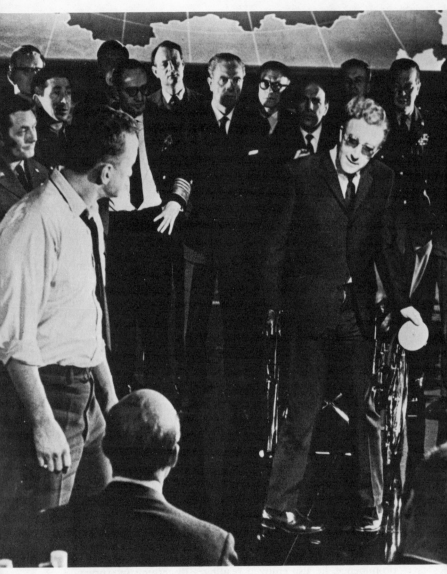

Dr. Strangelove, or: How I Learned to Stop Worrying and Love the Bomb, directed by Stanley Kubrick, 1963 (*The Museum of Modern Art/Film Stills Archive*)

Dr. Strangelove possesses a great many distinctions as a work of the imagination, but I should like to cite it, first and foremost, for valor: I think it may well be the most courageous movie ever made. It is certainly one of the funniest. A nightmare farce which proceeds from horror to horror, culminating in the annihilation of the human race after an American hydrogen bomb has been dropped on Russia, it is, despite its cataclysmic conclusion, a peculiarly heady, exhilarating experience. I can account for this partially by the fact that the movie pays absolutely no deference at all to the expectations of its audience. Artistic courage always soothes the spirit and makes glad the heart, but when this quality enters as craven a medium as the American film one feels curiously exalted, ineffably happy. Then, too, there is something extraordinarily liberating in the nature of the movie itself. It is the kind of total theater that Antonin Artaud would have admired, with its dark humor, its physical and anarchic dissociation. *Dr. Strangelove* is a plague experienced in the nerves and the funny bone—a delirium, a conflagration, a social disaster.

What Stanley Kubrick has done is to break completely with all existing traditions of moviemaking, both foreign and domestic. While the European art film seems to be inexorably closing in on the spiritual lassitude of certain melancholy French or Italian aristocrats, *Dr. Strangelove* invests the film medium with a new exuberance, expansiveness, and broadness of vision; compared with the sweep of this masterpiece, the weary meanderings of Resnais, Fellini, and Antonioni seem solipsistic and self-indulgent. Moreover, Kubrick's film is fun—this is its one debt to Hollywood. It is enjoyable for the way it exploits the exciting narrative conventions of the Hollywood war movie—say, *Air Force* or *Thirty Seconds Over Tokyo*—and even more, for the way it turns these conventions upside down, and cruelly scourges them. This is what is arrestingly new about the film: its wry, mordant, destructive, and, at the same time, cheerful, unmoralistic tone. We have heard this sound emanating from our comic novels, cabaret acts, satiric revues, living rooms, and dreams, but, although it rumbled a little bit under the conventional noises of *The Manchurian Candidate*, it has never before fully entered the mass media. With *Dr. Strangelove*, a subterranean vibration becomes a series of earthquakes, shattering cultural platitudes, political pieties, and patriotic ideals with fierce, joyous shocks. If the picture manages to remain open, it will knock the block off every ideologue in the country: even now, I suspect, Sidney Hook is preparing the first of fifteen volumes in rebuttal.

To avoid a repetition of Mr. Hook's embarrassing performance on behalf of *Fail-Safe*, where he wrote some eighty-odd pages of closely reasoned, technical argumentation to refute the premise of a cheap, best-selling fantasy, let me announce that *Dr. Strangelove* is frankly offered to the audience as a cinematic sick joke, and that it is based less on verifiable facts than on unconscious terrors. The film's source, a prototype for *Fail-Safe*, is Peter George's *Red Alert*, but the film writers have employed the novel very loosely, and the director has imposed on the finished screen play his own style and purpose. This style is Juvenalian satire; this purpose, the evacuation of fear and anger through the acting out of frightful fantasies. Kubrick has flushed a monster from its psychic lair—the universal fear of nuclear accident—and then proceeded to feed and nourish it, letting it perform its worst before your eyes. The consequence of this spectacle is, as the subtitle suggests, a temporary purgation: to witness the end of the world as a comic event is, indeed, to stop worrying and to love the Bomb.

The outline of the film is this: a psychotic right-wing general, convinced that the Communists are poisoning Americans through fluoridation, exercises emergency powers and sends a wing command to bomb the Soviet Union. The President, trying to recall these bombers, learns that the Russians have perfected a deterrent, a Doomsday machine, which is automatically triggered to explode the moment a bomb is dropped on Soviet soil, spreading a shroud of fall-out over the earth for a hundred years. After the general's base has been destroyed by American forces, and the recall code has been found, both nations cooperate to bring the bombers back or shoot them down. One damaged plane, however, its radio inoperative, manages to continue on to target. Through the invincible doggedness of the pilot and his crew, a hydrogen bomb is dropped on a Soviet missile complex—and apocalypse follows.

Kubrick handles this external action with ruthless documentary realism. The battle scenes, for example, which show Americans slaughtering Americans, are photographed through a gray morning mist (the same smoky tones so effectively used in Kubrick's *Paths of Glory*) with a hand camera shaken by artillery explosions; and the flight of the bomber over Arctic wastes is a terrifying journey into the frozen unknown. At the same time, however, Kubrick is evoking savage ironies through the conjunction of unexpected images and sounds: the bomber, for example, proceeds to its destination (and to the destruction of the world) over a chorus of male voices humming "When Johnny Comes Marching Home."

The same blend of farce and nightmare is found in other scenes. During the credits, a B-52 bomber is fueled in the air through a phallic hose, while the sound track plays "Try a Little Tenderness." A looming shot of two monstrous hydrogen bombs, triggered and ready to go, reveals two scrawled messages on them, "Hi There!" and "Dear John." And the epilogue is composed of a series of nuclear explosions (a sequence borrowed, I suspect, from a similar filmed skit used in *The Establishment*), which flower soundlessly while a female voice croons "We'll meet again (don't know where, don't know when)."

What these images suggest is that our heroic postures and patriotic reflexes have become hideously inappropriate to modern weaponry—the same thing is illustrated by the conduct of the crew on the lethal bomber. Kubrick has sardonically included among these crew members the various ethnic stereotypes of Hollywood war movies: a Negro bombardier, a Jewish radio operator, a Texas pilot, etc., all of whom behave, in crisis, according to preconditioned movie patterns— they engage in sexual banter, become comradely, grow steely grim and fighting mad. When the order is received to proceed over enemy territory and drop the bomb, the Texas pilot,

Major "King" Kong, takes off his helmet, puts on a ten-gallon hat, assumes an unctuous leader-of-men speaking style, and delivers an inspirational lecture to the crew about their duty to "the folks back home," while promising them all decorations, "regardless of your race, color or creed." When the plane is hit by a missile, he keeps it in action, flying low over jutting peaks; and when the bomb doors stick, he courageously climbs into the bomb bay, determined to fix the short circuit and complete his mission.

Kong finally clears the doors, and goes sailing down to target on the back of a bomb, waving his hat and whooping like a rebel. American heroism has become completely identified with American lunacy. So has American know-how—it is almost a structural principle of this film that our technology is wholly mad. Inside the bomber, for example, the camera peeks into complicated equipment and technical apparati—the instrument panel, the radar, the navigator's gear, the auto-destruct mechanism—all efficiently manipulated by this trained crew to create havoc and mass slaughter. The President's War Room, similarly, with its huge locating charts, is a model of gleaming competence and quiet decorum ("You can't fight in here," says the President to two dissidents, "this is the War Room"). Even the telephone works as an obstacle to survival. In one hilarious sequence, a British officer—having discovered the recall code—is trying to phone Washington with only minutes to go; but he lacks the necessary change, and the Pentagon will not accept collect calls.

If our technology is mad, however, then so are the technicians who create, control, and operate it. *Dr. Strangelove* is a satire not only on nuclear war and warriors, but also on scientists, militarists, military intellectuals, diplomats, statesmen —all those in short, whose profession it is to think about the unthinkable. Thus, the movie contains a large number of superb caricatures, all treated either as knaves or fools, but still recognizable as familiar American types.

These include two sharp profiles of General Walker-like military men: General Jack D. Ripper, played by Sterling Hayden in another of his stiff, interesting non-performances—

his eyes fanatically narrowed, his teeth clenched on a huge cigar, as he drawls to an aide about how he confines himself to pure alcohol and rain water and refrains from sexual intercourse to protect his natural essences against the Communist conspiracy; and General Buck Turgidson, Air Force Chief of Staff, played by George C. Scott in a fine frenzy of muscle-flexing pugnacity—stuffing his mouth with wads of chewing gum, and flashing an evil smile as he outlines his plan to obliterate the "commie punks" entirely ("I'm not saying we wouldn't get our hair mussed, Mr. President, but I do say not more than ten to twenty million dead depending on the breaks").

Then, there are three magnificent satiric sketches by Peter Sellers: Group Captain Mandrake, Ripper's befuddled British aide; President Merkin Muffley, a bald, bland, liberal Chief Executive, educated and slightly effeminate (a *merkin* according to the OED, is a "female pudendum," while *muffley* is an obsolete word for a pubic wig); and, finally, that eerie figure from the Bland Corporation, the German scientist, Dr. Strangelove.

Strangelove (formerly *Merkwuerdigichliebe*) is the most masterly character in the film, a composite portrait of Edward Teller, Werner von Braun, and Herman Kahn, played by Sellers with an excess of mischief, and conceived by Kubrick in an excess of fury. Imprisoned in a wheelchair, his mechanical hand gloved in black, his face fixed in a perpetual smile, he stares through dark glasses and sibilates through false teeth, suggesting emotion only through a slight emphasis on certain phrases, the word *human* being particularly distasteful to him. Strangelove is the perfect synthetic man, and he comes to us by courtesy of a Universal horror movie. In his person, the Mad Doctor and the State Scientist merge—Boris Karloff with a computer, calculating the proper use of deterrents and the half-life of cobalt-thorium–G.

This is extravagant enough, but towards the end, Strangelove goes completely haywire. So does the movie, as if Kubrick, having breathed the air of the outer limits for the first time, were suffering from stratospheric drunkenness. The

bomb has been dropped; the doomday shroud is beginning to
smother all life on earth; and Strangelove is outlining his plan
for preserving "a nucleus of human specimens" at the bottom
of mine shafts. His explanation is disarmingly rational but his
mechanical hand has gone out of control. It shoots up in a
Nazi salute, it punches him on the jaw, it strangles him, and
finally it propels him right out of his wheelchair—whereupon
he screams at the President, "*Mein Fuehrer*, I can walk!" The
lunatic inappropriateness of the remark somehow sums up all
the lunatic inappropriateness of the theatrics and celluloid
heroics that have preceded it; and it makes the devastation that
follows seem singularly fitting and just.

Dr. Strangelove is a work of comic anarchy, fashioned by a
totally disaffected and disaffiliated imagination: it is thus the
first American movie to speak truly for our generation. Kubrick has managed to explode the right-wing position without
making a single left-wing affirmation: the odor of the Thirties,
which clung even to the best work of Chaplin, Welles, and
Huston, has finally been disinfected here. Disinfected, in fact,
is the stink of all ideological thinking. For although *Dr.
Strangelove* is about a political subject, its only politics is outrage against the malevolence of officialdom. Conservatives will
find it subversive, liberals will find it irresponsible, utopians
will find it bleak, humanitarians will find it inhuman—*Dr.
Strangelove* is all these things. But it also releases, through
comic poetry, those feelings of impotence and frustration that
are consuming us all; and I can't think of anything more important for an imaginative work to do.

La Dolce Vita

Norman N. Holland, "The Follies Fellini"

ooooooooooooooooooooooooooooooooooooooooooooooo

Norman N. Holland's analysis of *La Dolce Vita* suggests strongly that a dominant strain in Fellini's imagination, from the earliest to the latest films, is the obsession with mythologizing humanity (see Edouard de Laurot's "*La Strada:* A Poem on Saintly Folly," which gives credence to this view). That *La Dolce Vita* is a study in modern decadence is sufficiently evident; yet Fellini's creative energy is rarely if ever put to the service of satire or ideology. He is an artist for whom imagination renders up artistic ideas and inventions freely and abundantly. In an interview with Gideon Bachmann, commenting on the making of *La Dolce Vita*, Fellini said:

> I just thought of it as a vast fresco—I saw it this shape [carving a Cinemascope screen out of the air with his hands] and then gradually characters and incidents emerged to fill it out, but several sequences, such as the "miracle" and the orgy, were almost entirely improvised in the course of shooting. I like to keep my mind open as far as possible to the miraculous gifts the world may bring: a face, a building, even a piece of clothing—look, that dress over there [pointing across the room], the green of it, the way it falls in three folds—that might be the germ of a whole sequence, a whole film. . . .

La Dolce Vita, directed by Federico Fellini, 1959 (*The Museum of Modern Art/Film Stills Archive*)

Fellini manipulates actors and decor to poetically concretize his viscerally felt—very unphilosophical, yet very compelling —vision of a distraught humanity, its dreams and reality. Mr. Holland probes many of the images in the film that are of seeing and hearing which, he argues, parallel and reinforce the setting off of men against women: "The women are goddesses, mythical, unreal *belles dames sans merci,* the sight of whom bewitches men into a kingdom of improvisation and illusion. Man is impotent, helpless; Marcello's dying father or Steiner, with his sounds and language, frozen, turned into stone by the fixity of his life. . . . Marcello, Everyman, is caught between these two alternatives, male and female, his mistress vainly seeking to play the role of goddess and petrify him into matrimony."

———————◆———————

THREE-HOUR, THREE-MILLION GROSS, triple-goddessed, Church-banned, myth-packed, and Totalscoped, *La Dolce Vita* amazes indeed the very faculty of eyes and ears. Eyes and ears are not just the targets, though, but recurring symbols for what author-director Fellini has on his mind. His protagonist, Marcello, is a reporter and would-be novelist, a man questing (admittedly, rather ineffectively) after truth in the form of sounds and language. Indeed, at one point, Marcello rather shame-facedly mumbles something of the sort. As against this basic stance for sound and language, Fellini shows his people pre-occupied with seeing, most obviously in the form of the ubiquitous *papparazzi,* the photographers who contrast with the verbal reporter Marcello—they swarm about virtually everyone and everything as though Sartre's flies had been out-fitted with flash cameras. Images of seeing and being seen run all through the film, as, for example, the sunglasses everybody wears. (If *It Happened One Night* ruined the men's undershirt industry, surely *La Dolce Vita* will turn prescription sunglasses into a major consumer item.) Sights in *La Dolce Vita* are mostly Ziegfeldian sights of women, culminating in Nadia Gray's striptease in the final party, but represented earlier, for example, by the pictures of female ancestors in the "haunted castle" sequence, the sight of the magnificently pneumatic Anita Ekberg, or the non-miraculous non-sight of the Virgin Mary in the televised "fake miracle."

Against these images of seeing and being seen, Fellini poises fewer, but far more striking, images of hearing. At the home of Steiner, Marcello's intellectual friend, we hear folk songs and poetry and a tape recording of the sounds of nature; conversation reigns supreme. Steiner himself had earlier gone into a church to practise the Toccata and Fugue in D Minor—after the rock 'n roll and other raucous cacophonies, you can almost feel the Bach soothe your ear. At one point, Marcello retires to the seashore to renew his work on the Great Italian Novel; he cannot write for the loudness of the song, from a jukebox played by a virginal blonde waitress he calls an "Umbrian angel." The song is "Patricia," which Fellini presses into service later as the music for the striptease; like the Bach, it, too, is played on an organ. The music of the film parodies itself, and the point of Fellini's images of sound seems to be that they fail. It was, of all people, Robinson Crusoe (though he was surely not the first) who pointed out that sound and language are the means by which human beings can achieve more than an animal relation with each other. Sound and language in *La Dolce Vita*, however, seem always to fail to create such a relationship. In the "haunted castle" sequence, Maddalena, one of Marcello's light o' loves, seats him in a room and goes outside to talk to him through a speaking-tube arrangement (a kind of "ear of Dionysius"). In the only serious moment of their relationship, we *hear* her propose marriage to him; we *see* her giving herself to another man.

The opening and closing bits (they are scarcely episodes) frame this recurring contrast of sight and sound. The opening (already, in the two fast years since the film was released, a classic among openings) shows a gilt image of Christ helicopter-borne over the Eternal City, which Fellini renders as a vast flux of running children and rising buildings; a second helicopter follows, carrying reporter Marcello and his photographer sidekick, apparently fishing for a story. Beneath them, they see a far more gripping sight than the Second, airborne,

Coming: four girls in bikinis sunbathing on a roof. As the helicopter hovers overhead, Marcello tries to speak to them, but they cannot hear one another over the noise of the chopper. The pattern is: the sight of a symbol; the sight of woman; the failure of sound. In the final shots, Marcello and assorted sodomites, usurers, grifters, and fornicators from the striptease party drift down to the sea (in shots reminiscent of Botticelli). At the sea's edge, some fishermen pull up a huge devilfish, and the camera closes in on its still-staring eye. As Marcello turns to go, the "Umbrian angel" appears on the shore nearby, but there is water between them, and though he sees her and she him, they cannot hear each other for the sound of the waves. He shrugs indifferently and leaves; she turns to watch him go. In a brilliant cinematic touch, Fellini pans the camera as she turns so that the final shot is an extreme close-up of the Umbrian angel staring out at the audience—or us staring at her: the audience has become image, and the image is the audience.

The rough beast from the sea, with its overtones of the birth of some mute and nameless horror from the depths of the unconscious, has provoked a good deal of speculation. Surely the most ingenious suggestion is *Sight and Sound*'s, that it represents Wilma Montesi. [Her body was found on an Italian beach; the press speculated that police were covering up for wealthy persons who seemed to be involved.] *Time*, following its current mythy bent, argues for the beast of the Apocalypse rising up out of the sea, the devilfish as antichrist; the opening bit is the Second Coming, and the film as a whole becomes an allegory of the seven nights of destruction in Revelation (the interpretation would be stronger if the film did not cover eight nights). Others have suggested an allegory on the *Inferno* with Marcello as Dante, his downward spiral through the sins of contemporary Rome culminating in the ninth circle with the devilfish as Lucifer, complete with three jellyfish dangling from his mouth. *La Vita Nuova* or the *canzonieri* [Dante's love lyrics] might be relevant to a film which so stresses the image of woman.

All are possible—what is not possible is to see *La Dolce Vita*

as "in the main a study of sexual manners," as simply "a
sensational presentation of certain aspects of life in contemporary Rome." Some critics want to impose on one Italian,
Fellini, the *neo-realismo* of other Italians. Behind this kind of
mis-seeing lies a nationalistic view of the film as simply the
expression of a particular time and place; also a notion of the
film like that of Siegfried Kracauer, the film as non-art, as
"the redemption of the real," a view which values in a film
only its formal realism. Fellini let himself in for the kind of
mis-seeing by basing the public episodes of *La Dolce Vita* on
items reported in the Italian press. He is, of course, formally
realistic, but that is not the important fact, any more than the
trappings of realism (non-professional actors, for example)
pasted on the sentimental plots of *Bicycle Thief* or *Umberto D.*
prevent those films from being as saccharine as O. Henry.
De Sica is still a sentimentalist, and Fellini still a mythmaker.

La Dolce Vita seems more tied to reality than Fellini's
earlier work, but only "seems." It really has that same strange
hankering after myth as his other films. His script for *The
Miracle* reached essentially toward the traditional mating in
the fields of sun-god and mortal woman. *The White Sheik*
with its horseplay on different kinds of hats balanced the
impotent male of church and marriage against the absurdly
sexual male of the *fumetti* [comic strips] (visual images again).
I Vitelloni constitutes a parody of the whole male pantheon,
while, in *Le notti di Cabiria*, a tawdry and pathetic image of
Venus renews herself in water after venal Adonises have
chosen and abused her. *La Strada* is the clearest of them all,
a classic *agon* [conflict] between *eiron* [the self-deprecator]
and *alazon* [the impostor] over a (more or less) mute woman
that could have come straight out of Cornford's *Origins of
Attic Comedy*. *La Dolce Vita* has the same theme and mythic
dimension as the others, men overpowered physically, morally,
or psychologically by the gorgon-like image of woman. As
Steiner says, "I am only this tall," and he holds up his finger.
In the "fake miracle" (an earlier form of which appeared in
Cabiria), an old woman gives us the tip-off. As the television
cameras and photographers close in on the two children who

have been gulled into saying they saw the Virgin, the crone says, "What does it matter whether it was the Virgin or not? Italy is full of strange cults." And indeed Fellini's Italy is.

The first one we see, the first full eposide in the film, is a kind of temple prostitution. The gilt Christ of the opening shots dissolves into the mute sinuosities of a gilt Siamese dancer in a night club where Marcello picks up a rich nymphomaniac, Maddalena (and the name, I take it, is not without significance). They ride off in her white Caddy convertible, boredly pick up a prostitute, and drive her home. Fellini goes out of his way to make them go out of theirs, go underground to the prostitute's basement apartment, cross the waters of her flooded basement, and there, in this doubtful chthonic sanctum, make love.

The second is the advent through the air from another land of an Aphrodite Pandemos, Anita Ekberg, cast as a Hollywood love-goddess, Sylvia (again, the name is not without significance). Ritually, she is offered the fruits of the Roman fields (in the form of a giant pizza); then, in a hilarious press conference, she is consulted as an oracle. During the day, she bounds up the endless stairs to the top of St. Peter's, dressed in a parody of a priest's gown. The true aphroditic rituals, however, took place on the tops of mountains or in caves, and that night, bobbling out of her evening gown, Sylvia leads a revel through the Baths of Caracalla, complete with rock 'n roll Orpheus and a faun in the form of a goatish American actor on whose shoulders she rides. "Why, Federico," Miss Ekberg is said to have remarked during the filming of these sequences, "you are making a fool of me." Despite this insight, Miss Ekberg can take comfort in the fact that Fellini was also making her a goddess. In some rituals, her celestial prototype did indeed ride a goat, and Marcello tells her she is mother, mistress, wife, home, "everything." They ride off in his Triumph, where he makes the old college try, but cannot find a place to go. (Throughout the film, blondes are unattainable—or at least unattainable by Marcello—unlike the brunettes, for example, Maddalena.) Our pandemotic love-goddess, however, seems (again, like Aphrodite) concerned as much with mothering animals as with mothering Marcello; anyway, she howls like a dog on a mountaintop, and in an exquisite sequence picks up a stray white kitten and, holding it before her like a monstrance, glides through the narrow corridors of midnight streets. She strides into the Trevi fountain; Marcello follows: "You're right—I'm on the wrong track—we all are." She puts water on his hair in a mock baptism, and to cap the parody, just then the fountain is turned off. They return to her hotel, where her opposite number, Lex Barker as a dipsoid American actor, awaits them, another mythic figure: "To think he once played Tarzan," sighs a *papparazzo*.

There are other "goddesses"—the missing Virgin Mary in the fake miracle; at Steiner's house, an old artist cries the praises of Oriental women, notably Mother Eve. In the haunted castle sequence, Maddalena standing before a row of matrilinear portraits puts a veil over her face; Marcello seduces a mysterious other worldly "Lady Jane" with streaks in her hair like antennae: the ghosts, nighttime, the cemetery, the surrounding plutocracy give the whole episode a persephonic aura. Finally, of course there is the "Umbrian angel," the virgin by the sea, image of a renewal and innocence, a kind of Aphrodite Urania, whom Marcello cannot accept.

In this matriarchal world, men become mere consorts, lover-kings, ridiculous, impotent. The clearest case is Marcello's father who turns up just before the necrotic haunted-castle sequence. An aging lecher, he gets his son to take him to an old-fashioned night-club, where the walls glitter like a temple's and everywhere there are statues of women. During the conversation, we find he was usually away from home, rather a philanderer and a wine merchant, indeed, "sold wine all up and down Italy." Playing vanishing parlor-tricks with one of the chorines, he is compared to a donkey. Meanwhile, the acts of the nightclub entertainers parody still other aspects of ass-headed Dionysus. The first routine shows a triad of mock-ferocious cat-women ridiculing their quite ineffectual male tamer; the second shows us girls in a Charleston routine out of the father's youth; finally, in an exquisite act, the clown

Polidor appears as a doddering Pied Piper, awed by the images of woman about him. A few pathetic notes of his almost limp trumpet and he shuffles out, trailing clouds of—empty balloons. Marcello's father goes to the chorus girl's apartment ("to eat spaghetti"), but suffers a stroke of some kind as they are making love. Pathetic, aging, his face always turned away, he wants only to return to Marcello's mother. In one of the most beautiful moments in the film, sick and exhausted as he is, he stoops and silently smoothes out the bed, removing his last trace; it is as though he had never been. So much for fatherhood.

Throughout the film, from the vulgarized Christ at the opening to the transvestite dance of the homosexuals at the end, man seems weak and helpless. Throughout, women lead men—Maddalena leads Marcello to the prostitute's apartment; Sylvia bounds up the steps of St. Peter's leaving behind clusters of exhausted Romans, and the haunted-castle sequence ends with the old *principessa*-matriarch leading the shamefaced "men" of the tribe off to Mass. Throughout, men seem awed, overcome by women, often trying to make themselves into women, sinking down into women. The men seem unable to get places; they have to clamber, grope, fly, break into places women seem to sink into effortlessly. When men do achieve heights, "rise above it all," they flag and gasp, revealing their impotency—Marcello climbing St. Peter's; Marcello's father up in the chorine's apartment; the camera-men's lights on high platforms shattering and popping in the fake miracle; the insignificance of the helicoptered Christ; the insignificance of our modern Mars—Marcello Rubini.

The exception (for a time, anyway) to all this is Steiner, Marcello's intellectual friend whose short unhappy life forms the most puzzling episode of the film. Unlike the other characters whose lives are dominated by sights and shows, Steiner lives in a world of sound and language. When we first see him, he is returning a Sanskrit text. He offers Marcello jobs in publishing, encourages him in his writing. Steiner, moreover, is a father with a lovely wife and charming children. Homespun, sturdy (Fellini originally wanted Henry Fonda for the part), he alone seems master of his fate. In fact, the whole situation is so goody-goody, it cloys. Then, inexplicably, Steiner commits suicide, destroying not only himself, but his children, destroying, in effect, his own fatherhood, his limited claim to be part of the flow of life, a total suicide. The film gives no particular reason for Steiner's suicide. It seems just one more in the long series of improvisations that make up *La Dolce Vita*. Impulse and improvisation are the ways the other characters work, however—not Steiner. In the first scene in which he appears, he starts to improvise jazz on the church organ, but at a gentle rebuke from the priest obediently shifts to the Toccata and Fugue, a frozen, "perfected" improvisation, as it were. At his house, he says, "In a work of art, everything is planned and perfect. We need to be a work of art, detached, perfect, in suspended animation," and yet, he also said his own life was too much so (the goody-goody quality of everything associated with Steiner). There seems to be no room in his life for the new, the unexpected. His suicide is the only improvisation left him and, at the same time, the closing or framing of his perfected life. It leaves his wife to be photographed by the *papparazzi*, she, now, image of the *mater dolorosa*. Quite the opposite is the only other sustained human relationship Marcello has in the course of the film, that with his mistress, Emma. Squabbles, flirtations, attempted suicides, reconcilations, their relation is one long series of improvisations as she tries to "catch" him, fix him into matrimony and fatherhood, a Fury valiently striving to be a hearth-goddess.

The film, then, uses its two central images, sight and sound, to set off men against women. The women are goddesses, mythical, unreal *belles dames sans merci*, the sight of whom bewitches men into a kingdom of improvisation and illusion. Man is impotent, helpless, Marcello's dying father or Steiner, with his sounds and language, frozen, turned into stone by the fixity of his life. (Indeed, sacred to Cybele was a small meteoric stone *acus*, supposed to have fallen from the heavens.) Marcello, Everyman, is caught between these two alternatives, male and female, his mistress vainly seeking to play the role of goddess and petrify him into matrimony.

These themes all come together in the final dreary episode, the despairingly hedonistic party that follows Marcello's appearance at the scene of Steiner's suicide. The subjugation of men culminates in the dance of the homosexuals and gigolos, and the image of woman culminates in the striptease (to the same song the Umbrian angel had played on the jukebox). Marcello presides over the dispirited merrymaking (the only case where a man is the "leader"), and as the party whimpers to its close he baptizes the departing revellers with feathers, as though he himself were plucking the chickens of Mother Carey *(mater cara)*, a grim parody of the earlier, Ekbergian baptism, just as his white suit is now the negative of the tuxedo he wore in the earlier episode. The effect is rather like snow, perhaps the snow of the ninth circle, perhaps also that "snow falling faintly through the universe and faintly falling, like the descent of their last end, upon all the living and the dead." This, the last party, gives way to the film's final image of man, a devilfish gasping in air, an eye caught in a net, and the final image of woman, the Umbrian-Uranian angel.

As with any important work, *La Dolce Vita* defines its own art. Fellini's concern about turning people into images finds its expression in what might be called the rotogravure style of the film. Fellini had both sets and costumes of *La Dolce Vita* designed to photograph in exaggerated blacks and whites, so that everything in the film would have the hard, contrasty look of a flash photo. The film itself seems almost to be composed as a series of stills rather than as a moving picture. Fellini's sense of the new, the unexpected, his theme of improvisation, finds its expression in the episodic structure (here, as in *Vitelloni*, this episodic quality seems a weakness of the film; only in *La Strada*, it seems to me, did Fellini overcome this his besetting vice). Fellini's brilliant use of dissolves also suggests a kind of impulse or improvisation (the best example being the opening dissolve where the gilt image of Christ suddenly, startlingly becomes a gilt Siamese dancer). This sense of improvisation, by the way, is not inappropriate for perhaps the only major director in the world who likes working on a chaotic set, who insists a script can only be an outline and "writes" his pictures by improvising on the set.

As in his earlier films, Fellini is essentially getting at a view of man as helpless and abject before the gorgon-like, all-powerful image of woman (in *Vitelloni*, for example, the gallant in the religious-goods shop surrounded by images of the Virgin, or—the most magnificent shot in that film—the half-wit worshipping a statue of an angel by the sea). Here, again, the theme fits a director who will look through thousands of photographs to get an actor with the right image; indeed he claims to have interviewed 10,000 actors for *La Dolce Vita*, truly a cinematic Ziegfeld. The good, gray *Times* insists on a Fellini "taking the temperature of a sick world," and that is no doubt true, but it is also a Fellini preoccupied with de-humanizing people, making them into things (*Cabiria*) or heroes (*La Strada*) or gods (*The White Sheik*), but in every case, dehumanizing them, making them into images—not an unnatural preoccupation for a man whose work in life is to turn people into celluloid.

Farrebique

James Agee, "Farrebique"

○○

Farrebique is the name of a farm in central France worked by a family whose possession of the property dates back to 1830. Georges Rouquier shot the film *Farrebique* in a period of one year, keenly and poetically observing the rhythms of nature and the human beings who depend upon it. There is the grandfather, his wife, their two sons, Roch and Henri, Roch's wife and her growing number of children. Rouquier shows the passing of time with lyric insight and feeling through the use of acceleration that depicts the waxing and waning of days and seasons. James Agee's review of the film is a sensitive appreciation of the film-maker's own sensibility and perception in creating the film. He concludes that "it is one of the finer works in the whole great line of rural art which extends backward through Van Gogh and Brueghel to the *Georgics* and to the *Works and Days.*"

───────♦───────

FARREBIQUE WAS MADE on a farm in southern France by Georges Rouquier, who was born and raised in the neighborhood, left home and became a linotyper, and ultimately got into movie-making because he couldn't keep away from it. Rouquier had made only one short film before this, a documentary about the making of wine vats. Both the subject of the new film and the particular kind of movie treatment happen to be obsessions of mine; so I cannot hope that many

Farrebique, directed by Georges Rouquier, 1946 (*Museum of Modern Art/Film Stills Archive*)

other people will be as deeply excited and satisfied by this film as I am. On the other hand, it is clear to me that because of the same obsessions I would be more merciless toward any mismanagements and betrayals, of the subject or in the treatment, than most people would.

Rouquier's idea is simply to make a record of the work and living of a single farm family, and of the farm itself, and of the surrounding countryside, through one year. I cannot imagine a better subject, or one that is as a rule more degenerately perceived and presented. In a sense, all that can be said of Rouquier's treatment of it is that it is right. That means, among other things, the following:

He realizes that, scrupulously handled, the camera can do what nothing else in the world can do: can record unaltered reality; and can be made also to perceive, record, and communicate, in full unaltered power, the peculiar kinds of poetic vitality which blaze in every real thing and which are in great degree, inevitably and properly, lost to every other kind of artist except the camera artist. He is utterly faithful to this realization; and it is clear in nearly every shot that he is infinitely more than a mere documentor, that his poetic intelligence is profound, pure, and vigorous; and it is clear many times over that he has the makings, and now and then the achievement, of a major poet. There is not an invented person or thing in the picture, and the reenactments, and invented incidents, are perfect examples of the discipline of imagination necessary under these difficult circumstances. One could watch the people alone, indefinitely long, for the inference of his handling of them, to realize that moral clearness and probity are indispensable to work of this kind, and to realize with fuller contempt than ever before how consistently in our time so-called simple people, fictional and nonfictional, are consciously and unconsciously insulted and betrayed by artists and by audiences: it seems as if the man is hardly alive, any more, who is fit to look another man in the eye. But this man is; and this is the finest and strongest record of actual people that I have seen.

Rouquirer's sense of the discretion and power of plot and

incident, such as they are, is just as sure and as rare. Even more remarkable is his ability with all the small casual scraps of existence which are neither plot nor incident nor even descriptive, nor revealing of mood or character, but are merely themselves, and of the essence of being. He never imposes poetry or rhetoric or special significance upon these scraps, and they are never left half-dead and helpless, as mere shots-for-shots'-sake: they are incredibly hard stuff to organize, but he has so ordered them that they are fully and euphoniously articulate in their own perfect language. He knows as well as any artist I can think of the power and the beauty there can be in absolute plainness: his record, for instance, of the differing faces of three men and two women as they stand in their home for night prayer; or the mere sequence of bedding down the cows. Much of the picture, and much of the finest of it, has this complete plainness; but raised against this ground bass Rouquier's sense of device and metaphor is equally bold and pure. He develops a wonderful communication of the rooted past, the flowering present, and the ungerminated future in about three minutes during which the grandfather tells the children the history of the farm and family, while the camera examines snapshots and mementos which are like relics from a primitive grave. He does a beautiful thing in showing the dreams of the old man, his son, his son's wife, wishes as touching and naive as those of a child: then hovers the dreamless face of the grandmother. His use of analogy and metaphor is Homeric in simplicity and force: the terrifying blooming of a sped flower, as an image of childbirth; the sound of an ax and of a falling tree as the camera watches a man's pulse die. He uses stop-motion as I have always wanted to use it: very plainly, to show the motions of darkness and light and shadow; and with complete freedom and daring, in his orgiastic sequence on spring, to show the jubilant rending and pouring upward and blossoming of the world. This sequence is as prescient and as primordially exciting as the *Pervigilium Veneris*. He also dares to add to it —almost whispered, as it should be—a poem of his own; and so well as I could hear, it is an extremely good poem. I'm not sure the picture wouldn't be still better without it; yet it adds a quality and full dimension of its own, and in principle I am for it. In one sense this film is a kind of Bible which expounds not only the grave kinds of discipline necessary to such work but also the kinds, degrees, and tremendous reaches of liberty and adventure which obedience to these kinds of discipline makes possible.

Bosley Crowther of the *Times* has written that *Farrebique* is "lacking in strong dramatic punch . . . not even a plain folk triangle," and that it will have to depend for support upon "the loyal, the very loyal." I don't feel that Mr. Crowther means ill by the film—though there is a certain patronizing air toward those who are poky and arty enough to admire it— and I thoroughly disenjoy derogation by name; but when a great work of art is dismissed so casually as not so good as "the classic French film, *Harvest*" (!), I find that I am loyal, very loyal. By no means all the great poetry in the world, especially the kind which is uniquely possible to moving pictures, is or can stand to be dramatic; and this picture is not for cultists, but for those who have eyes capable of seeing what is before them, and minds and hearts capable of caring for what they see. Others have complained that the film is repetitious. It is, exactly in the sense that the imitation and counterpoint and recurrence in a Mozart symphony are repetitious, and somewhere near as satisfyingly.

Rouquier's film is so far above and beyond the fat-headed "instructiveness" of most nonfiction films that I wish he had shown that even "instructive" material can transcend its kind. Even within his scheme as I understand it one should make clear just what the family lives on and just how it gets its living: but we don't know for sure, here, what is for sub- sistence and what goes to market. I wish also that there was a fuller record of the undomesticated natural year, as distinct from the farm; I learn that Rouquier wished so too, tried very hard for it, and could not get enough of what he was after—exactly the right shots of a fox, the flight of a crow, and so on. On "inanimate" nature and the differing lights of weathers and seasons, however, he was as right as it is imaginable to be. Whatever devices may have been used to help out the camera, they are used legitimately, that is, invisibly, and in order that the film may accept the exact light the world gives it; and in this the film is full of lovely achievements: subdued autumnal light in which the whole world is as scratchily distinct as trillions of little briars; the veiled shining of spring; the supernal light beneath impounded thunder; the holy light of snow. I would suppose, but am not sure, that with infra-red, or through stop-motion, luminous night images might have been had, of the woods and the open land, deep in the darkness—or throughout one night, condensed into a minute; of the luminousness of fallen snow in still, open woods during a cloudy night; of storming snow in the dark; of the stars. If these things were possible, I am very sorry not to see them here: sorriest, I guess, not to see what would have come of two shots: the stop-motion camera trained throughout one night upon the Pole Star, and upon the zenith on a moonless and starry night; so that in either case the whole sky turns, and bit by bit obliterates with morning. I think it is probable, too, that beautifully as the shots are articulated, and strong and rich as they are in poetry, they are seldom ordered into the definitive, unforgettable eloquence of the highest poetry which might have been made out of the subject. But it will take a good many seeings before I can be sure of that. I am sure already, however, of one thing. Whether or not this film is fully as great as it might have been, it is one of the finer works in the whole great line of rural art which extends backward through Van Gogh and Brueghel to the *Georgics* and to the *Works and Days*. It combines the cold deep-country harshness of Hesiod with a Vergilian tenderness and majesty; and its achievement is wholly of our time, through that reverence for unaltered reality which can be translated into a work of art only through the camera.

Gertrud

Elsa Gress Wright, "Gertrud"

ooooooooooooooooooooooooooooooooooooooooooooooooo

Although true generally with great films, the poignancy
and beauty of Carl Dreyer's *Gertrud* (1964) particularly
eludes verbal description. It is the story of a talented, at-
tractive woman. The wife of a politician, she refuses to
have her destiny absorbed into the dominating needs of his
career. After a disenchanting affair with a young musician,
she lives ultimately alone in deep spiritual isolation. This
rather commonplace bourgeois material is infused with tragic
emotion and meaning through Dreyer's subtle camera movements, his artful compositions, his revealing lighting, and his
direction of the studied speech rhythms of the actors. The
banal material with which he deals is not much different
from the stuff out of which cliché domestic-tragedy films
are made. But the genius of Dreyer is such that the film
communicates universal truth with deeply moving poetic
force. In her essay Elsa Gress Wright, a fellow Dane, surveys
some of Dreyer's previous work, and in discussing *Gertrud*
maintains that "Tragedy [in our time], he proves, is not
only possible, but possible in the most modern of contemporary media." A statement in the film directed to Gertrud,
"Love is all," is the message Dreyer genuinely and tragically
dramatizes.

———————◆———————

CARL TH. DREYER (now nearing seventy-seven) has for decades been considered a Difficult Dane, rather than a merely

Gertrud, directed by Carl Dreyer, 1964 (*Contemporary*)

melancholy one. But the main difficulty about Dreyer's work and personality does not consist in ideological or aesthetic incomprehensibility, for he is usually clear, if not simple, in his message and its form of expression. It consists rather in his uncompromising search for unpopular artistic and moral truths, and his unrelenting pursuit of his own way of expressing these truths. The extraordinary thing about his works is, perhaps, less their visual beauty and emotional strength, than the effect this beauty and strength has and has had on his contemporaries. He is, and always was, an artist who commands strong sympathies and provokes strong antipathies. He never lets his audience off the hook. He never repeats the obvious, but he always gives you *time* to see it. He makes everything plain, but nothing simple or easy. The strong emotional impact of his films is the one thing that unites them all, in spite of very striking stylistic differences.

All this has been proved true once more with the release of *Gertrud*, which was greeted (both in Paris, where it was first released, and in Copenhagen and Stockholm) with more attention and controversy than could possibly have been foreseen, for it was not just, as expected, among the initiates. The film set off a chain-reaction and made critical mechanisms go clicking at all levels, from that of the professional movie critics, some of whom were extremely hostile, while others were absolutely enchanted, to that of the man in the street who could not care less about aesthetic points. The film has been called everything imaginable, from a sublime elegy in pictures, to the trashy work of a dilettante; from a work utterly dead and antiquated in style and in ideas, to a vital work representing the height of modernity in both respects. And its heroine has been admired and loved as unreservedly as she has been despised and hated by people who are otherwise not given to strong expressions of emotion.

As for the epithets "antiquated," "stagnant," "unfashionable," and "reactionary" (a few of the designations used by the hostile critics who, at first, were in an absolute majority), they don't convey anything new in attitudes to Dreyer's works, as these are the exact terms that have been used about

his works ever since *The Passion of Joan of Arc* (1928), and
they have been used more particularly about those aspects of
his works that in retrospect seem most exciting and antici-
patory of important cinematic developments. Nor is it anything new that people walked out scandalized at the premiere
and that hisses and boos drowned out the dialogue. The
surprising thing is rather that the tide turned quicker than
has usually been the case with Dreyer's films. Within a few
weeks after the first avalanche of pans and protestations of
horror at the old master's final failure, more thoughtful
analyses started to appear in periodicals, and by the end of
the year the positive voices were much stronger, if not in a
majority. The objections were and are really to what a
certain type of critic has always been intensely annoyed at
in Dreyer's films: his absolute disregard of what is done or
not done in the films of the moment and to critical dogmas
of any kind, his stubborn sticking to his own artistic instincts
and convictions, which must of necessity be exasperating to
the people creating and following the fads of the moments.
The recognition, on the other hand, has been a realization
of those very traits as highly valuable, and of the fact that
his instincts were once more right. Apart from that the
subject of the film has aroused extra controversy, although—
or because—it is essentially the story Dreyer has always been
telling, with the moral he has always pointed: the story of the
individual pitched against organized repression, waste, and
cruelty, and of the pains and penalties as well as the necessity
of heresy.

This controversial effect of the film has to some extent
blurred the view of it as a work of art. And it is impossible
to treat the film without consideration of this effect for it is
part of the unusual character of this film, as well as of Dreyer's
works as such. I shall discuss *Gertrud,* first in terms of its
treatment of subject, next in terms of Dreyer's intentions,
and finally in terms of its timeless meaning. These three aspects are, of course, not separable in actual fact, but they
are useful categories when analyzing such an apparently
simple, but actually very complex, work.

The film is based on a 1907 play by the Swedish writer Hjalmar Søderberg (who based *his* work on true incidents in the lives of real people). It seems to follow the play closely, but more important is what Dreyer (who as usual has written his own scenario) left out and added than what he left in. The play is a minor, if competent, effort—a domestic drama with ironic overtones, heavily pessimistic, and with distinct undertones of animosity and contempt toward the heroine. It deals with a well-known adulterous situation: Gertrud is a mature career woman (a singer) married to a politically ambitious lawyer. Her marriage has become empty and meaningless, and she seeks love with a young composer, deciding to leave her husband for her lover. Her past emerges with the return of a celebrated poet, with whom she had lived before her marriage. At the end of the play she leaves all three men, none of whom can meet her demand for absolute love.

Out of this material Dreyer has made something much more significant. He has carefully removed all topical and satirical references to minds and manners of the time, and he has made Gertrud the unconditional heroine by removing all traces of contempt for her (or for woman as such) and emphasizing her superiority of intelligence and character. And he has added a fourth man as a stage in Gertrud's development and an epilogue that turns out to be a key scene, making it plain that Gertrud's "choice of herself" was right for her, but that it was costly. All this has been translated into a film of the usual majestic Dreyer slowness of speech and movement, and the usual Dreyer "purified realism" of milieu and carefully composed frames of great beauty. But it is a new departure in the handling of dialogue, which is more prominent than in Dreyer's earlier films, and in the extensive use of traveling camera and of semi-close-ups, rather than the *close* close-ups for which Dreyer is famous. The shots are very long, practically corresponding to entire scenes. The acting is stylized, but dictated by the cultural milieu, and convincing in its own way. "There was not a movement that Dreyer did not supervise and direct," says Bent Rothe, who performed superbly as the husband. "None of the acting was ours, it was all his, expressing his ideas." The whole adds up to a rare stateliness, which is miraculously so simple, direct, and austere that it entirely escapes pretense and pompousness.

The film-maker's intentions are, of course, interesting only in so far as they are realized convincingly, and in so far as the artist has an interesting mind. Both are the case here. Dreyer's purity of heart—or "abominable naiveté," as one critic put it—has once more baffled critics, who want to see satire, or even some diabolic attack on human values, in this film. (It has been ingeniously suggested that *Gertrud* is a Christian satire on the futility of materialistic ideas.) But Dreyer cannot, according to his own words, for the life of him see why he should be satirical about perfectly charming, cultured people, and he insists on treating with tenderness and respect an age (his own youth) and a milieu that are often ridiculed or vulgarized. Nor can he see why he should make propaganda for some idea or faith, when the human lessons he draws from the section of life he is showing are so interesting in themselves. He follows the artistic principle of "divided sympathies," so that nobody is let down completely and nobody unduly glorified, but he does this out of honesty and insight, not as a principle. With his usual passion for truth—artistic, moral, and even factual, in short anything but naturalistic verisimilitude—he has based his additions to the plot on the real life of the person who was a model for the play's heroine. It all serves his art, even when he is not entirely conscious that it does so, but is more concerned with other aspects.

This brings us to the timelessness of the film—nothing less will do. A French critic, Maurice Drouzy, who has carefully compared the play and the film, reaches the conclusion that Dreyer "has transformed a domestic drama into a spiritual meditation on the loneliness of the soul and the possibilities and impossibilities of human love." That sums it up neatly enough. The film does register—as did the play—that life is futile and love doomed and Dreyer uses Søderberg's text to say so, though he uses his own groupings and lightings and his power of making the very silence speak to say it more effectively. But he also shows that however futile life may seem, he never really believes in its futility. His interest in the futility itself is "a desperate registration of some instinctive belief that life might be, could be, indeed *is* full of significance." To him what makes things petty is an ever-present sense of their latent grandeur. Gertrud herself, in Dreyer's interpretation, is both very human, to the extent of stooping to folly, and not human at all, but somehow universal, a tragic embodiment of a longing for the impossible, a longing followed with terrible consistency to the truly inexorable loneliness that is not merely hinted at, but demonstrated: the film ends with a hypnotic sequence in which Gertrud's room is virtually changed into a tomb under your very eyes—by the closing of a door, a shifting light, and the distant sound of bells.

Dreyer himself has subtitled *Gertrud* "a period piece," and a period piece it is, rendered nostalgically and with tender irony. It is also, in his intention, a tentative effort in the direction of the tragic film poetry which he believes will come about when the truly cinematic tragic style has been formulated. The question is, however, whether he himself is not the tragic film poet he is waiting for. The style he has developed, and with modifications dictated by his choice of milieu and theme has used in *Gertrud*, is certainly so close to film tragedy that probably only he himself could see any distance to the goal. It is an Apollonian kind of tragedy, in the vein of Euripides, the first "modern" tragic poet, but austere, almost Doric, in style. By creating it, Dreyer has refuted the words of his compatriot and contemporary, Isak Dinesen, to the effect that tragedy is no longer possible in modern times. Tragedy, he proves, is not only possible, but possible in the most modern of contemporary media.

Gertrud is an autonomous work strikingly different in style from Dreyer's earlier works, particularly from *Ordet*, his previous film, though reflecting a steady continuity of mind and feeling. But the film is also more than an indication that Dreyer's plans for a *Medea* (in non-naturalistic color) and his other projects that have remained so long undone for lack of funds will be worth anybody's time and money. It will certainly be a mystery to the future if at this point nobody turns up at the eleventh hour to allow Dreyer to create more films; for even a failure of his would be infinitely more interesting than the successes of most movie-makers. And this in itself is a true measure of his greatness as a film poet.

Hiroshima, Mon Amour

Wolfgang A. Luchting, "Hiroshima, Mon Amour,
Time, and Proust"

○○

In *Hiroshima, Mon Amour* (1959), his first full-length
feature, Alain Resnais created a new kind of cinema. He
transcended the conventional mold of action in time and
space by commingling with it the reality of the complex and
subtle dimension of memory in human experience, memory
interacting with the continuum of the present. Art that
focuses on such content is an attempt to express the pris-
matic, multiple character of reality. In the modern fictional
styles of Marcel Proust, James Joyce, Thomas Mann, and
more recent writers, various rhetorical inventions effect dis-
locations of time and space. Wolfgang A. Luchting explores
the comparable effort of Resnais to find equivalent modes
and techniques to break up the surface of the chronological
present in order to deal with its relation to the realities of
other times and places, real and psychological. The depth of
communication in the film is evident by the way in which
the technique of flashback functions. Ordinarily flashback
has been employed to clarify character motivation in the
context of present action, to supplement the exposition of
character. Mr. Luchting observes that "In HMA, action (on
the level of real time) and flashbacks (onto the plane of
psychological time) are not essentially independent of each
other. There could be no action if there were no flashbacks,
because the latter cause the former and the former causes the
latter. Past and present are a sort of emulsion, little drops of

Hiroshima, Mon Amour, directed by Alain Resnais, 1959 (*Zenith*)

past time being suspended in the present, and vice versa." According to Mr. Luchting's analysis the "message" or "messages" of *Hiroshima, Mon Amour* are substantial. His examination of style and technique is ultimately an assertion that they are inextricably one with theme and meaning. And in order to effect his analysis of the film he establishes Resnais' complex debt to the author of *Remembrance of Things Past:* both are preoccupied with the human and philosophical question of time, Proust to eternalize the moment past, Resnais to forget it.

What follows is a greatly shortened version of Mr. Luchting's article published in *The Journal of Aesthetics and Art Criticism,* Spring, 1963. The translations of French passages have been provided by the author.

———————◆———————

I AM CONVINCED THAT *Hiroshima, Mon Amour (HMA)* is one of the very best pictures ever made. It is of the same significance to modern film-aesthetics as Griffith's use of the close-up was for silent pictures. *L'année dernière à Marienbad* shows in which direction Alain Resnais' breakthrough will lead.

Before looking into the aspects that make *HMA* an epochal work, I should like to resume in a few words what, to my mind, constitutes a great work of film-art—or any great work of art: It is given when what is seen on the screen demonstrates that the intellect has formed a matter in a way that opens the final product to the existential or essential problems of *la condition humaine* and gives man an opportunity to see these problems in *a new light*[1] and thus with a new hope for their solution. A great work of contemporary art is, and not only in the cinema, that which shows us the same old reality

---

[1]Compare Brecht's words: "The estrangement effect occurs when the thing to be understood, the thing to which attention is to be drawn, is changed from an ordinary, well-known, immediately present thing into a particular, striking, unexpected thing. In a certain sense the self-evident is made incomprehensible, although this only happens in order to make it all the more comprehensible." *Versuche 11,* p. 102 (translation by R. Gray).

under a new aspect, possibly under one that receives its illumination from a contemporary understanding of the world.

I. THE STRUCTURE OF TIME

What kinds of time are there in *HMA?*

1. To begin with the least important, there is what may be termed the *exterior time:* the ninety minutes or so the film lasts. This time the film has in common with the theater, with music. It is one which is imposed upon us. In literature, the exterior time, although it exists, is not a condition of literature's existence: We can begin a book, read some pages, leave it.

2. Next, there is what may be termed the *interior time:* the time of the central action we see, whose development the film follows and presents to us. This interior time in *HMA* has as its collateral "space" two principal settings in which the psychological action and the physical actions take place: *Nevers*, the girl's hometown, and *Hiroshima*, where the love story takes place.

3. Both the exterior and the interior time are, if seen as wholes and, as it were, at a distance, dramatic *continua*. But while the interior is dependent on the exterior time, the latter is not dependent on the former. No single entity could (in this film; and in good films in general *should* not be able to) express its meaning without being in the place it has been assigned, without the complementary function of the other— foregoing or subsequent—entities of the same dramatic series. In short: each part of the *continuum* is valid only in function of all others. The ensemble of all the parts constitutes the story of the film. The story, in turn, not being Aristotelian, consists of individual actions, of sequences of happenings. Where there are several actions, there must be several times—even though they may be simultaneous—because in their subjective experience they must needs follow one another. These times in their aggregate make up the interior time. Each one by itself might also be called a *specific* time, a circumstantial fraction of the interior one.

4. These specific times, the circumstantial components of the interior *continuum*, are in *HMA* subdivided into two categories:

(a) One is *le temps réel*, the time in which the action in the city of Hiroshima takes place. *Le temps réel* is, then, the time in which the love story between the Japanese architect and the French actress develops.

(b) The other category is *le temps psychologique*—or even *le temps proustien*, for obvious reasons. This *temps psychologique* comprises the memories of and their effect within the *temps réel* on both hero and heroine. For him the memories are, primarily, *concentric*, that is to say: revolve around the complex of what Hiroshima as a historical fact means today, what the city's moment of destruction was like. Secondarily, his memories are *excentric*, in so far as they participate in her memories. For her, the memories of *le temps psychologique* are, primarily, *concentric* around her experience in Nevers. Secondarily, they are *excentric* in so far as they participate in his memories of Hiroshima.

Two things have to be mentioned here. First, that *le temps réel* and *le temps psychologique* interact. In fact, *HMA* would not be possible without this interaction. The interaction is the film's substance—though not its theme, which, instead, deals with the attitude both hero and heroine and, *in extenso*, man in general, take towards this interaction between memories and both the events that cause them to arise at a given moment and those that created them. In other words, the substance of the film, the matter Alain Resnais set out to mold into a work of art, is the interaction between past and present. The spiritual effect of his work is to make us aware of the importance this interaction has on human behavior. This might be called the cathartic effect of the film, which does not, however, arise out of any climax, but out of the total, the accumulative impression the film makes: it is an epic film.

Here is one example of how complicated this interaction can become: Part of the story is the fact that the heroine, a French actress, has come to Hiroshima in order to do a picture about Hiroshima. Resnais' film also is about Hiroshima. We see, at the beginning, how a film-company shoots a picture about Hiroshima (the historical fact) in which the heroine acts. The people caught in the act of filming are Resnais' own people: Resnais thus films himself filming a film about Hiroshima. This is not so gratuitous as it may seem, for this procedure reminds one of Proust who also wrote seven volumes about how Marcel came to write seven volumes about how he came to write seven volumes. In both cases, with Resnais and with Proust, we find the creator describing how he created or came to create (often a topic of modern art). With Resnais the cause of the creation and the creation itself are the psychological complex of Hiroshima and what it represents in the history of mankind. At the same time, the heroine of *HMA* comes to Hiroshima and thus to the locale of her love-and-time-dilemma because of the film-within-the-film's topic, which, again, is Hiroshima.

The second thing to be mentioned in connection with *les temps réel et psychologique* is that there exists a kind of diametrically opposed movement within the heroine and the hero from the above mentioned concentric to excentric memories. The motors of this movement are empathy and sympathy. Remarkable is the reverse direction of the movement in him and her: *she* takes part, empathetically and sympathetically, as if in a secondary memory, in *his* primary memories of Hiroshima and its implications for *him* publicly and privately. This, her participation, comes *before* his participation, empathetically and sympathetically, as though in a secondary memory, in *her* primary memories of Nevers and its implications for *her* publicly and privately. Expressing it differently, one might say: as the lovers' story develops—on the plane of *le temps réel*—there takes place an almost symmetrical interchange of the intensity of their respective primary and secondary memories. While *his* memories are strongest at the beginning of the film, they become weaker in the same degree that *her* primary memories come to the surface and influence their relationship and the love between them.

From these opposed movements arises one of the decisive scenes of the film: they meet head-on when, in the famous restaurant scene, he slaps her. The meaning of this climactic moment might be described thus: intense experience—the progressively stronger love between hero and heroine—can either further forgetfulness of earlier suffering, or repress it.

It may be remembered that, before it comes to the slap, there creeps into the lovers' conversation a somewhat maudlin aspect of insanity. She, while recounting her love affair with the German soldier, speaks to her Japanese lover as if *he* were the German. She says, at first: "We used to meet at the river" and, then: "*You* used to wait for me," etc., projecting into her new lover an identity with her old one. This highly poetic "gimmick" shows, to my mind, that Resnais and Mlle. Duras were trying to have the Japanese "catch up" on the formation of his secondary memory, because her secondary memory is way ahead since she knows more about Hiroshima than he about the German lover.

5. Turning now from particular details in *HMA's temps réel et psychologique* to a more general survey of interior time, attention must be drawn to one of its highly interesting dramaturgical aspects: the action of the film becomes progressively slower. The scenes change less in their thematic contents. The locations tend to remain more and more the same. The rhythm of individual sequences softens. At the same time, in order to give depth of association to what he wishes to say, Resnais resorts more and more to flashbacks. Also, on the plane of *le temps réel*, the more detailed, lengthier scenes gain in poetic quality, aiming less and less at impact (as did the scenes beginning the film) and more and more at a serenity of understanding on the part of the spectator.

6. The endeavor to cause associations in the viewer is, of course, again channelled by Alain Resnais and Marguerite Duras into the expanses and inexhaustible possibilities of time. They use what I should like to label time-perspectives. These time-perspectives are like aids for placing the story in, as it were, sudden temporal dimensions, for heightening some

element of the story, making us fathom the invisible depths of
the images visible on the screen. As a rule, the elements thus
heightened are meant to show, from various points of view,
the essence of human ephemerity as the succeeding stages
of the story on the screen demonstrate it.

What then are some of these perspectives of time? According to their emphasis, the following are worth mentioning:

(a) The film opens with images that immediately call to
mind some sort of *Ur*-creation, some cosmic creative process:
the heaving of crude, raw, unformed masses, convulsions, it
seems, of matter in the process of evolution. As the images
becomes clearer and refine themselves, as words spoken by
human beings become audible, we realize that those *Ur*-masses
in movement are nothing but the bodies of a man and a woman
engaged in the sexual act. Resnais creates this association with
something *Ur*- by photographing in close-up the planes of
two human bodies. What he evidently wishes to express by the
gradual transformation of convulsing masses into recognizable
human forms is that the sexual act, the physical expression of
human love, is something "eternal" and perhaps redemptive.
The clearer the images become, the more the situation is revealed for what it is and the more Resnais adds the romantic,
sentimental decor and the intellectual superstructure mankind
and time have elaborated around the same physical fact. The
perspective we are meant to glimpse is that of man and woman in love across mankind's, possibly life's, existence—in spite
and because of Hiroshima.

(b) Another perspective is this: the convulsing masses seen
at the beginning also lead the spectator to think of a human
body suffering from the effects of an atomic explosion. Some
of the expanses of human flesh shown in the first passages seem
to bear resemblance to burnt flesh. In view of the title of the
film we have come to see, what is more likely than that we
associate immediately the burnt flesh, the bubbles of shrinking
skin, with all the photos we have ever seen of Hiroshima
victims? Directing thus the audience's associations through the
memories of Hiroshima and Nagasaki towards their immediate
consequences in human destruction, visible here and now, be-

fore us, Resnais states one of the *leitmotive* of his film: namely, that hearing of H-bombs and A-bombs and similar products of human genius, of their destructive power, and of all the horror that legend has accumulated since 1945 around the mere mention of them, is and has become so much of an everyday experience for us that we no longer associate it with its real consequences, of which burnt, shrinking, and stinking human flesh is one infinitesimally small part.

That the initial sequence, which reveals the present in its aspect of eternity by associating *Ur*-masses in movement with the sexual act, is not an accidental time-perspective, can now clearly be seen. For, placing present events (love-making) in the perspective of the past (*Ur*-masses) is as much a *leitmotiv* in this film as bringing the viewer face to face with the atomic age in terms that he can understand and shudder at—in terms of what it can do to *him*.

Life not being a handful of clearly and cleverly separate, separable, definable, or defined strands of *leitmotive*, it can be assumed that those mentioned up till now will sooner or later be fused or will recur in other constellations, constantly forming new patterns. Indeed, they do, revealing always other facets of Resnais' and Duras' "messages." One of the facets— and it is interesting to note its proximity to Proust's preoccupations in *A la Recherche du temps perdu (RTP)*—is: No matter how intense a human experience, is, it is always situated in time and therefore subject to oblivion, both by man as a historical *continuum* and by the individual as its manifestation in the present. In fact, this is one of Resnais' *universalia*. It teaches that forgetting is as necessary as living—which, among other things, consists precisely of experiences that seem unforgettable—is inevitable for man.

But this facet of Resnais' "message," this *universalium*, is also meant to contain an application *ad hoc*. By giving us to understand that man is the creation of forces that have been at work since "the beginning of time" and by using the same images that convey this information to associate in us the realization of man's vulnerability (the burnt flesh) as well as his disregard for this vulnerability in his fellow men, Resnais projects into the initial sequence a prophecy of man's destiny: for anybody who approaches man without prejudices, not even pragmatic ones, it comes as no surprise that man should be himself but a particle in a greater process entirely indifferent to him.

What other perspectives are there?

(c) There is, of course, always the perspective of the atomic explosion in Hiroshima in 1945. It serves as a sort of middle ground before which both hero and heroine enact their story.

(d) Another, extremely "Proustian" time-perspective is the projection of art into life: to participate in the creation of a work of art—the film about Hiroshima—the heroine of *HMA* came to Hiroshima, where now, as we see throughout the film, she experiences all the intensity of her existence as a human being, put into relief by the proof of the very opposite of existence—death—which surrounds her and which lurks for her, as for any human being, in the very name of Hiroshima. In this context, the title of Resnais' film gains a new depth— *Hiroshima*, on one side, the very memory of death; *Mon Amour*, on the other, an expression of the affirmative forces of life, those that perpetuate it. The actress, in other words, is led through the fact that somebody wishes to create a work of art (the film within the film) to simultaneous suffering and enjoyment, to death—for part of her dies when she begins to love the Japanese; and to life—for something new is born in her while she forgets her past, the part that dies.

This brings us to a rather interesting aspect of the film: the strangely neglected social problem that one would expect to arise immediately out of its love story, namely that both protagonists are married. Their married life belongs to *le temps psychologique*, to the plane of memories. Its implications hardly ever manifest themselves in *le temps réel*. In fact, only once are they touched upon—when the Japanese and she find themselves in his apartment. Almost brutally Resnais dismisses it and makes the two adulterers dedicate themselves to adultery. This harsh suppression of a socially still-explosive fact and its strange absence in the rest of the film are, of course, not due to any absent-mindedness of Mlle. Duras or M. Alain Resnais. They are intended. They are meant to reveal another *leitmotiv* of the film:

(e) I have said that both protagonists' *état civil* belongs to their memories. But so does the heroine's love affair with the German. Why then should the German lover be so intensely present in the *temps-réel* action, and the French husband, who waits for the heroine in Paris, so very little? I believe the answer is the following: their *état civil* is an integral part of their ordinary life. Not so their present love affair which is part of an extra-ordinary life. They are both different people. This change in their characters, too, is a highly Proustian element, for in his work, also

Notre MOI armoureux ne peut même pas imaginer ce que sera notre MOI non amoureux. (André Maurois, *À la Recherche de Marcel Proust* [Hachette, 1949], p. 170).[2]

What an effect being in love has with reference to time has been described by Proust himself:

Le temps dont nous disposons chaque jour est élastique; les passions que nous ressentons le dilatent, celles que nous inspirons le rétrecissent, et *l'habitude le remplit*.[3]

[2]Our *I* in love [MOI *amoureux*] cannot even imagine what our *I* will be like when not in love.

[3]The time we have at our disposal each day is elastic; the passions we feel dilate it, those we inspire shrink it, and habit fills it.

Cf. *Esprit*, June 1960, p. 962: "le temps est au centre des films de Resnais, de Varda, de Tati, non pas le temps qui passe et qui presse, mais au contraire celui qui ne passe pas. . . ." and p. 963: "il se dessout au contact du monde, il n'est plus qu'un éspace, des rues, des routes, un village . . . où tout semble s'étirer et s'arrêter en de longs plans immobiles et silencieux . . ." and "leur rencontre ne trouve pas d'autre issue que l'incertitude finale des dernières heures où le temps s'étire sans pouvoir cependant cesser d'être." (p. 962: "Time is at the center of the films by Resnais, by Varda, Tati; not the time that passes and presses, but on the contrary the one that does not pass. . . ." and p. 963: "It dissolves upon contact with the world, it is nothing any more than a space, streets, highways, a village . . . where everything seems to stretch and come to a standstill in long immobile and silent images [plans]" and "their encounter finds no other issue but the final incertitude of the last hours where the time stretches without, however, being able to cease being.")

But love not only changes time, it also changes people—apparently. Here is what André Maurois says about this same phenomenon in Proust:

> ces nouveaux MOI sont parfois si différents qu'ils devraient porter un autre nom. On verra, dans le roman, Swann, Odette, Gilberte, Bloch, Rachel, Saint-Loup, passant successivement sous les projecteurs . . . des sentiments, en prendre les couleurs comme des danseuses dont la robe est blanche, mais qui paraissent tour à tour jaunes, vertes ou bleues. (*Op. cit*, p. 169.)[4]

and

> "En vérité [dit Proust], la désagrégation du moi est une mort continue" et "la stabilité de nature que nous prêtons à autrui est aussi fictive que la nôtre." (*Ibid*.)[5]

All these experiences are present and shown to us by Resnais in hero and heroine of *HMA*. To name only the most striking example: At the end of the film, when they say good-bye to each other, he calls her "Nevers," she calls him "Hiroshima"— both, then, *do get other names*. Love has transformed them and made them die a little. Their love affair is carried on in their extra-ordinary life, outside of routine, even *hors la loi*. It is an extreme situation, *un instant privilégié*. And it is in extreme situations that the doors are pushed open to the dusty attic full of experiences in our past, that time becomes alive, past becomes present, and the fear of the future is lost. For both—but more for her—love is what opens these doors as the mirrors open for Cocteau's poets. In other words, events in *le temps réel* break through to *le temps psychologique*. Proust has similar thoughts and convictions:

[4]These new *I* [MOI *nouveaux*] are sometimes so different that they should carry another name. One will, in the novel, see Swann, Odette, Gilberte, Bloch, Rachel, Saint-Loup, passing successively under the projectors . . . of sentiments, take on the colors of these like the *danseuses* whose costume is white but who appear one after the other yellow, green or blue.

[5]"In reality [says Proust], the disaggregation of the *I* is a continuous death" and "the stability of character [nature] with which we endow our fellow man [*nous prêtons à autrui*] is as fictitious as our own."

il a eu, en certains instants privilégiés, "l'intuition de lui-même comme être absolu." (André Maurois, *op. cit.*, p. 169.)[6]

and, giving us time, art, and love in their perishable and their eternal meaning for man,

Il y a autonomie entre son angoisse à sentir que tout s'écroule . . . et sa certitude intime qu'il y a en lui quelque chose de permanent et même d'éternel. Cette certitude, Proust l'a éprouvée en des instants très courts où, soudain, un moment du passé devenait réel et où il decouvrait . . . qu'ils étaient capables de réapparaître. (André Maurois, *op. cit.*, p. 179.)[7]

The same conviction *(certitude intime)* and the same fear that everything is ephemeral are the impulses that motivated Resnais to make the film here analyzed; they are the material of *HMA*. The difference between him and Proust is that the latter accentuates in his novel the ephemeralness (although the writing of the novels is proof of his "secret conviction" that there is something eternal), whereas the former, Resnais, puts rather more emphasis on the very *necessity* of this ephemeralness in order that there *be* a continuity. The juxtaposition, then, is that of routine as over against exception, the ordinary as over against the extra-ordinary situation. Leaving out the fact that both hero and heroine are married causes us to become aware of the ramifications that are contained in the juxtaposition between ordinary and extra-ordinary situations. The protagonists' love is both *hors la loi* and *hors du temps*, or if one wishes: *hors la norme*.

The latter fact opens an interesting vista on man's preoccupation with time, if we remember that, to mention only

[6]He has had, in certain privileged instants, "the intuition of himself as an absolute being."

[7]There is a contradiction between his anguish at feeling that everything vanishes . . . and his secret conviction [*certitude intime*] that there is something in him that is permanent and even eternal. This certitude Proust has sensed in very fleeting instants when, suddenly, a moment of the past became real and when he discovered . . . that they were capable of reappearing.

literature, most novels that deal with time have as heroes "outsiders" (until some years ago, at any rate; of late, this dedication to time has spread to comprehend even what before were not considered "outsiders"): Proust himself, Hans Kastorp in Thomas Mann's *Der Zauberberg*, and Darley and Pursewarden in Durrell's books; Ulrich in Musil's *Der Mann ohne Eigenschaften*, etc. That Alain Resnais should have worked for this "time" effect in his film is of course not surprising: he must make his protagonists' love "timeless," untroubled by the mediocrity of their married life, because he wants to achieve an effect that permits him to progress on to another of his *leitmotive:*

(f) *Time asserting its rights:* If we observe closely the "timelessness" of his protagonists, we notice that there is one way in which their past and their future (i.e., routine) may be permitted to intrude on it: paradoxically enough, through intensity, i.e., where earlier intense experiences equal or surpass their present intensity in *le temps réel:* her first love affair; his experience of the atomic explosion. This intrusion of intensities from the realm of *le temps psychologique* into that of *le temps réel* serves a very definite purpose. Resnais wishes to demonstrate that there exists a sort of cohesion of *situations extrèmes* across ordinary time. Again we enter the terrain of Proust, who also, in his novel, meant to save certain intensely experienced moments from the corrosion caused by the flux of time. In his *Carnets* he writes

> ne pas oublier . . . qu'il est un motif qui revient dans ma vie, plus important que celui de l'amour d'Albertine, et peut-être assimilable au chant du coq du Quatuor de Vinteuil. . . . Tasse de thé, arbres en promenade, clochers, etc.[8]

and, we might add—for it is, after all the decisive remembrance —the sensation of the uneven cobble-stone before the Hôtel de

---

[8]Not to be forgotten . . . that there is a *motif* in my life that recurs, more important than that of Albertine's love, and perhaps assimilable to the cock's crow of Vinteuil's Quartet. . . . Cup of tea, trees on promenade, church steeples, etc.

Guermantes. Maurois sums up this cohesion of intense moments like this:

> [à ces moments] le temps est retrouvé et, du même coup, il est vaincu, puisque tout un morceau du passé a pu devenir un morceau du présent. Aussi de tels instants donnent-ils à l'artiste le sentiment d'avoir conquis l'éternité. Cette nuance "nouvelle de la joie, cet apel vers une joie supraterrestre," il ne les oubliera jamais. (*Op. cit.*, p. 173.)[9]

—they are never forgotten because they are proof, for Proust, of the fact that art is justified, for its attempts to transcend ordinary life. Proust's thesis was that human memory, through a cohesive tendency, adds up all the experiences of beauty, all "transcendental" moments which thus accumulatively become the impulse that leads man to perpetuate himself in his works of art, i.e., by another most intense form of self-expression. In the canons of traditional philosophy, such intense forms of self-expression also are defined as partaking by their very nature of the absolute; in fact, they achieve their value because, and to the degree, of their participation in the absolute, the "timeless," the divine. Just as Proust's Marcel sees in the distance the church steeples jut forth like boulders in the inexorably passing river of time, so Resnais' couple in their love transcend their own lives and their quotidian norms. But there is one decisive difference: the couple's love is as timeless *to them*— and not to Marguerite Duras or to Alain Resnais—as the promenade below the trees was *to Proust*. In Proust, objective experiences—such as Marcel's were to Proust—and subjective experiences—such as the writing of Marcel's story—are, for all practical purposes, the same. In fact, they must be the same, because he uses the cyclic structure: a circle whose circumference is joined where life joins literature—a movement, by the way, that characterized French 19th-century literature in

---

[9][At such moments] time is found again and, simultaneously, it is conquered, for a whole fragment of the past has been able to become a fragment of the present. Also, such instances give the artist the feeling of having conquered eternity. This "new nuance of joy, this call to a supraterrestrial joy," he will never forget it.

general (Frères Goncourt). It is no wonder, then, that, as was said before, Proust makes his Marcel decide at the end of *À la Recherche . . .* to write the very book that Proust has just finished. In Resnais' film this juncture between life and literature remains entirely literary; in other words, he and Mlle. Duras, the author of the libretto, were so aware of this cyclic structure that they treated it as a topic, at the same time distancing themselves from it. I refer, of course, to the film-within-the-film-sequence towards the beginning of *HMA*: A manifestation is being filmed. Schoolchildren with banners march through the streets. The heroine, in this sequence of the film-within-the-film, has no function to fulfill. So she—and the hero—watch the procession and then, suddenly, run away from it. What this signifies is obvious: They run away from the cyclic structure of Resnais' film and, by doing so, flee from literature into life—their own life: the subject of *HMA*. On the level of artistic probability, the flight is motivated, seemingly, by the incompatibility of their love with the memories of Hiroshima, of something intensely alive with something that recalls people intensely dead.

7. Above, when writing about some of the characteristics of the "interior time," I pointed out that the film becomes progressively slower. I called this a dramaturgical aspect of the *temps-réel* component of the "interior time" and emphasized its formal purpose, which is to dilute the *leitmotive* instead of repeating them. In *HMA*, action (on the *temps-réel* level) and flashbacks (onto the *temps-psychologique* plane) *are not essentially independent of each other*. There could be no action if there were no flashbacks, because the latter cause the former *and* the former causes the latter.[10] Past and present are a sort of emulsion, little drops of past time being suspended in the present, and vice versa. The phenomenon mentioned above might be described as the prevalence in so much "time-art" of

[10] It is interesting to note that Resnais, in the interview the above-mentioned number of *Esprit* printed, mentioned himself that in certain moments his collaborators believed the whole story of *HMA* to be only "a dream of the heroine." Later, when *L'année dernière à Marienbad* came out, Resnais again stated that the film can be interpreted as a "dream of the heroine."

a *perpetual present*. We find it in Lawrence Durrell, in Proust, in Robert Musil's *Der Mann ohne Eigenschaften*, in the new French school of the *antiroman* (Nathalie Sarraute, Michel Butor, Alain Robbe-Grillet—the latter Resnais' collaborator on *L'année dernière à Marienbad*) and, of course, in Alain Resnais himself. The method by which this effect of a perceptual present is achieved may best be circumscribed as a "flattening" of past and future into an even present. Undoubtedly, this denotes mankind's—or its antennae, the artists'—constant endeavor to fight against its becoming past and, by implication, to hold at a distance the approaching future, including, for them, that of Hiroshima's past.

8. We see now that Resnais' flashbacks are so organized and interwoven with the narration in the *temps réel* as to annul the normal time perspective and to create an effect of simultaneity. The most interesting use of the "flattening" of time is made in the museum-sequences of the film and in the way the topic of Hiroshima is developed throughout the film. The museum is, as it were, a flashback frozen into the present, blasted into the rock of time the same way that contours of a human being were found to have been engraved into a wall near the center of the explosion of Hiroshima. And yet, the topic of Hiroshima, so forcefully pressed upon the minds and the emotions of the spectators in the beginning, recedes more and more as the action of the film progresses, both by becoming more and more absent as a pictorial element, succeeded instead by long shots of the new Hiroshima, and by being overcome more and more as an impediment to the couple's love. This slow fading of the primary psychological presence of Hiroshima is of course nothing but the symbol of the process of forgetting that time imposes on the couple. It is a parallel symbol to the oblivion the heroine imposes on her first lover, the German soldier.

9. But could all this preoccupation with time not simply be overlooked? No. For, if we do, we do not understand the film: Time and its manifestations in man, forgetting, are the very theme of the film, as they were to be again in *L'année*. . . . In *HMA*, Resnais investigates above all the phenomenon of obliv-

ion. In scene after scene he circles around this so essentially "timely" element of human life: forgetfulness—and its ethical implications. The film, it is true, does not have as its message "Thou shalt not forget!" Nor does it dictate "Thou shalt forget!" It simply does research on the subject of time as it becomes petrified in oblivion. The film, just as Proust, is *à la recherche du temps qu'on a perdu* . . . and shows how with this loss also the lessons are lost that human experience has drawn and draws each day, incessantly, only to forget them. Resnais' film, in this light, represents a statement about man's attitude towards his history: history is the concrete record of all the lessons drawn from the experience of mankind, lessons whose usefulness for the present has been forgotten. In short, Resnais implies that it is wrong to say that history *teaches* anything. It never does, it never has. History only *explains*. The only "lesson" we can draw from this insight is that we never heed the lessons we have "learned."

To exemplify this, *HMA* has to interweave past and present, must show how the past affects the present and how the present even affects the past. Nowhere can this better be seen than in the restaurant scene. The heroine threatens to become mad again the very moment when past and present touch each other, when her memories become so strong that she confounds past and present. The Japanese architect slaps her! This is, theoretically, the most important moment of the film, for here Resnais leaves Proust behind, or at least goes further than he. How much further can be measured, as it were, if we remember the scene of the hand of the Japanese on the bed-cloth. This sight recalls a similar one: the hand of the German soldier who lies dead in the street of Nevers. It is the madeleine all over again. In the restaurant scene, however, the evocation of an impression of the past by events in the present, is, so to say, brusquely short-circuited: by slapping the heroine, the Japanese lover becomes the executor of Resnais' ultimate statement about time and man. The empirical order of things—i.e., past belongs to the past and present to the present—is reestablished, must be reestablished, else we become unfit for life—mad.

The order of things as we understand them asserts itself and its rights by all means: either we accept it and thus become capable of meeting life on our terms, or we refuse it and become insane, as the heroine did after the death of her first lover. In passing, mention may be made of one particularly original symbol that Resnais uses to drive this point home: up until the slap the flashbacks to Nevers always show the town as peopled with human beings. After the slap, Nevers is shown in the dimension of a ghost-town, empty of human figures. The heroine can return to her home-town now and find it empty of significance. She has conquered her past.

10. Forgetfulness, then, its necessity and its tragedy, are what the story of the film is about. In it Resnais and Mlle. Duras see an aspect of *la condition humaine*. In *HMA*, they decline the word "forgetfulness" in the forms of human grammar, exemplifying a universal quality in particular lives. That is why their film is a great work of art. Let us look at some of the implications of their theme:

(a) The actress, by giving in to her present love, fears that she is betraying her earlier love. At the same time, she remembers that the loss of her first lover drove her mad. May not the memory of that loss together with the degree of intensity her present love manifests drive her mad again?

(b) The architect and she live and love each other in a place where one of the most horrible and most symbolic crimes of mankind against itself has taken place. It is like making love in a graveyard. Instinctively man shrinks away from such proximity of death to love. And yet, here they are, both, loving each other physically and talking about what Hiroshima was like. Resnais underlines their state of mind and their emotions skilfully by making—while the soundtrack gives us the lovers' conversation—the tour through the Hiroshima museum, by showing sequences of the film the French actress has a part in, by visiting the hospital, by stills of the victims, by the gruesome remnants of the catastrophe: the ruins and the molten expanses of the city. This is the stage on which the hero and the heroine have come to love each other. Parallel to this exposition, the progress of their love is shown, its oscillations between shying away from it because of the reasons mentioned, and forgetting them in order to give the present its due, in order to validate their love. Both can say "yes" only by saying "no": "yes," to themselves, to this moment, to their love; "no," to all that unites against it and them. The ethical implications are never resolved, a characteristic that only very great works of art have. Chekhov asked: "Am I not fooling the people, if I don't know all the answers?"

(c) But there is one aspect that is more important yet: If the heroine loves the Japanese and resigns herself to relegating her first lover to the gallery of inoperant memories, does she not also, implicitly and in the future, depreciate her present love? For, if in face of her present love she comes to renounce or to neutralize her earlier love, does this not imply the ephemeralness of love in general, no matter how strongly it may be felt?

(d) But Resnais does not come to a halt there. He draws the conclusion on a universal level: if the heroine of the film can forget her first lover and, by implication, one day will surely forget her second, is this not proof that one day mankind, the Japanese nation, the people of the city of Hiroshima itself, will forget the disaster that befell them?

(e) Applying this conclusion to the question of time, we come to the insight that, in accepting the power of the present we admit also the right to the future to *become* present. One might say: a sorrow (the heroine's forgetting of her first lover) and a joy (her acceptance of the present one) make for the reestablishment of the order of time and thus of history. This may be considered as Resnais' most memorable comment on modern time-consciousness.

11. We can turn now to what was set out above in connection with the "time-perspectives" and see how everything in this film, in one way or another, complements everything else and how from these complementary elements arise two important formal principles of *HMA*.

First, on the active side, the atomic explosion is symbolically equalled to the heroine's love for the German and the consequences of this love: insanity.

Second, on the passive side, her first love was a forbidden

love, forbidden by the society she lived in. As in Greek tragedy the gods, so here, in Nevers, society reestablished its rights and its order by killing the German and thus driving the young girl to insanity. Only *time* heals her, i.e., forgetting. Japan, too, recuperates through time, as the last sequences of the film clearly indicate.

II. PROUST, RESNAIS, AND TIME

In conclusion, it seems advisable to point out the difference between Proust and Resnais in relation to their common subject, time.

Proust puts the emphasis on the change in people wrought by time. This change he records and saves from oblivion by remembering. *Resnais* cannot put the accent on the same elements—although he certainly shows his awareness of them—because he portrays a love story. Lovers cannot live or love in the consciousness of forgetting. From this arises the film's problem. *Proust's* two main themes are, first, the time that destroys; second, the memory that conserves. *Resnais* treats these themes, too, but the other way round: first, for his protagonists, memory destroys; second, time restores. *Proust* is interested in memory. *Resnais* studies forgetting. In *Proust*, memories cause joy—the madeleine. In *Resnais'* film, memories cause sorrow and even terror—the hand. In *both* artists the raw material of their works is the same: the tension between past and present. But *Resnais* investigates two things: that which is being forgotten and why it is forgotten. *Proust* mainly studies that which has been forgotten. Besides, *Resnais* has a socio-political dimension in his film. *Proust* concentrates on the sociological dimension.

Using a metaphor, the difference between the two artists can be described as the way in which they see the texture they have woven: *Resnais* sees the back of the tapestry, *Proust* only the front. Proust's is a tapestry with many motifs; Resnais' is one with many variations on the same motif.

Resnais does not wish the past to reside in the present, he

pushes it back into its own realm. Proust celebrates the past, searches it, makes it into the present, and lives in it: *Le temps retrouvé* is the title of his last book.

Proust, although he knew of course as well as Resnais that the past cannot be revived except in memories, prefers the memories and finds his redemption in them. Resnais believes one can keep on living only by forgetting, no matter how important is that which we have experienced and are going to forget—sooner or later.

Last Year at Marienbad

Jacques Brunius, "Every Year in Marienbad: or The Discipline of Uncertainty"

○○○

In *Last Year at Marienbad* (1961) Alain Resnais intensified his search for a literary cinema attempted in *Hiroshima, Mon Amour* (1959). Whereas for the earlier film he requested Mlle. Duras to provide "a love story set in Hiroshima which would not look too absurdly trivial in the context of the atomic bomb," in *Marienbad*, for a script, Resnais turned to Robbe-Grillet, a writer whose ideal is "to construct a purely mental space and time—those of dreams, perhaps, or of memory, those of any affective life—without worrying too much about traditional relations of cause and effect. . . ." *(Last Year at Marienbad*, Grove Press, p. 8). As a leading exponent of "The New Novel," Robbe-Grillet's own fiction is impeccably objective about subjectivity. While in *Hiroshima, Mon Amour* the realities of divergent times and places is a serious preoccupation, *Marienbad* is a study in the timelessness of the mind's action. As in the earlier film there are shifting time sequences, but now sequences are repeated (sometimes with variations) and sequential relationships between elements are absent. The substance of the film is the labyrinth of human thoughts, recollections, and fantasies that engross the viewer in their kinetic unfolding.

There has been great disparity of opinion among critics regarding *Marienbad*: some have dismissed it as nonsense, a deliberate effort at obfuscation; some have found it an interesting but careless attempt to imitate a mental process; some

Last Year at Marienbad, directed by Alain Resnais, 1961 (*Museum of Modern Art/Film Stills Archive*)

others have imposed on it a conventional "narrative" interpretation that is distorting and oversimplifying; and yet
numerous others have convincingly opened vistas for further
viewing, appreciation, and interpretation. Jacques Brunius
belongs to this last group. He argues that Resnais made the
film with a definite structural order, simple but difficult to
perceive, from which emerges a comprehensible reality. His
essay is an argument for the view that "the narrator is giving
us his recollections *as they come*, and does not appear to be
himself in a position to discriminate between these emotional
fragments. He does know himself which are dreams and
which are shreds of lived reality."

———◆———

L'ANNÉE DERNIÈRE À MARIENBAD has by now produced an
amount of critical literature which, collected in volume, would
easily outweigh the original script and dialogue. Yet there is
no other film about which so little has been said in so many
words.

I don't think a single critic has missed recording the now
famous difference of interpretation between the two authors,
and many of them have used this "difference" to attack the
film. Those who gloat over it fail at the same time to emphasise
that Resnais and Robbe-Grillet have proclaimed their complete
agreement about the construction and the style of the film.
Moreover, the "gloaters" grossly exaggerate this "difference of
interpretation." As so much was made of this trifle, let us
reduce it once and for all to its proper dimensions.

Resnais said he was inclined to believe that something really
did happen last year in Marienbad (but he never said what!),
Robbe-Grillet wrote in his Preface that the Narrator "gives
the impression of making it up." (Incidentally, this is
slanted in the published English translation, where "on a l'impression" is rendered by "we sense.") As they have carefully
constructed a film based on doubt—where the nearest thing to
a story is precisely the story of a doubt, where even the character who attempts to persuade the other is not quite sure of
every detail—it would be a failure indeed if they had not

managed to maintain at least that amount of uncertainty. I am by no means certain that Resnais and Robbe-Grillet are absolutely sincere about this so-called difference of interpretation. Even if their guesses, relative to what happened or not, were identical, pretending to differ would still be the best hint they could give of a right approach to their film; and would be sufficiently justified by this consideration.

The critics should rather thank them for their courteous refusal to explain any more. Any additional information or explanation would sound like a slap in the face of the critics and an exposure of their emotional and intellectual inadequacy. As it is, Resnais and Robbe-Grillet have already said too much.

Another important point to note is that most "anti-Marienbad" reviewers misleadingly state that the film presents three characters, X, A and M—thus betraying that they are not really talking about the film, where these initials are never spoken, but about the published script, where they are used for the purpose of convenience. Such a lapse explains why so many have failed to let the sensuous impact of the film, both visual and aural, affect their sensibilities. Theirs are literary reactions to a printed film script.

There is not much point in trying to convert those who refuse to be moved or interested. Some of my best friends, and some of the people I most respect, simply state that the film bores them. They are not likely to make the effort to see it again and offer themselves to its strange fascination. The obvious conclusion, if you are bored, is that the film must be "pretentious nonsense."

In another category are those who, in spite of both authors' protests, try to understand what *Marienbad* symbolises. Their discoveries are stupendous, especially if one takes into account that their excavations are attempted without first examining the object submitted to their investigations. I mean that they start unveiling symbols before they have described and clarified the film's *structure*. This might be fruitful if it were a conventional film with a conventional story line. It happens to be a very unconventional film where the content can only be discovered by consideration of the structure. I wouldn't go so far as to say that the form and content are totally identical—this would fail to take into account the margin of uncertainty left deliberately in this structure, where interpretations factual, psychological or symbolical, are permitted. However, it can safely be said that *Marienbad* is probably the first film where, to a very great extent, the content *is* the form, and would not exist outside this particular form. Any attempt to construct valid interpretations must be postponed until the structure has been studied, described and understood. Only thus can we map the few certainties contained in the film and delineate the shadowy zones left to our imaginations.

I confess that when I saw the film for the first time I was completely defeated by a few apparent inconsequences. I was of course quite prepared (by my own writings on the subject, and my own experience as a film-maker and viewer) to accept a "mental continuity," a continuity of thought, instead of the usual factual-spatial continuity—after all we are familiar with the flashback—but I could not see clearly the line of thought justifying the breaks in continuity. I suspected that a certain number of them might be arbitrary. Yet I could not resist the hypnotic fascination, the visual beauty and dignity of the film, the purity of writing. It induced me to caution.

A second viewing forced me to take sides, convinced me that here was *the* film I had been waiting for during the last thirty years. A brief glance at my own writings on the cinema reminded me that I had advocated the making of films following a mental process, and shown that it was not only possible but desirable. A number of films indicated the way: *Caligari, Sherlock Junior, Peter Ibbetson, Berkeley Square, Un Chien Andalou, L'Age d'Or, Citizen Kane, La Règle du Jeu*[1] and a few others perhaps. But here was a film which carried their lesson to its logical conclusion.

After a third and fourth viewing I discovered that I was more and more interested each time, my pleasure and fascina-

---

[1]Richard Massingham's *And so to Work*, less known, must be mentioned separately. Massingham's own notion of film-continuity was almost exactly that of Resnais, who probably knew his films through the Cinémathèque Française.

tion increasing with familiarity. I am now quite prepared to claim that *Marienbad* is the greatest film ever made, and to pity those who cannot see this.

Those who start from the premise that the authors have deliberately, maliciously, arbitrarily, upset the chronology of events, and even those who obligingly try to put it right in their minds, are blinding themselves to the relative simplicity of the film. It is this simplicity that must be perceived before going any further. There never was any chronological order to upset, as there never was any certainty about any single episode described by the Narrator.[2] The only order is the order in which these events, real or imaginary, remembered or invented, come to his mind. The film is constructed in order to build up the gradual increase of his conviction, which is reflected by a weakening of the girl's resistance to persuasion. From time to time a doubt brings a temporary regression in this process of persuasion, but both the build-up and the setbacks result in an increase of tension between them. I feel in *Marienbad* a far more riveting suspense than in any Hitchcock thriller.

Let us try to define more precisely what is the architecture of this "story of a persuasion."

First a point on which I think everybody can agree: this film is presented as a process of recollection. Secondly, it has the atmosphere and the form of a dream. The opening droning recitative is obviously intended to put us in the mood and to warn us of what to expect.

Whether it is the dream itself—or a recollection of a dream —or the recollection of actual events presenting themselves in the memory as if they might have been a dream—or even mixed recollections of dreams and actual events—this is at the

[2]Although this film could rightly be called "anti-narrative," does not give us a story in the conventional sense, that is rationalise *a posteriori*, I shall persist in calling the man "The Narrator," because to narrate is exactly what he is trying to do, even if to a large extent the film is devoted to his failure to do so. Alain Resnais pointed out that Albertazzi's Italian accent in French is meant to show that his narration is *not* an interior monologue.

moment idle speculation, and anyway it is irrelevant, because the narrator is giving us his recollections *as they come*, and does not appear to be himself in a position to discriminate between these emotional fragments. He does not know himself which are dreams and which are shreds of lived reality. This uncertainty is essentially the subject of the film.

At this point we cannot ignore the possibility that this dream is not *his*, but *hers*. While the bulk of the film follows the Narrator's recollections, some sequences follow *her* mental processes and show events as *she* imagines them, even confronting their different memories of the same object (is there a painting or a mirror above the mantelpiece?). Sometimes the Narrator's voice seems to be trying to guide or influence her recollections or imaginings, as we see them on the screen. (Her delay in reproducing the posture he describes—her groping along large mirrors—his insistence that she goes to the bed—the door open or shut, etc. . . .)

This again does not really affect the general structure. If it is *his* dream it can include his guesses about what she dreamt or imagined. If it is *her* dream, it is a dream in which his voice is the main leading thread and she inserts her own dreams or memories or imaginings within *his* recollections. What is important is that most of the time their dreams or recollections do not coincide, with a few exceptions, when the persuasive voice seems to shatter her insistence upon not remembering, and she sometimes admits glimpses of recollection.

However, the main body of recollections or imaginings takes place in the mind of the narrator. As both hypotheses give finally the same result I shall from now on accept the first as simpler and more convenient for the sake of analysis.

The next point—and it flows from what precedes—is that whoever is dreaming or recollecting, there are several dreams or recollections within the main narrative. This fact amply justifies the sudden changes of costume and breaks in continuity. It only requires a small amount of attention to see that such apparent ruptures of continuity are simply passages to another time, another idea, another recollection, or sometimes, to the same thing as imagined by the other character. The changes of costume, far from being arbitrary, are clearly intended to be of some help to the spectator. How ungrateful of some critics to denounce them as puzzling and gratuitous!

It will be noticed here that I have not yet mentioned the possibility that the film might be describing present events in the large hotel, during which the Narrator, meeting the girl, tries to persuade her that they met last year. I have not done so because although I originally believed it I dismissed this belief after seeing the film a second time and after verifying my impression by reference to the script. My reasons for pushing aside this hypothesis are as follows:

(*a*) The Narrator starts, it is true, in the present tense, but soon abandons it before any action takes place and speaks in the past tense until the end, except, of course, in the scenes with other characters.

(*b*) The whole of the end scene, showing the girl finally persuaded to follow him, is equally narrated in the past tense.

I do not see how any part of the film could be taken as describing the present when these two sequences, which constitute a frame for the whole film, are both situated in the past. They establish clearly that the entire film is a recollection of past events, dreams or imaginings.

The illusion that some scenes are set in the present comes from what Robbe-Grillet's preface defines in these words: "The essential characteristic of the cinema-image is its present-ness." The same could be said of the dream-image.

Robbe-Grillet also remarks in this preface: "There is no last year, and Marienbad is no longer to be found on any map. This past too has no reality beyond the moment it is evoked with sufficient force; and when it finally triumphs it has merely become the present, as if it had never ceased to be so." The contradiction with what I have just said is only apparent. In the realm of dreams and imaginings we necessarily observe time from above. One might as well consider some of the episodes of *Marienbad* as happening in the future. Perhaps some of the action takes place next year? We are outside the flow of time and the usual notion of time has become meaningless.

This will help me to go a step further. I had up to now considered simultaneously several possibilities:

1. Recollections of actual facts.
2. Recollections of dreams or day-dreams.
3. Invention on the spur of the moment.
4. A blend of the three.
5. A possible difference of nature between: *(a)* scenes illustrating these recollections or inventions, representing the past; and *(b)* scenes of persuasion representing the present.

We can now dismiss the last distinction. If he was just inventing it *now*, he would not *conclude in the past*. How could she have already eloped with him before having been persuaded?

There is not much point either in maintaining any longer the distinction between recollected dreams or reality. Whatever it is that the Narrator recollects—real facts, imaginings or dreams—the mental process is the same. The film is conceived as a clinical report of such a mental process, and carefully avoids establishing whether any of the events recollected are real or imagined, past, present or future. This is perfectly legitimate. When we try to remember certain events, especially of an emotional nature, we sometimes find it difficult to be sure that they really happened, that we did not dream them. Perhaps we *only* dreamt them. Perhaps we *also* dreamt them. The reverse is true in any attempt to remember a dream: we sometimes introduce some memory of a real event into our memory of a dream.

We can therefore consider *Marienbad* one way or the other. I shall from now on talk about it as if it were a dream. There are enough mentions of dreams in Robbe-Grillet's preface and in Resnais' various statements to justify such a choice. Furthermore it is easy to recognize in *Marienbad* all the familiar mechanisms of the dream: disguise, displacement, condensation, dramatisation. What follows will add further justification.

There is a category of dreams which are more likely to induce in our minds the kind of confusion with real events

I was referring to previously. Such are *recurring* dreams. After we have dreamt the same event several times, it is only natural that we should begin to believe the last dream was inspired by some real happening and not only by some previous dream or series of dreams. This is further complicated by the well-known phenomenon of false recognition, by which, whether in dream or in our daily life, we have the fallacious impression of having been here before, or of having seen before what is happening now.

In one of the best articles published about *Marienbad* (in *Positif*, No. 44, March, 1962) Robert Benayoun, suggesting the explanation of a meeting in a dream, attributes to this phenomenon the Narrator's illusion of having met the girl before. This hypothesis fits quite well with the assumption that the "present" scenes in the film are really supposed to show what is happening *now*, but I have more or less rejected this idea, and furthermore I do not see how the phenomenon of instant fallacious recollection can help in analysing the structure of the film. On the other hand the *recurring dream* pattern seems to fit better. Before accepting this, however, let us see what reasons I have for suggesting it.

The idea occurred to me the second time I saw the film. While the credit titles are unfolding, we hear the Narrator's voice, sometimes near, sometimes fading away, repeating the same ideas and the same words like a repeating groove, or a loop, but not quite the same, since each time they reappear in a slightly different grouping: "Once again—I walk on, once again, down these corridors. . . . I was already waiting for you. . . ."

Not only are these words "once again" stressed here by repetition, but they crop up later in the film. In conjunction with the repeating groove cum variations, this suggested to me not only the dream, but the recurring dream. The hint was so convincing that I could not help seeing the rest of the film as if it were a recurring dream. Instead of being puzzled, as I had been the first time, by a suspicion of the arbitrary, everything now looked clear, simple and not only legitimate but strictly necessary. When I heard *"And once again* I was walking on down these same corridors, walking for days, for months, *for years,* to meet you . . ." (italics are mine) I was definitely convinced. The various people to whom I suggested this explanation do not seem to have experienced any difficulty in following the continuity of *Marienbad* when they saw it for the first time; and this shows that there is at least *one* approach to the film which eliminates the apparent inconsistencies in continuity.

The fact that, in the Narrator's recollection, several successive dreams are sometimes combined to reconstruct a single sequence of events, is of course sufficient to explain some sudden changes of light and unexpected changes of costume. They always signal the passage from one dream to another. But this is not the strongest argument in favour of my hypothesis, as anyway these changes would be acceptable in an ordinary dream, although they could, with some reason, be considered as relatively gratuitous.

The fact that the characters of the film appear first in the early scenes in frozen attitudes, as photographs in a family holiday album, suggests that these scenes—which might be taken for the present reality, framing as it were the dream recollection—are in fact already dream scenes remembered. The identity of situation in the play being performed and between the characters of the film—to such an extent that in the dialogue on the stage, the Narrator and the male partner of the play can relay each other—is another pointer hinting that we are already in a dream. What the actors on the stage are playing is the final scene of the film. Most of the snatches of conversation overheard in the various lounges of the hotel are in some way pre-echoes of episodes which we shall see later (the couples discussing problems similar to the Narrator's and the girl's situation—the broken heel—the mysterious Frank who was "a friend of her father's and had come to keep an eye on her," etc. . . . .).

This does not supply any conclusive interpretation. They can be taken as the rough material from which the Narrator constructs his dream or day-dream or invention. On the other hand he may have picked them out simply because they have a more or less direct bearing on his own situation. They could also be a disguise for his obsessive preoccupations, as it often happens in dreams (and especially in recurring dreams) where the same material can give birth to different dramatisations. In any case, if they do not specifically confirm the recurring dream hypothesis, they fit easily in its pattern.

There are, however, several oddities in the film which nobody has tried to explain, and which I believe cannot be satisfactorily explained by any other hypothesis.

First there is the fact that some recollections of the same event are presented in several different ways, none being more certain than the others. The most blatant case is that of the several different endings, including the murder of a woman by the man who may be her husband. The Narrator rejects the endings he does not like, especially the murder one which is incompatible with taking her away ("No, this is not the right ending. . . . I must have you alive. . . ."), and only accepts the final one, which represents his burning wish. He does not even want to have raped her. He wants her to follow him. But the only possible origin of the various twists in his story is in a series of dreams (or day-dreams) which did not always turn the same way. It has become difficult for him, now, to remember which was, or should have been, the right one. It may be objected that these various endings might all have been part of a single dream, and that they may be dreams within a dream. (Some of them may even be *her* contribution to the dream.) This is possible, but less likely, and does not tally so satisfactorily with the words "once again." Let us not forget that the Narrator seems to think that his waiting quest has already lasted "for years."

We shall find further proof and confirmation in an analysis of the most disturbing discrepancies in chronology. There are at least two very puzzling cases—that is, puzzling unless my hypothesis is accepted.

For clarity I shall henceforth number the years. The time of persuasion, which we are tempted to call the present, will be Year Zero; and last year will be Year Minus One.

Let us remember the scene where the Narrator says: "What

proof do you still need? I had also kept a photograph of you taken in the park . . . but when I gave it to you, you answered again, that it proved nothing. . . ." So he has not given the photograph to her just now. When then? Let us assume it was a few days before the Year Zero scene shown at the moment. It must therefore have been taken last year in Marienbad or elsewhere. He then goes on evoking their meetings the year before (Year Minus One), in the park, in her bedroom, and, on a certain evening, a visit of the supposed husband to her bedroom, during which the photograph in question *is already in her possession* (which gives rise to questions from the so-called husband: "Who took it? When was it taken?").

From the wording of the Narration, one seems to be justified in assuming that this whole sequence is an evocation of the preceding year (Minus One), which would mean that the photograph was not taken last year (Minus One) but two years ago (Year Minus Two) or even before (Year Minus Three), and given to her last Year (Minus One), in a previous attempt at persuasion. However, in the hypothesis of a recurring dream, an apparent discrepancy becomes perfectly natural.

There was another similar instance (although less noticeable because no prop was involved) in a previous scene. The Narrator and the woman are sitting in a hotel lounge. The other guests have left them. She sits on a small sofa on the right of the frame. He sits on a chair at a table on the left. This scene obviously takes place in what one is tempted to call the "present," that is Year Zero. He says, talking to her about the preceding year:

"You never seemed to be waiting for me—but we kept meeting at every turn of the paths, behind every bush, at the foot of each statue, near every pond . . . we were talking about anything at all . . . or else we weren't talking at all. . . ."

From these words we are led to expect an evocation of these meetings, and true, it comes in a series of shots of them in the park. In the last shot of this sequence (which we assume represents another meeting of Year Minus One) he says: "But you always stayed at a certain distance. . . ." In the past tense!

So it appears that last year, Year Minus One, he was already trying to remind her of previous meetings having taken place the year before: Year Minus Two—or Year Minus Three . . . who knows?

If you insist on regarding *Marienbad* as a series of arbitrary inconsistencies, you will no doubt conclude that this is just another gratuitous whim of the editor or the director (or indeed the scriptwriter, as this follows the published script). I happen to believe that such a carefully polished work is not likely to be unnecessarily arbitrary. The possibility must be considered, of course, that this is part of a deliberate ambiguity: that the authors have just reverted without warning to Year Zero at the end of a sequence which appeared to take place in Year Minus One, and that they do so again in the sequence about the photograph. I am more inclined to believe that within this ambiguity, there is a rule, a "rule of ambiguity" as it were, and that this rule is so chosen that it allows a certain kind of logic to be respected without dispelling the ambiguity necessary to the style and mood of the film.

A last example for good measure: the recollection of the meeting at the foot of the ambiguous statue occurs twice. The first time the Narrator recalls it: "Remember: quite near us there was a group of stone . . ." and he continues: "The others around us had come closer. Someone gave the statue's name. . . ." So they were not alone. But *we do not see* the scene. The second time we *see* the meeting, including their discussion about the meaning of the statue, but this time the Narrator and the woman are alone.

It is clear that this scene would not have happened twice, but could have been dreamt or imagined twice, in different circumstances. Such a difference cannot possibly be a failure of memory. If you remember such a striking episode in your relationship with a girl, in such detail as to be able to recall the conversation, you also remember if there were other people around. It is again typical of a recurrent dream.

I had reached this point in my reflections, and was already convinced that such an hypothesis was the only one to account totally for the film's structure and for the various statements made by the authors, when I read by chance (I had given up reading about this film) the interview given by Resnais and Robbe-Grillet to Claude Ollier. There suddenly appeared confirmation by Robbe-Grillet himself of the preceding deductions.

"It is possible that past episodes, like present ones, may be partially or even completely imagined, or dreamed, or reconstructed askew. There may have been several stories in the past which the hero confuses and tangles up. There may never have been anything but a desire which takes shape little by little under the influence of words, by persuasion and suggestion. But this does not exclude the possibility, after all, that there was indeed a meeting, last year at Marienbad." (So much for the famous difference with Resnais!)

The words *recurring dream* are not pronounced, but the hint is clear. It will be noticed that in my series of observations I have never definitely stated that *Marienbad is* a recurring dream. My purpose was to show that the recurring dream pattern is the most convenient image to describe the structure of the film and to facilitate its understanding. All apparent discrepancies become natural in such a pattern, where the dreamer (or day-dreamer) is more or less aware of his previous dreams, in which he already remembered some anterior dreams, and so on, as in a mental corridor of mirrors.

In the article quoted above, Robert Benayoun came very close to a description of this structure when he compared *Marienbad* to Raymond Roussel's *Nouvelles Impressions d'Afrique*, which is written in a series of parenthesis within parenthesis within parenthesis, and so on, like Chinese boxes. This is a different image to denote the same structure. Resnais' allusion to "degrees of reality" is another.

Of course this interpretation leaves a number of ambiguities and uncertainties. They are precisely characteristic of such a tale. They are the stuff dreams are made of. They also appear in recollections of deep emotional crises, where the boundaries between facts and fancies, actions and desires, become blurred. They are necessary, indispensable in this film.

Resnais has asked several times for the spectator "not to

reconstruct a story coldly from the outside, but to live it at the same time as the characters, and from the inside." Indeed the authors of this film never adopt the god-like omniscient attitude, usual among authors who know everything about their characters. They have put themselves in exactly the same position as their main character. As for us spectators, we can identify ourselves completely with the Narrator, because we know what he knows, what he remembers, never more or less. We can also identify ourselves with the girl, because it might after all be her dream and because the Narrator sometimes identifies himself with her. So do we in dreams where we can be ourselves or someone else, where we can be ourselves and at the same time *see* ourselves from outside.

Seen from this point of view *Marienbad* is no longer obscure or mysterious. At least there is no longer any mystery at the level of the film's shape. There is no more need to look for deep symbolism in order to enjoy the film with a small high-brow minority. It can be enjoyed, and immensely enjoyed, for what it is, once you see clearly what it is.

The mystery and the symbols, if you insist, must now be excavated from a deeper stratum. Before indulging in such exercises, however, I contend that a closer examination of the characters of the film is indispensable. It has been said that they behave like puppets, or androids, or robots. I am not so sure of that. They are certainly withdrawn, secretive, but inhuman—no. They only appear so because we do not know all their motives. In everyday life we are often in the same position of being puzzled by our best friends' behaviour when we are not in their total confidence.

As I have taken great pains to show that the so-called differences of interpretation between Resnais and Robbe-Grillet were nothing of the sort, I hope I will not be accused of perversity if I bring to light a really important difference, a major departure in Resnais' film from Robbe-Grillet's script. (There are not many really significant ones.)

I was saying earlier that I find it easy to identify myself with the Narrator. With the elusive character played by Sacha Pitoëff I feel no immediate identification at all. With the girl, I suppose a female spectator can find identification possible. I find it difficult as a man, of course, but mainly because if I were she, I should know who is this enigmatic character referred to as "Your husband, perhaps." To which she never answers.

Now, is he her husband? I do not think the hero believes he is, or he would not put it that way. Living in the same hotel, and claiming as he does to have met them last year, and being so obsessively in love with her, he must have enquired discreetly, of the other guests, of the porter, the receptionist, the chambermaids, even bribed them to discover more. (You will notice that I am now talking as of a real story, but once having admitted the particular shape of the story as happening in the mind, I see no reason now not to treat it as any other story, which also happened in the mind of its author.)

The Narrator has not discovered the real status of the girl's companion or their exact relationship. Why is it so secret? Why is she so noncommittal? Would the explanation be that this relationship is uncommon, unconventional, perhaps reprehensible or likely to call for reprobation? Personally I never thought he behaved like a husband, but he does not even behave like a lover or a suitor, at least not like an ordinary lover or suitor. What is he then? Would he be like the Frank who appears only in people's conversations: "Frank had convinced her he was a friend of her father's and had come to keep an eye on her. It was a funny kind of eye, of course. . . ."

To me he behaved much more like a brother. I was so puzzled that I thought of looking up the script to find his description, at his first appearance. And it reads: "A man of about fifty (tall, grey-haired) with a good deal of style. . . ." Everyone will agree that Sacha Pitoëff, who has a good deal of style, is not grey-haired and does not look fifty—not even a well-preserved fifty.

So Robbe-Grillet originally intended this character to look like an ageing husband, lover, or suitor, or guardian, *old enough to be her father*. He took further care to preserve a very odd suspicion about their relationship, a suspicion which was even bound to imply that *he might be her own father*. Written as it was, the suggestion of possible incest was unmistakable. I am surprised that no reader or critic has yet noticed it.

In the film this suggestion is modified by the choice of a younger actor to play the part. Is this pre-censorship of a scabrous situation by the producers? Or forced upon them by submission of the script to the censorship committee? Whatever it is, it has obviously been accepted by Resnais and Robbe-Grillet—let us see what they made of it.

I have already said that Pitoëff's acting suggested to me a brother rather than a husband. This was probably a devious way of finding a substitute for the original ambiguity in the situation. But that is not all. There is a detail in the film which was not specified in the script. (A surprising thing when one thinks of the meticulous descriptions in which Robbe-Grillet indulges.) When the camera, twice in the film, arrives near the room where the theatricals take place, the script describes: "Lastly a framed theatre poster for a play with a foreign, meaningless title." In the film, this poster is seen twice: the title of the play is foreign, but *not* meaningless. It is ROSMER.

Rosmer . . . Rebecca West . . . Dr. West . . . Kroll. . . .

It is not the usual title of Ibsen's play *Rosmersholm,* but it could easily be. One recalls instantly the most intriguing scene of the play when Kroll, brother of the late Mrs. Rosmer, reveals to Rebecca West that her adoptive father, Dr. West, the man who took care of her after her mother's death, might have been her own father. Rebecca seems upset far beyond her alleged concern not to be an illegitimate daughter. She never admits any clear motive for her torment, but the spectator cannot help remembering that Rebecca, on the threshold of triumph, has unexpectedly turned down Rosmer's offer to marry her, and in her last scene with Rosmer she refers to "her past" to convince him that marriage is impossible. There are several allusions to this mysterious event in her past, strongly suggesting that she has been Dr. West's mistress. There is never in the play any open assertion of incest, but

Ibsen's intention of planting it indirectly in our minds is obvious enough. Several commentators have noted it, and Freud, following Otto Rank, has tried to relate it to the father-daughter relationship between Rebecca and Rosmer—but this is another story.

I feel absolutely unable to accept such a coincidence as fortuitous. Only Resnais could tell us whether the choice of the title *Rosmer* was unconscious or deliberate, but the fact that Robbe-Grillet's suggestion of incest is replaced by another hint to the same effect cannot be attributed to chance. We must therefore take it as significant—slightly more recondite, but nevertheless detectable. The brother-sister incestuous relationship is a perfectly acceptable substitute for the father-daughter one, in this case where the general attitude of the "brother" is more that of a guardian than that of a lover. It is even more satisfactory, as it avoids the age discrepancy which could be visually repellent to some spectators. The girl's fear of love, her hesitation until the last minute, become much clearer. The last scene on the bed between her and her guardian, which was moving but obscure, becomes far more upsetting. We understand better why she still loves him as a brother, while she does not love him any more as a "husband," and is already prepared to leave him. The whole relationship, oddly distant and yet intimate, now makes sense.

Another peculiarity of the film has been pointed out by several critics: the disturbing contrast between the frozen atmosphere of the setting and postures, and the latent hysteria perceptible under the restrained dialogue in the convulsive attitudes of Delphine Seyrig. This is probably one of the most fascinating aspects of *Marienbad*, but it remained also one of the most intriguing. If, as I believe, the relationship between the three main characters is derived from such an incestuous situation, the mood of artificially stilted emotion becomes not only understandable but fitting and necessary.

The game of matches, cards or dominoes, not only echoes the triangle situation (like the trees and alleys of the park) but it also parallels the guardian's position. He always wins, but at the same time he loses, and the game expresses his forebodings; his adversary always takes the last match, as he will in the end take the girl away.

Does all this preclude other interpretations of *Last Year in Marienbad?* I don't think so. I only mean that any valid interpretation must take into account the relative amount of certainly contained in the preceding pages. My only purpose was to eliminate the apparently gratuitous, and to push back uncertainties as far as possible into their last entrenchments. There and only there, not before, begins the realm of shadow where speculations are permitted. Many have been suggested which do not necessarily clash with my theory. The "incestuous" theory may even lead to another interpretation according to which the character played by Pitoëff could be the Narrator himself under another dream-disguise (perhaps his Super Ego!)

I shall not venture into symbolic interpretations myself, although I would welcome some more. But do we really need them? When we have exhausted all the possible interpretations that are at the moment only faint gleams in our minds, we shall be tempted to dismiss *Marienbad* and forget about it. I still enjoy being haunted by this film as I never was by any film; I still hope to see it many times and preserve its polyvalent ambiguities. They are the ambiguities of life itself.

Lola

Joel Siegel, "I Found It at the Nudies:
Jacques Demy's Lola, At Last"

ooooooooooooooooooooooooooooooooooooooooooooo

Lola (1961), Jacques Demy's first feature, is a film of
unique freshness and artful technique that, in spite of its
charm, grace, and subtlety, is nonetheless somewhat slighted.
Conditioned by fanciful and sentimental Hollywood musical
comedies, moviegoers who would normally respond to an
exceptional film have tended to dismiss Lola without recognizing Demy's attainment in creating something unusual and
artistically noteworthy—a "musical" that contains both sweetness and light, entertainment and meaning, joy and sorrow,
fantasy and reality. Although framed in the context of
the issue of the neglect of Lola by American audiences, Joel
Siegel's essay is principally an interpretative analysis of the
film. He states that it is "a fable about ideals and illusions,
those sustaining fancies of romance and success in which
all of us indulge and which become for us a second 'reality.'" Among other considerations, Mr. Siegel observes that
Demy structures the film on "a cycle of love and abandonment," and discusses how Demy alludes to old Hollywood
movies to symbolically communicate the theme of illusion.

———————◆———————

. . . There are certain things I believe in profoundly. I
prefer French provincial cities—Nantes, where I was brought
up, or Cherbourg or Nice—to Paris. Here are simple, gentle
people of dignity, who seek to better their lives. I have

Lola, directed by Jacques Demy, 1961 (*Contemporary*)

the same idea in my picture, and I avoid themes of death and evil. I prefer blue to black, births to funerals, red wine to Vichy water, the sun to the rain.

Jacques Demy

Now THAT THE NEW WAVE of French film-making has ended, that burst of cinematic energy between 1959 and 1963 when more than one hundred directors made their first feature films, it is apparent that Jacques Demy's *Lola* deserves to be ranked with the finest of these directorial debuts, alongside Godard's *Breathless*, Truffaut's *The 400 Blows* and, perhaps, Rivette's maddening *Paris Nous Appartient*. Though of indisputable historical importance, *The 400 Blows* and *Breathless* have lost some of their once-stunning impact with the passing years, years that have seen Godard (*My Life to Live, Contempt*) and Truffaut (*Jules and Jim, Shoot the Piano Player*) develop artistic powers quite beyond anything suggested in the promise of their first efforts. In contrast, *Lola* (1960), with its charm, intricacy and formal elegance, has grown in stature and would now appear to be the carefully wrought creation of artistic maturity, after which Demy's subsequent films, the Jeanne Moreau vehicle, *Bay of Angels* (1963) and the "film en chante," *The Umbrellas of Cherbourg* (1964), seem only encouraging beginnings. Sadly, Demy's most recent films are largely unsuccessful; the musical *The Young Girls of Rochefort* (1966), though entertaining, is painfully coy and badly miscalculated, and *Model Shop* (1969), the director's American debut and something of a sequel to *Lola*, is a desperate and disastrous attempt at self-imitation which makes one fearful for Demy's future.

Despite a most favorable critical reception in both France and England, two years elapsed before *Lola* surfaced in New York. Because it was not a money-maker in Europe, the American distributor promoted the film half-heartedly and, when the daily reviews proved hostile, *Lola* was pulled after a brief run and didn't fare much better when made available for non-theatrical showings. After a few more years in limbo, *Lola* improbably turned up on the "nudie" circuit, receiving its Chicago premiere on the crowd-chasing half of a twin bill at the Monroe Theatre, a musty showcase for dubious Krafft-Ebing divertissements. Hyped by such absurdly misleading blurbs as "Confessions of a Sensual B-Girl" and "Ninety Minutes of Hot-Blooded Pleasure," I had found *Lola* at last.

As is sometimes the case with films of unique vision, many of the European critics who hailed *Lola* seemed rather confused about its meaning; one, in particular, thought it an attempt to tell about all of a woman's life without employing flashbacks. *Lola* is essentially a fable about ideals and illusions, those sustaining fancies of romance and success in which all of us indulge and which become for us a second "reality." Experience teams up with society, sometimes in the person of the psychoanalyst, in an attempt to strip us of these illusions, forcing us to "adjust" by proclaiming that maturity cannot be achieved until those youthful dreams have been compromised. Demy is at once simple and quite profound in recognizing the importance, even necessity, of illusion as a part of our humanity, suggesting that in any compromise with "reality," we can never be sure that, by holding out a bit longer, we might not have been able to strike a better bargain. Implicit in this idea is a bittersweet optimism based upon the belief that once in a while the dream really does come true. Many will regard such notions as old-fashioned and rather embarrassing and with good cause; in the popular arts, one seldom finds positive themes developed without the mawkishness of *The Sound of Music* or the outright cynicism of TV situation comedies. Demy's artful and intelligent treatment of a generous, optimistic subject is responsible for much of *Lola's* freshness.

Although *Lola* is not a particularly comic film and seldom attempts to make us laugh, it nonetheless has firm structural roots in the classic comic tradition that begins with Menander, Plautus, and Terence and finds perfection in the comedies of Shakespeare. Surely everyone is familiar with some of the formal devices and conventions which Demy employs: the immediate introduction of the various characters, the reliance upon chance encounters to set these characters in motion, an emphasis upon the themes of Spring and rebirth, first love and childbearing, the presentation of a spectrum of lovers, presupposing a common and cyclical response to the problems and pleasures of loving, and the increasing stylization and simplification of action as the inevitable, optimistic resolution approaches. To these traditional comic devices, Demy adds elements from other genres: the wish-come-true of the fairy tale, the magic of the fable—ending up with a new form unlike anything offered to us before, at least in movies.

Except for Roland, the moody, unsatisfied wanderer who reappears in *The Umbrellas of Cherbourg* as Genvieve's diamond-merchant husband, each of the central characters of *Lola* is part of a common, shared life—a cycle of love and abandonment which is repeated, with only slight variation, from generation to generation. Lola, a dance-hall girl in Nantes, has waited seven years for the return of her lover Michel, the father of her son. She has a casual affair with Frankie, an American sailor who reminds her of Michel, but in doing so, she remains faithful to her lover's memory, guiltless in the event of his return. Because of the emotional strength of her first love, and her faith that, all evidence to the contrary, Michel will return to her, Lola rejects the marriage proposal of Roland, a childhood friend whom she meets again after many years. Mme. Desnoyers' daughter Cecile, a fourteen-year-old, meets and falls in love with Frankie at a carnival on her birthday, in the same setting and at the same age that Lola met Michel. Like Lola, Cecile wants to be a dancer; in fact, Lola's given name was Cecile. Mme. Desnoyers, a dancer in her youth, has been abandoned by Cecile's father and her loneliness indicates the emptiness of Lola's future if Michel does not come back to her. However, the first shot in the film is one of Michel returning to Nantes, dressed in a dazzling white suit and driving an enormous American convertible. By the middle of the film, we know that the stranger is indeed Michel and so the inevitability of reunion is established for us, though not for Lola. Knowing this, we wait to see whether Lola will be able to sustain her battered illusions until Michel decides to present himself.

There are a number of similar character correspondences that could be mentioned, but these should be enough to suggest the various relationships which, when seen collectively, provide the sense of a common life central to Demy's conception of the film. In using this structure, and in choreographing the action so that one character leads us to another, Demy dedicates *Lola* to Max Ophuls, whose *La Ronde* is similarly constructed. Ophuls' presence is also felt in the character of Lola; his *Lola Montez,* a dancer who likewise gives her body but retains her soul, was also an influence on Godard's creation of Nana in *My Life to Live.*

In designing his celebration of illusion, Demy draws heavily upon the Hollywood movies of the Thirties and Forties. The American sailor and his shipmates are all the Gene Kelly of *Anchors Aweigh* and *On The Town:* friendly, amorous, fond of children. The dance hall–brothel where Lola works is not the whorehouse of Genet or Godard, but the "saloon" of the American Western, the night clubs of Vincente Minnelli. To replace those harsher aspects of living which would surely undermine our acceptance of his fable, Demy selects those qualities of the Hollywood movie that, until the middle Fifties, were most engaging: directness, heartiness, generosity, the desire, or necessity, to overlook unpleasantness—in short, the essential flavor of the Hollywood film when it was in its most "mythic" phase and the movies were an entertainment which most Americans had in common. America itself seems to hover over the lives of this handful of people in Nantes: Roland lived in the United States as a child, Cecile is eager to learn "American" and is delighted when Frankie teaches her the word "birthday." Because Demy's knowledge of the United States stems from Hollywood movies, America becomes, for his characters, a world of infinite possibility. Even if, as Mme. Desnoyers supposes, there is nothing in Chicago but gangsters, they are surely Bogarts and Cagneys and not the petty swindlers of Paris.

Visually, *Lola,* filmed entirely in Demy's birthplace, is haunted by sunlight; it floods the arcades and streets with an overpowering brightness, forcing its way through the dusty windows of shops and apartments as if intent upon ridding the town of shadows. Apart from a single night sequence, in which the camera pans slowly past Lola to reveal an endless boulevard shimmering in lamplight, *Lola* happens in sunshine, as appropriate a visual metaphor for the film's theme as Demy's suggestive use of things American. Raoul Coutard's cinematography is exquisite, once again reminding us of his key role in the creation of a new French cinema. Coutard feels that *Lola* contains his best black-and-white cinematography, and regrets that the film's stock, Gevaert 36, is no longer being manufactured for he now finds himself unable to recapture "those unsaturated blacks, those extraordinary whites, that grainy texture of real and unreal." Though there is little use of the hand held camera, many other characteristic devices of New Wave film-making are in evidence, particularly an iris-in and iris-out effect to open and close the film (a Demy trademark) and a breathtaking slow-motion sequence of Cecile and Frankie at the fair in homage to Jean Vigo. (This unforgetable sequence is, curiously enough, mentioned by Charlotte in a love-making scene in Godard's *The Married Woman.*)

Demy has included a number of allusions to earlier films which, like his visual tricks, are carefully integrated, adding an interesting texture to a film that might seem too pure without them. Elina Labourdette, the Agnes of Robert Bresson's *Les Dames du Bois de Boulogne,* exhibits a snapshot of herself in a dancing costume, a photo which first appeared in the Bresson film. She also tells of her abandonment, using several lines of the Cocteau dialogue of *Les Dames.* Lola's song number is photographed in the manner of Sternberg and, in it, Anouk Aimée strikes Dietrich's famous Lola-Lola pose from *The Blue Angel.* (The lyrics of the song are by Agnes Varda, Demy's wife and herself a New Wave director—*Cleo from Five to Seven, Le Bonheur.*) Through these allusions, Demy pays tribute to those films which have inspired his own first effort. And there are allusions-in-the-making. Marc Michel will soon return as Roland in *Cherbourg*, and the Michel Legrand theme which accompanies his appearances in *Lola* will become his "Once I loved a woman named Lola" aria, accompanied by an insert of the Nantes arcade.

Although up to this point I have stressed *Lola*'s cheerfulness and optimism, the film ultimately evokes a bittersweet response. Elements of shattered illusion and regret are carefully woven into the film's texture, piercing the surface at times to remind us of the risk run by those who refuse to surrender their illusions. A note of sadness is sounded in Mme. Desnoyers' emptiness as she bids Roland farewell (a beautifully handled moment by Elina Labourdette) and in Lola's apology to Roland for her brief lapse into self-pity. (Anouk Aimée performs throughout with a kind of selfless radiance. Unhappily, nine years later in *Model Shop*, Miss Aimée had become an important international movie star and her Lola reduced to little more than a showy, narcissistic star turn.) There is even a hint of sadness in the fact that when the now-wealthy Michel is reunited with Lola, he is no longer the dashing sailor of her memory but appears to us jowly and plump, a bit past his prime.

Lola's optimism is also muted by the audience's knowledge that life seldom resolves itself so neatly and happily. Lola's dance-hall friends weep when her lover returns as though they were watching a movie—one of Demy's most enchanting inventions. Demy has anticipated this divided response, heightening the tension between our desire to see everything turn out pleasantly and our awareness that such cheerful resolutions are unlikely to occur in our own lives. Several sequences in the film make us slightly apprehensive. When the American sailor befriends Cecile, there are several uneasy moments before we are assured of his intentions. When his underworld employer is nabbed by the police, it appears, for a few moments, that Roland's life has suddenly been placed in danger. The discrepancy between the doubts and fears that impede our relationships with others in our own world, and the unity, trust and gentleness which inform *Lola*'s, causes us to regret that our experience cannot be the same. Moving us in this way, *Lola* has something of the same effect as Prospero's famous dream speech in *The Tempest*, about which critic Northrop Frye observes:

> We spend our lives partly in a waking world we call normal and partly in a dream world which we create out of our own desires. Shakespeare endows both worlds with equal imaginative power, brings them opposite one another, and makes each world seem unreal when seen by the light of the other.

It is finally in the character of Roland that we see the worlds of experience and desire in conflict. He is the wanderer, the poet, the alien who senses too much of himself and tries to see too deeply into the workings of the world around him to join quite so easily as the others in the dance of life. Too romantic to be contented and yet not knowing how to create his own contentment, he finds himself forced to withdraw. The film ends with Lola, Michel and their son driving out of Nantes. Suddenly she sees Roland, the man who loved her but for whom she could not compromise the memory of her first love, as he hurries with his suitcase toward the ship that will take him to South Africa and, hopefully, to the fulfillment he so desperately seeks. For a moment, Lola's joy is tinged with pity for him, with sorrow that Roland cannot share her happiness. Then Michel speaks to her, she smiles and they drive on, forgetting Roland.

How can a movie like *Lola*, overflowing with intelligence, grace and charm, fail to find an audience in this country? Certainly not because it is too remote or difficult. If anything, Demy sometimes risks over-explicitness in his effort to make sure that we transcend the literal level of his fable. Perhaps it is because *Lola* goes against the grain of the best serious art of our time, an art characterized by alienation, neuroticism and negation in which even the mask of comedy is usually displayed in blackface. More likely, *Lola* has been passed over as a result of what Pauline Kael calls the "fantasies of the art house audience"—the demand for films of "significance" and "committment" to reinforce this audience's liberal prejudices. Movies like *Lola, Singin' in the Rain* and *The Five Day Lover* are generally held suspect, for their lack of didacticism seems to imply a complacency, compounded by annoyingly "aristocratic" associations. This audence feels more at home with *The Pawnbroker, West Side Story* and the witless but doggedly working-class comedies of Richard Lester —artistic botches that have "something to say."

Like ideals and illusions, some very good films can get lost somewhere along the way unless we watch over them closely. With no special social or moral axes to grind, *Lola* inhabits the realm of what Nabokov calls "aesthetic bliss, that is, a sense of being somehow, somewhere, connected with other states of being where art (curiosity, tenderness, kindness, ecstasy) is the norm." The failure of Demy's film to find an audience suggests that acceptance of cinema as "aesthetic bliss" has yet to become a reality in this country.

Marnie

William Johnson, "Marnie"

ooooooooooooooooooooooooooooooooooooooooooooooo

Although Alfred Hitchcock is recognized as a great film-maker, his admirers divide sharply and incontrovertibly over the question of the specific quality of his genius. On the one hand there are, generally speaking, the American critics who see him as the model director in his supreme mastery of technique which is always in the service of suspense. For them he is the creator of perfect thrillers offering boundless artistic inventions in pacing his plot—controlling, sustaining, and manipulating it; in achieving exquisite economies of shots and scenes; and in arriving at the triumph of good over evil without being moralistically or aesthetically offensive. And on the other hand, there are the more avid admirers of Hitchcock, generally European. They not only praise his technical mastery but also claim that his films consciously deal with themes of philosophical depth. Eric Rohmer and Claude Chabrol (*Hitchcock*, Classiques du Cinéma, 1957), for example, find Hitchcock in film after film conveying specific themes that lend themselves to universalization. In his essay on *Marnie* (1964) William Johnson discusses the film by alluding to a broad range of technique, plot, and characterization from Hitchcock's earlier films that surface in *Marnie* in new combinations for the same effects—the sem-blance of realism, the generation of suspense, the cleansing of the heroine "of all but her sweetness." Obviously Mr. Johnson sides with those who, like Hitchcock himself, take him less

Marnie, directed by Alfred Hitchcock, 1964 (*Universal*)

seriously than those who find his films dramas of great thematic import. "As a popular director, he recognizes that well-rounded plots are still in demand, even if they have to be hammered violently into shape."

———————•———————

In The Birds, Hitchcock tried two things he'd never done before—suspense derived from non-human agents, and an unresolved ending. Since hardly anybody outside the *auteurs* club liked *The Birds*, it wouldn't be surprising if he retreated to familiar ground for his next film. At first sight, *Marnie* seems to be just such a safe retreat.

The agents of suspense are human, if not slightly superhuman: the Bird woman meets James Bond. Tippi Hedren makes up for all that inane smiling in *The Birds* by pouring her nervous energy into the title role, and the result is surprisingly commendable. It's Sean Connery who tends to smile too much (he doesn't have the outlets for action that he had against Dr. No), but his performance is more than adequate. As for the ending of the film, it's a thumping big red exclamation mark.

The plot seems like a potpourri of earlier Hitchcock films. It begins with Marnie lighting out for a fresh city after robbing an employer (shades of *Psycho*). This isn't her first theft, and now, changing her identity and appearance (*Vertigo*), she gets a job with another prospective victim, Mark Rutland. Her thievishness is bound up with a childhood trauma that sends her into a fit whenever she sees a red-and-white object (*Spellbound*) and also makes her crave love from her mother (who suggests what the mother in *Psycho* must have been like when she was alive). The plot thickens when Mark not only discovers that Marnie is a thief but falls in love with her, so obsessively (*Vertigo* again) that he forces her to marry him as the alternative to prison. They then lead a strained marital life (*Rebecca*, *Suspicion*) while Mark tries to find out the whole truth about Marnie before she kills herself or is caught by the police.

It isn't only the plot that reminds one of earlier Hitchcock.

The dialogue, which has more wit and bite to it than in Hitchcock's most recent films, echoes his John Michael Hayes scripts of the mid-fifties. The color is well controlled, with smoky blues and greens for the exteriors and pale or neutral tones for the interiors, all these serving as foils for the traumatic reds; but they reflect the palette of *Vertigo* without matching its shimmering virtuosity. Similarly, Bernard Herrmann's music is a matter-of-fact echo of his lyrical *Vertigo* score.

It would seem, then, that Hitchcock has reached back beyond the offbeat melodramatics of *The Birds* and *Psycho* to the more subdued tensions of *Vertigo*. Of course, this alone would hardly offer a safe retreat, since *Vertigo* fared little better with the public than *The Birds;* so he has neutralized all supernatural overtones, weighting the film down to earth with a heavy plot mechanism *à la Spellbound*. In *Marnie*, Hitchcock has gone all out for realism.

At this point the film sounds well and truly condemned, for everyone knows that Hitchcock's realism is only skin deep. "I have to make films about something," he says, "but I don't really attach all that importance to what it is." Through his career he has skillfully adapted his themes to fit the prevailing fashions. In the thirties he could take a simple, Buchanesque attitude toward life, because that was what the majority of his public ultimately believed in. World War II added sternness to this attitude—one can see the change actually taking place in *Foreign Correspondent*. As the horrors of war entered the public consciousness, Hitchcock made his protagonists more complex and more corrupt: the widow-killer of *Shadow of a Doubt*, the youth-killers of *Rope*. The old simplicity and romance were becoming something of a liability, and Hitchcock began to disguise them: in *Notorious*, for the first time, he ventured to portray a "tarnished" heroine. By the fifties, the public view of reality had been embittered by the cold war and other disillusions, and Hitchcock became more overtly amoral, as in *Rear Window* and *The Trouble with Harry*. Even his most thirties-ish script of the period—the remake of

The Man Who Knew Too Much—took on a skeptical anti-authority note. The contrast can be seen still more clearly in *North by Northwest*, a reworking of *The 39 Steps:* the attitudes and experience of Eva Marie Saint are poles apart from those of the virginal Madeleine Carroll. Yet, at the end, the old romantic simplicity emerges briefly as the heroine reverts to straightforward femininity. And so it is with Marnie, who represents the conventional clichés of the sixties woman—chic exterior, sexual problems, and amoral resourcefulness—until the dénouement cleanses her of all but sweetness.

The point is, of course, that Hitchcock's realism is a means, not an end. It is a tool for shaping suspense, and a more supple tool than is usually recognized. He may accept the over-all conventions of the time, but he often gives them a sharp edge by carving them across the grain. Amid the stereotypes of *Lifeboat*, for example, his characterization of the Negro can still be watched without embarrassment—which cannot be said for most other Negro characterizations of the forties. One of Hitchcock's favorite devices for quietly jolting the audience is to add a sympathetic touch to a villain: the tormented murderer in *Rear Window*, world-weary James Mason in *North by Northwest*, and so on. In *Marnie*, where there are no villains, Hitchcock refines this device to the point of turning it inside-out: he adds *un*sympathetic touches to characters who have right and reason on their side.

If contempt for Hitchcock's realism shouldn't obscure its piquancy, it certainly shouldn't lead to moral indignation. In his calculated manipulation of characters and events, Hitchcock is doing nothing more reprehensible than (say) Antonioni does in his later films. The main difference is that Antonioni has a "serious" purpose in imposing his particular paradigm on reality, while Hitchcock is "merely" creating suspense. Antonioni's thesis of the vacuity of modern life leads naturally to intellectual discussion, while Hitchcock's suspense leads nowhere: it can be analyzed, but that is about all. Attempts to link it to a Heraclitean as opposed to a Platonic view of existence, et cetera, et cetera, may accurately reflect the viewer's own preoccupations, but there is no evidence that they reflect Hitchcock's, and usually they are simply a justification for enjoying so unphilosophical an experience as suspense.

In *Marnie*, this experience is rich indeed. Most Hitchcock films have only one main source of suspense, though the wily man may divert us from it by means of extensive red herrings (the opening of *Psycho* and *The Birds*) or a firework train of episodes (*Rear Window, North by Northwest*). *Marnie* does have one most emphatic source—the mystery of the red trauma —but Hitchcock's subdued brand of realism, paraphrasing the complexity of life, gives us three other major sources as well. There is Marnie as a criminal: will she be exposed, or will she get away with it? There is Mark's obsession with Marnie: will love or fury win out? And finally there is the sexual conflict: this involves not only Mark and the traumatically frigid Marnie but also a brunette (Diane Baker) who is in love with Mark and is determined to find out the truth about his mysterious wife.

Naturally, this proliferation of sources would not by itself ensure suspense. It all depends on how they are handled. Here we approach another misleading truism about Hitchcock: his technical mastery. It so happens that there are certain departments of technique in which Hitchcock has a patently blind eye. These include the phony backdrops that grate like TV commercials (especially in color), the bits of rapid montage that do not quite fit together, and the two-shots that are held so long that they almost ossify. All of these are conspicuous in *Marnie;* and Hitchcock even aggravates the crassness of the dénouement with some clumsily contrived shots.

Hitchcock's technical mastery—unlike his realism—operates on a deeper level. His handling of suspense depends above all on movement and timing. Movement enables him to generate a basic neural excitement in the audience. In some of his films he goes so far as to maintain a continual undercurrent of tension by gearing the action to a moving vehicle: the train journey of *The Lady Vanishes* (where the tension reaches its climax when the train unexpectedly stops), the voyage of *Life-*

boat. At the other extreme, but with similar effect, he may send his camera roaming continually through a single static setting (*Rope*). *Marnie* has a sophisticated mixture of the two: occasionally the camera goes on a long, slow prowl, while the "moving vehicles" include cars, a cruise ship and runaway horse.

As in most of Hitchcock's recent films, the movements in *Marnie* are generally slow. A rapid pace is easier to maintain and avoids the risk of boredom; but a slow pace, if it comes off, can build up a greater potential energy of tension. This is where Hitchcock's timing comes into play. In *Marnie*, with its four sources of suspense, he works continual variations on the tension to prevent it from growing stale. The audience is periodically keyed up to expect an outburst from one quarter or another; and from time to time Hitchcock allows a partial release—a flaring of temper, a moment of panic when Marnie runs into a former employer-victim—that briefly gratifies the audience while increasing the over-all tension.

One extended and rather melodramatic sequence illustrates the way Hitchcock uses movement and timing to manipulate suspense. (The sequence contains at least two obvious technical lapses, but the tension passes through them unscathed.) Marnie is riding in a fox hunt when she "sees red" and frightens her horse, which bolts away with her—and with the camera. The horse tries to leap a wall, stumbles, and breaks a leg. Now the camera takes over the movement, following Marnie in close-up as she goes off hysterically for a revolver, and then following the revolver in close-up as she returns to shoot the horse. Having pushed this particular line of tension as far as it will go, Hitchcock allows a respite—a static shot of Mark being warned on the phone of what has happened. But the tension snaps back when the camera follows Marnie into the house, still carrying the revolver, and all the way up and down the stairs. Only when she has left the house again are we sure that she isn't going to shoot Mark—at least, not just yet!

This sequence illustrates another of Hitchcock's devices for keeping the audience on tenterhooks. In the first half, the gun goes off; in the second, it doesn't. The former shocks, the latter agonizes, and the two together are doubly agonizing because there's no telling which is going to be which. Most of Hitchcock's films contain some equivalent of this gun, the most powerful being a mentally or emotionally unstable character who threatens to explode into violence. *Marnie* has two such threats—Marnie and Mark—aimed at each other the whole way through.

Marnie's behavior is especially unpredictable because we don't know the truth about her. Mystery is the bluntest instrument in Hitchcock's arsenal of suspense, but here he handles it with the delicacy of—well, not a scalpel, but certainly a sculptor's chisel. At the beginning, Marnie is smiling and self-possessed; then Hitchcock starts to chip away at her, putting her through a long series of minor transformations as she tells new lies about herself or unwillingly reveals new facets of the truth. In this respect, *Marnie* is even subtler than *Vertigo*, for the mystery that surrounds Kim Novak is simply a mask, unchanging until the final fifteen minutes. Unfortunately, it's in the final fifteen minutes of *Marnie* that Hitchcock's mystery reverts to bluntness. The subtlety of his build-up seems to promise not just an explanation but an apocalypse; the bathos he actually gives us seems like a slap in the face.

Of course, this mystery is precisely that "something" which is the pretext for Hitchcock's film-making and to which he doesn't "really attach all that importance." All of his films involving mysteries have something ludicrous about them, though this is less noticeable in films like *Psycho*, where he is half spoofing, than in *Vertigo* or *Marnie*, which appear to be serious. While the plot of *Vertigo* is even more ludicrous than *Marnie*'s, its full outrageousness doesn't become apparent until one thinks it over in retrospect. *Marnie* enjoys no such protection.

I would like to think that Hitchcock chose this pathetic dénouement as a dig at those who rhapsodize over his *Weltansicht*. The rest of the film offers all sorts of temptations to the critic who likes to discuss reality and illusion or the problem of identity. But one shouldn't be deluded by its veneer of modish situations—even to the limited extent of being indignant at the plot beneath. The mature Hitchcock has attempted only one film without contrivance—*The Wrong Man*—and (regardless of its merits) its fortunes would not encourage him to repeat the experiment. As a popular director, he recognizes that well-rounded plots are still in demand, even if they have to be hammered violently into shape.

Both the worst and the best of Hitchcock jostle for attention in *Marnie*. Because the weaknesses are so conspicuous, they tend to outweigh the strengths at a first viewing. But those who enjoy Hitchcock for his suspense shouldn't be disappointed. After all, they will already know that with Hitchcock one must take the smooth with the rough, the glib contrivances with the tension.

Masculine Feminine

Pauline Kael, "Youth Is Beauty"

ooooooooooooooooooooooooooooooooooooooooooooooo

The movement in French film-making known as *la nou-
velle vague,* "the new wave," belongs to the period of the
late fifties and early sixties. François Truffaut's *400 Blows*
and Jean-Luc Godard's *Breathless* are two of the best known
of these films and, in many respects, best represent the spirit
and energy of the movement. Characterized by a wistful,
playful use of the camera that, in its surprises, suggests a
certain arbitrariness of purpose and direction and by an
equally irreverent violation of the viewer's narrative expectations, the work of the new wave directors brought new
vitality to French and international film-making. Like all
creative movements, however, it spent itself as a collective
ideal and force, expiring as individual directors developed
their talents variously and individually, voiding the group
identification. In the mid-sixties the dynamic of the movement continues in the work of the prolific Jean-Luc Godard.
Sometimes shooting and/or editing two films simultaneously,
since 1962 he has made *Vivre sa Vie, RoGoPaG, Les Carabi-
niers, Le Mépris, Alphaville, Band of Outsiders, Pierrot le
Fou, Made in USA, Masculine Feminine, Weekend,* and
others.

The title of Pauline Kael's analysis of *Masculine Feminine,*
"Youth is Beauty," the shifting of Keats's "Beauty is Truth,"
suggests the capacity of Godard to render to his audience
with force and immediacy the ideologies, the obsessions, the

tensions of the age, the decade, the current year. His aesthetic involves a yielding to rather than a controlling of the complexity of life: the details of his films seem only as random, unrelated and chaotic as the reality of modern life itself. In order to express the immediate experience of contemporary life, Godard relentlessly invents departures from the style and tradition of the well-made film. Asked by one critic whether he subscribes to the Aristotelean principle in art of a beginning, a middle and an ending, Godard answered, "Yes, but not necessarily in that order."

———•———

MASCULINE FEMININE is that rare movie achievement: a work of grace and beauty in a contemporary setting. Godard has liberated his feeling for modern youth from the American gangster-movie framework which limited his expressiveness and his relevance to the non-movie-centered world. He has taken up the strand of what was most original in his best films—the life of the uncomprehending heroine, the blank-eyed career-happy little opportunist-betrayer from *Breathless,* and the hully-gully, the dance of sexual isolation, from *Band of Outsiders.* Using neither crime nor the romance of crime but a simple romance for a kind of interwoven story line, Godard has, at last, created the form he needed. It is a combination of essay, journalistic sketches, news and portraiture, love lyric and satire.

What fuses it? The line, "This film could be called The Children of Marx and Coca-Cola." The theme is the fresh beauty of youth amidst the flimsiness of Pop culture and Pop politics. The boy (Jean-Pierre Léaud) is full of doubts and questions, but a Pop revolutionary; the girl (Chantal Goya) is a yé-yé singer making her way.

It is fused by the differing attitudes of the sexes to love and war even in this atmosphere of total and easy disbelief, of government policies accepted with the same contempt as TV commercials. The romance is punctuated with aimless acts of aggression and martyrdom: this is young love in a time of irreverence and hopelessness. These lovers and their friends,

Masculine Feminine, directed by Jean-Luc Godard, 1966 (*Museum of Modern Art/Film Stills Archive*)

united by indifference and disdain toward the adult world, have a new kind of community in their shared disbelief. Politically they are anti-American enough to be American.

They are also Americanized. This community of unbelievers has a style of life by which they recognize each other; it is made up of everything adults attack as the worst and shoddiest forms of Americanization and dehumanization. It is the variety of forms of "Coca-Cola"—the synthetic life they were born to and which they love, and which they make human, and more beautiful and more "real" than the old just-barely-hanging-on adult culture. Membership is automatic and natural for the creatures from inner space. The signals are jukebox songs, forms of dress, and, above all, what they do with their hair. Americanization makes them an international society; they have the beauty of youth which can endow Pop with poetry, and they have their feeling for each other and all those shared products and responses by which they know each other.

There are all sorts of episodes and details and jokes in the film that may be extraneous, but they seem to fit, to be part of the climate, the mood, the journalistic approach to this new breed between teen-agers and people. Even if you don't really like some pieces or can't understand why they're there, even if you think they're not well done (like the episode out of LeRoi Jones, or the German boy and prostitute bit, or the brief appearance of Bardot, or the parody of *The Silence* which isn't as ludicrously pretentious as *The Silence* itself, or the ambiguous death of the hero—the end of him like a form of syntax marking the end of the movie) they're not too jarring. The rhythms, and the general sense, and the emotion that builds up can carry you past what you don't understand: you don't need to understand every detail in order to experience the beauty of the work as it's going on. An Elizabethan love song is no less beautiful because we don't catch all the words; and when we look up the words, some of the meanings, the references, the idiom may still elude us. Perhaps the ache of painful, transient beauty is that we never can completely understand, and that, emotionally, we more than understand. *Masculine Feminine* has that ache, and its subject is a modern young lover's lament at the separateness of the sexes.

Godard has caught the girl now in demand (and in full supply), as no one else has. Chantal Goya, like Sylvie Vartan (whose face on a billboard dominates some of the scenes), is incredibly pretty but not beautiful, because there is nothing behind the eyes. Chantal Goya's face is haunting just because it's so empty: she doesn't look back. Her face becomes alive only when she's looking in the mirror, toying with her hair. Her thin, reedy little singing voice is just as pleasantly, perfectly empty, and it is the new sound. There's nothing behind it musically or emotionally. The young girls in the movie are soulless—as pretty and lost and soulless as girls appear to a lover who can make physical contact and yet cannot make the full contact he longs for, the contact that would heal. The girl he loves sleeps with him and is forever lost to him. She is the ideal—the girl in the fashion magazines she buys.

Possibly what flawed the conception of *My Life to Live* was the notion of the prostitute giving her body but keeping her soul to herself, because there was no evidence of what she was said to be holding back. Now, in *Masculine Feminine*, Godard is no longer trying to tell just the girl's story but the story of how a lover may feel about his girl, and we can see that it's not because she's a prostitute that he gets the sense that she isn't giving everything but because she's a girl, and (as the camera of *My Life to Live* revealed though it wasn't the story being told) a love object. A lover may penetrate her body but there is still an opaque, impenetrable surface that he can never get through. He can have her and have her and she is never his.

The attraction of this little singer is that she isn't known, can't be known, and worst of all, probably there's nothing to know (which is what we may have suspected in *My Life to Live*). The ache of love is reaching out to a blank wall, which in this case smiles back. This male view of the eternal feminine mystery is set in the childlike simplicity of modern relations: before they go out on their first date, the boy and girl discuss going to bed. Easy sex is like a new idiom, but their talk of the pill is not the same as having it, and the

spectre of pregnancy hovers over them. The old sexual morality is gone but the mysteries of love and isolation remain;
availability cancels out the pleasurable torments of anticipation, but not the sadness afterward. The lover is surrounded
by blank, faintly smiling walls.

With the new breed, Godard is able to define the romantic
problem precisely and essentially. This approachable girl who
adores Pepsi—the French cousin of Jean Seberg in *Breathless*—
is as mysterious as a princess seen from afar, *more* mysterious
because the princess might change if we got close. The boy
says, what's in "masculine"—mask and ass, what's in "feminine"
—nothing. And that's what defeats him. Worse than losing a
love is holding it in your arms and not finding it.

In *Masculine Feminine* Godard asks questions of youth and
sketches a portrait in a series of question-answer episodes that
are the dramatic substance of the movie. The method was
prefigured by the psychiatric interview in Truffaut's *The 400
Blows* (Léaud, now the questioning hero, was the child-hero
who was quizzed), the celebrity interview in *Breathless*, and
cinéma vérité movies by Jean Rouch and Chris Marker. It is
most like Chris Marker's rapturous inquiry of the young
Japanese girl in *The Koumiko Mystery*. There are informal
boy-to-boy conversations about women and politics; there is a
phenomenal six-minute single-take parody-interview conducted
by the hero with a Miss Nineteen, who might be talking while
posing for the cover of *Glamour;* and there are two boy-girl
sessions which define the contemporary meaning of masculine
and feminine. These dialogues are dating-talk as a form of pre-
liminary sex-play—verbal courtship rites. The boy thrusts with
leading questions, the girl parries, backs away, touches her hair.
Godard captures the awkwardnesses that reveal, the pauses,
the pretensions, the mannerisms—the rhythms of the dance—as
no one has before. *Masculine Feminine* is the dance of the
sexes drawing together and remaining separate. He gets the
little things that people who have to follow scripts can't get:
the differences in the way girls are with each other and with
boys, and boys with each other and with girls. Not just what
they do but how they smile or look away.

What can a boy believe that a girl says, what can she believe of what he says? We watch them telling lies and half-truths to each other and we can't tell which are which. But, smiling in the darkness because we know we've all been there, we recognize the truth of Godard's art. He must have discovered his subject as he worked on it (as a man working on a big-budget movie with a fixed shooting-schedule cannot). And because he did, we do, too. We can read all those special fat issues of magazines devoted to youth and not know any more than we do after watching big TV specials on youth. But even in the ladies' lounge right after the movie, there were the girls, so pretty they hardly seemed real, standing in a revery at the mirror, toying with their shiny hair. Godard has imposed his vision and experience confirms it. What more can one ask of an artist?

There is a question that remains, however: Why haven't more people responded to this movie? Maybe because *Masculine Feminine* is not only partial to youth but partial as a view, and movie hucksterism has accustomed people to big claims (and movie experience to big flops). Maybe because Godard has made so many films and critics have often urged the worst upon the public. I would not recommend *The Married Woman* or *Pierrot le Fou*: Godard loves the games and style of youth but does not have the same warm feeling for older characters. He presents them as failed youth: they don't grow up, they just deteriorate, and those movies become cold and empty. But there's life in *Masculine Feminine*, which shows the most dazzlingly inventive and audacious artist in movies today at a new peak.

Miss Julie

Richard Rowland, "Miss Julie"

ooooooooooooooooooooooooooooooooooooooooooooooo

Alf Sjoberg's *Miss Julie* is a superb filmic rendering of August Strindberg's long one-act play. Richard Rowland perceptively calls attention to the many artistically effective means by which Sjoberg adapts Strindberg's play. Mr. Rowland considers the play "anti-cinematic in its evocation of claustrophobia." The art of the film is seen in the imaginative use of flashback to express the vivid presence of reminiscence in Strindberg's play; the smooth and sustaining pace of the film; inventive, fitting camera work; the functional use of sound; the relevation of character owing to the sensitivity of the actors for the roles they play; and the audience-involving point of view of the camera's eye. Mr. Rowland maintains that the Julie of the film is a richer, more humanly convincing characterization than the woman Strindberg created. And finally he acknowledges the poetry of many visually lyrical shots in the film that can only be introduced in a play by suggestion, "the visual equivalent of the moments in drama when a gesture or a sentence catches an event and transmutes it into a symbol to echo in one's memory."

———◆———

IT IS RARE indeed that one leaves a film with the gratified feeling that here is a whole work of art, something complete and thought out and meaningful, something one can think of as one thinks of a play by Shakespeare or an opera by Puccini

Miss Julie, directed by Alf Sjoberg, 1950 (*Janus*)

or a novel by Henry James. Usually one says "That was a fine bit of acting," or "How cleverly he uses his camera," or "There was more of the book's meaning left than I expected"; we appreciate the films with reservations which we do not make for the other arts. When a film appears which makes us forget these reservations, the feeling of discovery is intense. But how often has it happened? The judgment is personal: I can name four or five Chaplin films, Carl Dreyer's *Passion of Joan of Arc*, and, for all its crudities, Von Stroheim's *Greed*. Now, for me, it has happened again with the Swedish film, *Fröken Julie*, adapted by Alf Sjoberg from the famous play by Strindberg.

Nothing had prepared us for this brilliant film. Sjoberg's only other film known to English-speaking audiences was *Hets*, shown in England as *Frenzy*, in America as *Torment*; it was a melodrama of adolescence, filled with over-simplified psychologizing and moody shots of stairways, good of its kind but in a lugubrious Germanic tradition considerably beneath the first-rate.

Strindberg's *Miss Julie* is, like all his plays, tight, enclosed, anti-cinematic in its evocation of claustrophobia. It has only three characters; it is aimed with relentless singleness toward a didactic point, the assertion at the heart of most of Strindberg's plays that warfare and hatred are the only possibilities between the sexes, that woman is a devil in whose hands man and all decency are powerless. No one can deny the brilliance or power of Strindberg's best plays; few would dare to credit them with much understanding; they dramatize a state of mind any of us recognizes as the borderline of sanity; the world *can* look like this to a man, but it is a disastrously incomplete vision of life beside which Baudelaire's and Webster's and T. S. Eliot's, for all their various limitations, seem complex and many-sided and humane.

But from this cinematically unpromising material Sjoberg has built up a film rich, deep, truly moving, a film which uses every resource of the screen to create a picture of life so delicate in its perception, so singing in its beauty, that we emerge from the theater shaken as only a few artistic experiences can shake us.

One must go back to the play to appreciate what a truly creative act this has been. The play tells how Miss Julie, daughter of a Swedish count, brought up by her feminist mother to hate and distrust men, is stirred by the peasant celebrations of Midsummer Eve to fling herself at the head of her father's valet, Jean. After the shame of her seduction, their conflicting desires to master and to be mastered—his based on a caste system and hers on her mother's sexual theories—drive them implacably on to her suicide at his command. In this bald outline the plot seems arid and tendentious; such is never the feeling one gets from the film. Part of Sjoberg's change is mere multiplicity; new characters have been imagined with extraordinary completeness, so that, for instance, the father, in the play a vague off-stage shadow, has here been endowed with more pitiful life, perhaps, than the heroine. The mother is a monster, but she has been elaborately developed from hints in other plays of Strindberg's; we believe in her more than we ever do in the Laura of *The Father*, who is seen only in one setting and one situation.

Much of the play was built up in reminiscences, through which Jean and Julie described their past to each other, these the film has expanded and pictorialized into some of the finest moments of the story. The cinema flashback has become a hackneyed and boring device, but here it is used with fine and novel effect. There are none of the conventional dissolves; the reminiscent voice speaks, and on the screen, behind the speaker, the figures of the narrative appear in the same room; casually the camera moves to them, forgetting the narrator. So we see the terrible mother leading the frightened child off into mental servitude while the shattered girl that she is to become fills the foreground of the screen, and we think "here—in this room" and shudder in sympathy. The freshness and power of this device is uncanny; the past haunts a scene as it does so often in reality.

Part of the film's power is the result of its freedom from interruption. It is unflagging, our interest absolutely sustained. Scene moves into scene brilliantly and effortlessly; the brawling peasants overturn a keg of beer which merges into the peasants themselves spilling into the farmyard, which merges into a burst of fireworks; not since Hitchcock's scream which became a train whistle has so showy a metamorphosis been contrived—yet how much more central and meaningful this one is than Hitchcock's can only be felt by seeing the film. Even during the credits the screen is filled with Miss Julie and her canary in the window, watching the peasants lighting their fires; on the left side of the screen her eyes are restless and hungry behind the lines of credit; the canary, unobscured, fills the right-hand side of the screen. When later, Jean, in wanton self-assertive cruelty, kills the canary, we feel it as deeply as Julie does, for Sjoberg's device has imprinted the canary on our mind as something of importance; in the play we did not know of the canary's existence until just before its death and the effect was less strong.

Although movement is incessant, never does Sjoberg resort to moving the camera merely to create interest; never does the camera look at things eccentrically without some clear reason. In one scene the camera, emphasizing Jean's essential servility, looks up at Jean and Julie from behind the count's boots; he kicks the boots angrily away, turns and stands in the same position, so that we see Julie against the wall beneath the towering threat of his masculinity. When Jean is exploring the mansion as a child, the camera moves slowly, wonderingly, caressingly around the portraits and the formal statuary and rich gardens. When Julie is describing her mother's madly farcical experiment in exchanging the duties of the sexes on the farm, the camera rocks and seesaws wildly.[1]

Sound, too, is used with great suggestive power: the mother's hysterical laughter rings wildly through the house, the drunken folk music suddenly twists out of shape into something frenzied and hideous during the seduction, the trembling bell whose silence has been too loud bursts into frantic summons.

But most of the film's strength comes from its insight into character, an insight resulting from interpretation of the Strind-

[1] It is worthy of note that Sjoberg's cameraman was Goran Strindberg, the dramatist's grandson.

berg play, not from the letter of it. Sjoberg's actors have
helped him greatly; Anita Bjork brings great understanding to
Julie's variety; she shows us her tremulous virginity and her
cold ferocity; it is not easy to forget the wanton gesture with
which she puts her hand on Jean's hip, the harsh accents her
voice assumes when she addresses Christine and later its
honeyed cajolery when she tries to persuade Christine to share
their honeymoon with them, her shaking despair when the
canary is murdered. Even better is the way in which Nef
Palme's subtle coarseness reveals the valet's soul and its pathet-
ically limited dreams.

We are always somewhere within this film, not standing
outside as an observer; we can always say not only what we
see but how we see it, through whose eyes. The childhood
episodes have a springtime wonder throughout Jean's reminiscences—it is uncanny how lovely the rococo privy looks to us
as well as to him—and also absolute terror in Julie's reminiscence; the scene of her father's abortive suicide is appalling:
the fallen body fills the foreground; far in the corner of the
room the forgotten child huddles. The camera's eye is the
child's eye, emphasizing the distance between death and life;
as the flashback ends we return to the grown Julie's perception and watch the black-gloved hands of her mother close in
with terrible finality about the thin shoulders of the terrified
child in the white frock. When Christine, the servant girl,
orders back to the stable the coach in which Jean and Julie
had planned to elope, the camera moves off and looks at the
neat farmyard and Christine's stiff, self-righteous, church-
bound figure with Christine's own unrelenting severity. At
the end of the film the camera moves from the dim uncomprehending eyes of the father and wanders vaguely over the
lovely limp form of Julie, the razor, and halts shockingly on
the trumphant portrait of the mother; as the lights go up, we
are aware that at last we are ourselves again and can emerge
from this strange haunted world of Julie and her father, a
world whose external sunlight and grace was so significantly
shadowed.

In Strindberg's preface to his play, he expressed his aware-

ness of the limitations of the dramatic form and then went on
to say:

> In explanation of Miss Julie's sad fate I have suggested
> many factors: her mother's fundamental instincts; her fa-
> ther's mistaken upbringing of the girl; her own nature, and
> the suggestive influence of her fiancé on a weak and degen-
> erate brain; further, and more directly, the festive mood of
> the Midsummer Eve; the absence of her father; her physical
> condition; her preoccupation with the animals; the excita-
> tion of the dance; the dark of the night; the strongly
> aphrodisiacal influence of the flowers; and lastly the chance
> forcing the two of them together in a secluded room, to
> which must be added the aggressiveness of the excited man.

It is hard to imagine a performance of the play perfect enough
to justify all this; its Julie is really less complex than this suggests. Strindberg's hatred of women, turned against the mother
and Julie's own aggression, dominates the play; Sjoberg's film
seems at once gentler—Strindberg's harsh phrase "a weak and
degenerate brain" is his and not Sjoberg's—and truer. Perhaps
Strindberg put all those things into the play; it is not possible
to feel them as they pass, except as occasional flat statements; in
the film, they are there as constantly evoked actualities or as
poetic images; flat statement is unnecessary. The film is, indeed,
an answer to Strindberg's ambitions; not only has it escaped
the limitations of the theater,[2] it has escaped the often crip-
pling limitations of Strindberg's ailing mind. Julie, her father,
Jean, Christine, are all real and pitiful—even the mother's dark,
brooding figure has pathos in the terrible wedding-night scene.
One pities each of them because they are doomed and because
their humanity has worth in it in some form, however unlov-
able it may often be. Strindberg's play too often sounded like
the knowing child who says "It's not my fault I'm a heel; it's
my parent's fault." Here the parents and children and environ-

---

[2]Strindberg wanted a theater without intermissions, with limited
and suggestive scenery, without footlights blotting out the individuality
of the actors' faces. All these have been accomplished for him by the
film.

ment are entangled in responsibilities; the result is life itself at its most pitiful.

But—and here is the miracle—at its most beautiful, too. For the lyricism of this film is what is finally unforgettable—the grace of the small boat racing down the stream as Julie and Jean flee the laughter of the peasants, the halo of light above the hay, the knowing grace of the garden statues at night, the heavy joy of the folk dancers. These moments are pure lyricism, the visual equivalent of the moments in drama when a gesture or a sentence catches an event and transmutes it into a symbol to echo in one's memory: Vittoria's lines in the last act of *The White Devil*, Mme. Ranevsky's gesture of farewell in *The Cherry Orchard*, any of scores of lines in *Othello* which transfigure that sordid tale of jealousy and violence. Such things are the opposite of realism but they do not falsify; they bring depth to details, making us see things with new fullness. Life can be seen so by the observant eye; certain writers have had special skill in bringing it to the written page —Homer, Chaucer, Shakespeare, Turgeniev, Chekhov (not Strindberg) are names which spring first to mind. The cinema is exquisitly able to achieve such effects; how rarely it bothers to. Flaherty and Chaplin and René Clair have occasionally achieved such lyricism; usually the cinema is too busy merely telling a story, creating suspense, painting portraits (all of which *Miss Julie* does brilliantly) to pause over the significant detail in this way. But in Mr. Sjoberg is a talent which can do much more than that; here, for instance, is someone who could bring the troubled harmonies of Chekhov to life on the screen if he chose to. It will be exciting to watch for more films from him.

The French language has a word for the direction of a film that is far more meaningful than the English term—*réalisation*. Even in English this carries fuller meaning. Certainly it describes the process here perfectly; the text has been made real, flesh has clothed the bones, meaning has been made plain. Two recent attempts (both admired in some quarters) to make short stories into long films have shown the pitfalls in doing so. In neither *The Fallen Idol* nor *The Rocking Horse Winner*, in spite of all the characters and incidents added to the bare originals, was any new meaning discovered. It was quite simply a spinning out of a terse story into a repetitious and attenuated film. Here, Strindberg's play must have been doubled in length, but it seems stripped and spare, meaningful in every moment. This is a true realization. Few films have ever been so stamped with the unifying mind of an artist as *Miss Julie* is.

Monsieur Verdoux

James Agee, "Monsieur Verdoux"

○○

W. H. Auden's fascination for the film criticism of James Agee typifies the response of many movie and non-movie-goers to his regular commentaries in *The Nation* in the 1940's. Auden once said that he eagerly awaited each new issue of *The Nation* to seize upon the latest Agee review, while—at the same time—acknowledging a lack of enthusiasm for motion pictures. In writing about movies Agee's prose is shot through with passionate concern for and insight into his subject. The heat and excitement of his mind discovering new thoughts and the honesty with which he probes his own response to a film are reflected stylistically in the racy, immediate quality of his prose rhythm. With the release of Charlie Chaplin's *Monsieur Verdoux* in 1947, he obtained extra space which permitted him to discuss "this great poet and his poem" over a stretch of three issues of *The Nation*. In the first part Agee exhorts his readers to disregard what they have heard about the film and rebuts briefly many of the charges against it—immoral, tasteless, wanting the figure of the tramp, poor direction, inferior production, etc.—and he summarizes the story situation: "Henri Verdoux, a French bank teller of the thirties who has lost his job in a depression, works out a business of his own whereby he can support his crippled wife (Mady Corell) and their little boy. He becomes a professional murderer of women of means. He courts them, marries them, finesses their fortunes into his possession;

murders them and eliminates their corpses; plays the market with the whole of his profits. We see him at work on four such women. . . ." The subsequent parts of the review, which here follow, are a penetrating character analysis of Verdoux (part II) and a dynamic search for the meaning of the film (part III).

———◆———

JUNE 14, 1947
MONSIEUR VERDOUX-II

CHAPLIN'S PERFORMANCE as Verdoux is the best piece of playing I have ever seen: here, I cannot even specify the dozen or so close-ups each so great and so finely related and timed that withdrawn and linked in series they are like the notes of a slow, magnificent, and terrifying song, which the rest of the film serves as an accompaniment. I could write many pages, too, about the richness and quality of the film as a work of art, in fact, of genius; and as many more trying, hopelessly, to determine how Chaplin's intellect, instinct, intuition, creative intelligence, and pure experience as a master artist and as a showman serve and at times disserve one another, for intellectually and in every other kind of self-exhaustion this seems incomparably his most ambitious film. And since the film is provocative of so much that cannot be examined as fun, I wish I might also use the many thousands of words I would require to do it adequate honor, purely as fun. And all the more because I love and revere the film as deeply as any I have seen, and believe that it is high among the great works of this century, I wish I might discuss at proper length its weaknesses as a work of art and of moral understanding. I have reluctantly chosen, instead, to suggest a single aspect of its meaning, which seems to me particularly important. And this itself, I fear, I may have reduced beyond usefulness.

Chaplin's theme, the greatest and the most appropriate to its time that he has yet undertaken, is the bare problem of surviving at all in such a world as this. With his usual infallibility of instinct he has set his story in Europe; Europeans

Monsieur Verdoux, directed by Charles Chaplin, 1947 (*The Museum of Modern Art/Film Stills Archive*)

are aware of survival as a problem, as we are not. As rightly, he has set aside the tramp, whose charming lessons in survival are too wishful for his purposes, for his first image of the Responsible Man, and of modern civilization. (For Verdoux embodies much of the best that can be said of modern civilization, whether democratic-capitalist, fascist, or communist: whatever he may lack in the way of conscience, he does have brains; and whatever crimes he commits, they are committed, or so he believes, out of compassionate love and in uncompromising discharge of responsibility.) The tramp is the free soul intact in its gallantry, innocence, eagerness for love, ridiculousness, and sorrow; we recognize in him much that is dear to us in ourselves. Verdoux is so much nearer and darker that we can hardly bear to recognize ourselves in him. He is the committed, dedicated soul, and this soul is not intact: we watch its death agonies. And this tragic process is only the more dreadful because it is depicted not gravely but briskly, with a cold savage gaiety; the self-destroying soul is rarely aware of its own predicament.

The problem of survival: the Responsible Man. Chaplin develops his terrible theme chiefly as a metaphor for business. But the film is also powerful as a metaphor for war: the Verdoux home as an embattled nation, the wife and child as the home front, Verdoux as expeditionary force, hero in the holiest of causes, and war criminal. But it is even more remarkable and fascinating as a study of the relationship between ends and means, a metaphor for the modern personality—that is, a typical "responsible" personality reacting to contemporary pressures according to the logic of contemporary ethics.

In the terms of this metaphor the basic cast is small. Verdoux, his wife, and their son are differing aspects of a single personality. Verdoux is the master, the intelligence and the deep unconscious; he has estranged his soul and his future. He has made the assumption that most people make, today—one of the chief assumptions on which modern civilization rests. That is, that in order to preserve intact in such a world as this those aspects of the personality which are best and dearest to one, it is necessary to exercise all that is worst in one; and that it is impossible to do this effectively if one communicates honestly with one's best. Accordingly the personality which, until the world struck that living down, lived in poverty and docility, but happily, is broken and segregated.

The wife and child are shut away in a home which is at once a shrine and a jail; and there, immobilized, and cut off from the truth, they virtually cease to exist as living objects of love; they become an ever more rigid dream. For when the worst and the best in the personality are thus segregated, and the worst is thus utilized in the nominal service of the best, it is inevitably the good which is exploited; the evil, which thinks of itself as faithful slave, is treacherous master; and evil, being active and knowledgeable, grows; and good, rendered motionless and denied knowledge, withers. Like most men obsessed with the world's ruthlessness, Verdoux carries his veneration of innocence to the extreme; he is determined that it shall never be touched, shall never change (the song of how many million homesick soldiers: "We want to find everything at home just as we left it"). But change is inevitable, and uncontrollable. Ruthlessness and the murderous adoration of static innocence enlarge each other; and the ruthless man becomes the more ruthless because he has broken all communication with innocence. And innocence itself is altered. At the moment Verdoux tells his wife that they own their home at last, she dares to remember sadly that they were happier when they were poor. Her face shows the terrible drugged passiveness of the oversustained, the still more terrible intuitive guilt that comes of all that is uneasily apprehended, untold, and unasked. Small wonder that she has become a cripple; the wonder is that she continues to breathe. Passiveness was forced on her, truth was destroyed, love was undermined, her own love became pity, as surely as her husband's, and in pity and in fear she failed to question what was being done. As is so often true, it was not she who wanted to be so well provided for; that was her husband's desire, the one desire he might hope to satisfy; so she let him satisfy it.

As for Verdoux, he is irreparably committed. All the heart he has left prevents his confessing to his wife, and prevents his changing trades. He could only have chosen his course through defect of love—vengefulness and self-pity masked as pity, pity masked as love; the love-destroying, monstrous arrogance it requires to make the innocent answerable for your guilt—and the constant necessity of deceiving love has damaged love still more profoundly. Like many business men who feel unloved, or incapable of full enough love, he can only propitiate, and express, his love by providing for his family as handsomely as possible. (He can desire this of course, rather than the bare subsistence his wife prefers, only because he respects the standards of the world he thinks he despises. During his docile years, remember, he served at the high altar of modern civilization, breathing year in and year out The Bank's soul-dissolving odor of sanctity, all day, every day, touching the sacred wealth he must never dare touch with his conscious desire. When he was thrown out of his job, this ruthlessness released the tremendously impounded ruthlessness in him.) But that is never well enough to satisfy him—and only *his* satisfaction really counts, in this household—for his wife and child scarcely exist for him except as a self-vindicating dream, which he must ceaselessly labor to sustain, improve, perfect, be worthy of. A vicious cycle is established. Only through the best good-providing possible can Verdoux at once express his love, quiet his dying intuition that his love is defective and that he is wrong even in the little that he believes to be right, sustain the dream that is all that remains of love, require of himself ever more obsessive industriousness in crime, and silence his wife.

As good, by his will, is ever more stonily immobilized, evil becomes ever more protean in disguise and self-disguise, ever more mercurial in its journeyings. (The personality is also a constant metaphor for modern civilization—in which, for one instance, creative power is paralyzed except in the interests of gain and destruction; in those interests it is vigorous as never before.) Verdoux cannot bear to sit still, to stop work, long enough to realize his predicament. He cannot feel "at home," at home. He has to act his roles as perfect husband and father, dearly as he wants merely to *be* both, just as he acts all his other roles. All that he loves is saturated in deceit; and he in self-deceit as well. He gets home seldom, apparently never longer than overnight; the divided spirit can only assert its unity, even its illusion of unity or its desire, in twilight contemplation or in dreams; and the pressure of business is always on him. The pressure of business indeed! Verdoux's family is almost lifeless; such piteously cherished life as it retains, he is hopelessly estranged from. All that requires his intelligence, skill, and vitality, all that gives him life, is in his business. He is the loneliest character I know of: he can never be so desperately lonely as during these hours among those dearest to him, when he must deceive not mere victims, or the world at large, but those he loves. The only moments during which this appalling loneliness is broken, during which he ever honestly communicates, however briefly, with other human beings, are those few moments during which he can know that his victims realize they are being murdered. No doubt he loves his wife and child—there are two of the most heart-stopping, beautiful close-ups ever made, to prove that—but in the fearful depths into which he cannot risk a glance he loves their helplessness; and deeper, only the idea of love; and that only because it consecrates his true marriage, which is to murder.

June 21, 1947
Monsieur Verdoux-III

(*Monsieur Verdoux has been withdrawn and will be released only after a United Artists' build-up which will, I hear, try to persuade people that they will kill themselves laughing. I will take care to notify readers of this column of its return, and of changes, if any are made. I am grieved to be so late—or early—with this review, but not very; this film has too long a life ahead of it. It is permanent if any work done during the past twenty years is permanent.*)

The most mysterious line in the film, Verdoux's reference to having "lost" his family, becomes clear if the three are seen as members of a single personality. The wife whom segregation and deceit so inevitably paralyzed was dying a slow death from the moment she became uneasy and failed with her own kind of misguided tenderness to beseech her husband's confidence; and the child could not long have survived his mother.

With their death Verdoux all but dies himself. He becomes old, bent, sore, stiff, not only through heartbreak or because all that he most cherished in his nature is destroyed, but because their death has deprived him of the one motive he would recognize for his criminality. The third meeting with Miss Nash, for all its handsome prospects, revives him only to an old man's charming glimmer; but as soon as danger once more requires work of him and, after showing how effortlessly he might escape, he casually surrenders himself to society's vengeance, he limbers up and shines like a snake which has just cast its winter skin. All that remains now is memory and the pure stripped ego, the naked will to survive which discovers, with ineffable relief, that there is no longer any point in surviving.

With his soul dead at last, it is no wonder that Verdoux asserts himself so proudly, in the courtroom and death cell, in terms of his dream of himself. He would have explained himself less proudly and with greater moral understanding to his wife, but he had successfully avoided that possibility, at the cost of their marriage and her life. His dream of himself is urgently challenged only once, by the girl whose life he spares; and he successfully resists that challenge in the strangest and, I think, most frightening scene ever filmed.

I had expected this film to be the last word in misogyny; but although there is a good deal of it about, Verdoux's handling of his victims is in general remarkably genial and kindly. The one really hair-raising moment of that sort is the chance second meeting with the girl, the scene in which he brushes her off. After all, Verdoux risks nothing against the poor frumps he kills or tries to kill, except his life. But the girl is infinitely more dangerous. She is the one human being with whom he holds in common everything he regards as most important. Both have known love as passionate pity for the helpless, both could kill for love; both would be capable of maturer love, if at all, only with their own kind. The girl is much closer to Verdoux than his own wife, or his murdered wives; in sparing her he has betrayed both his marriage and his vocation. Since he is above all else a family man and an artist, she threatens the very structure of his soul. But the deranged and deadlocked will which has made and sustained Verdoux is never so strong or so ruthless as when it faces the threat of cure; and I know of no moment more dreadful or more beautifully achieved than that in which Verdoux veers from the girl, the sun on his suddenly shriveled cheek, and mutters in the shriveled, almost effeminate little voice of more than mortal hatred and terror: "You go on about your business."

But *why* does Verdoux become a murderer? One good answer is: why not? Verdoux is a business realist; in terms of that realism the only difference between free enterprise in murder and free enterprise in the sale of elastic stockings is the difference in legal liability and in net income. And if the film is regarded as a metaphor for war, we may blush to ask Verdoux *why;* or if it is regarded as a metaphor for the destruction of the soul, murder is almost too mild a vocation. Yet we may still ask why, and wonder why Chaplin's only direct statements, most of which are made through Verdoux, are so remarkably inadequate. Verdoux, to be sure, is grandly in character in holding "society" accountable and in absolving the individual; but is this all that Chaplin knows? If so, he is as surely a victim and dupe of evil as Verdoux or the civilization he excoriates, and all that goes deeper in the film is achieved intuitively, as if in a kind of waking dream. If he knows better, then he is gravely at fault, as artist and moralist, in making clear no more than he does, still worse in tossing the mass-audience so cynical and misleading a sop; and one of the purest and most courageous works I know of is, at its climax, pure and courageous only against the enemy, not in the face of the truth. For the answers to why and how criminality can be avoided, we can look inward more profitably than at the film; for all that is suggested in the film is operant in each of us. If Chaplin had illuminated these bottom causes more brightly than we can see them in ourselves, *Verdoux* would be a still greater work of art than it is. But in proposing so richly suggestive an image of process and effect in the world and in the personality, and in proposing it so beautifully, the film, with all its faults, is one of the few indispensable works of our time.

It even contains and implies the beginning of the answer. Good and evil are inextricable, Verdoux insists. But his fatal mistake was in trying to keep them apart. If the film is regarded as a metaphor for the personality, and through that metaphor, as a metaphor for the personality as the family as business as war as civilization as murder, then this is certain: if the man and wife had honored their marriage with more than their child, the murders would never have been committed, the paralysis would never have imposed itself or would have been dissolved, and the wife and child would never have been shut into that exquisite tabernacle of a closed garden, but all three would have lived as one in that poverty for which the wife was forlorn, in the intactness of soul and the irresponsibility of that anarchic and immortal lily of the field, the tramp, the most humane and most nearly complete among the religious figures our time has evolved; whom for once in his life Chaplin set aside, to give his century its truest portrait of the upright citizen.

Ordet

Jonas Mekas, "Ordet"

○○

Like Robert Bresson whose reputation is great but whose number of films over many years of film-making is slight, Carl Dreyer has made fourteen feature-length films in nearly fifty years. Age cannot wither his artistic imagination; at seventy-nine Dreyer continues to pursue his muse with projected literary adaptations that could keep him active for some time to come—*Medea* in color, Faulkner's novel *Light in August*, and O'Neill's *Mourning Becomes Electra.* He regards *Ordet* (1955) as one of his most successful films. Jonas Mekas, who, in another context, has said that "unlike Bergman, Dreyer never asks questions he can't answer," discusses *Ordet* as "a highly accomplished work of cinematic art," a seemingly hyperbolical statement about a film that climaxes with a veritable biblical miracle. Dreyer's authority over his material and the infecting build-up in the film of a real but remote universe is such that the resurrection of a dead woman, fully manifested to the characters present and to all who behold the perceptions of the camera's eye, is powerful and moving.

———◆———

But really is everyone in my generation capable of making the movements of faith, I wonder?

Søren Kierkegaard
"Fear and Trembling," 1843

By any standards, *Ordet* is a highly accomplished work of cinematic art. Dreyer's formal and technical mastery, the seeming simplicity of his style, and the depth of the film are overpowering. However, *Ordet* is in no way a modern film, neither in a strict nor in a popular sense, and, viewed in an atmosphere of cool jazz, super-markets, and satellites, could be easily misunderstood, despite its artistry—the more since it comes to America preceded by reviews of several European critics who have called it a "fraud," who have accused Dreyer of mysticism and of believing in miracles in the age of science.

Let us turn to the film itself. The cause of most misunderstandings being the surface plot, let's relate it briefly:

A young theology student, Johannes, after an intensive study of the New Testament and contemporary philosophers, loses his memory and believes he is Christ come back to earth. He is kept in his father's house, where there are also living his younger brother, Anders; another brother, Mikkel; and Mikkel's wife, Inger. This younger brother, Anders, loves the tailor's daughter, but marriage is impossible because their parents belong to antagonistic religious sects. Two symbols of a total confusion where no one knows the truth, they denounce each other fervidly. Meanwhile, Inger, a kind and good woman, has a miscarriage, the baby dies, and she herself lies dying. Now Johannes states that if only some one person believed that he could perform miracles, he could save her. Since no one believes him, Inger dies. The grief unites the two quarrelsome neighbors, the tailor brings his daughter to Anders. "But Inger is dead!" cries Mikkel. "Because nobody thought to ask her back from death," says Johannes. "She will rot because the times are rotten." But there is one, Inger's little daughter, who, in her simple childish mind, believes in Johannes' words. Thus, it is for her, or because of her, that Johannes performs his miracle: he pronounces the word which recalls Inger to life, and there the film ends.

Now, if this film means only that Dreyer is propagating nothing but a belief in miracles, as some critics have said, it would be really a limited work of art. However, this simple plot is only the surface frame. On its deeper level, or on its

Ordet, directed by Carl Dreyer, 1955 (*Contemporary*)

true level, the film transcends its plot and becomes a parable. We know parables told to children: realistic content presented through fantastic happenings. No child believes them, but everyone gets their simple moral messages: courage, endurance, or whatever it may be. *Ordet* is a modern parable, and its message—or, let us say, one of its most obvious messages— is a plea for man's faith in our time of confusion. Not a cry of desperation or pessimism, but a trembling, anguished, searching cry—a cry of a man who takes his life and his death seriously and who still believes that there must be a WORD.

On its surface, the film seems just another Christian parable. As a matter of fact, I don't know any other film in which the spirit and symbol of Nordic puritan Christianity are so well integrated. And it is Dreyer's faithfulness to the back- ground of his parable that helps sustain the film on all other levels of interpretation. Its foundations are not Dreyer's alone: they are the foundations of the entire culture that produced him.

Perhaps the worst misinterpretation of this film has arisen with "realist" critics. This is regrettable, but also historically understandable. For decades now we have been exposed to various brands of naturalism in the arts without fully coming to understand or define realism. There is a growing effort here and in Europe to discover the true meaning of realism, a realism which is not bound to externalities, but to essences. Such an attempt was Edouard Laurot's article "Towards a Theory of Dynamic Realism" (*Film Culture*, No. 1, Vol. I, 1955): a definition used in the article could serve us now: realism as "content dictated by a dynamic perception of reality, reflecting the development of the human conscience within its historical context." Too many artists and critics confuse realism with a pedestrian surface description, with naturalism, thus depriving art of the use of creative imagina- tion to its fullest extent. It is for this reason that, for instance, De Sica's film *Miracle in Milan* was misunderstood by critics of both the left and the right, as was Rossellini's *Europe 51*. Critics who are not familiar with the poetic license of the

creative imagination have interpreted the flight of the under-
privileged people in De Sica's film as an act of escapism. They
could not see that, artistically, this was a positive act (positive
in its negativism, so to say). In stating through an image of
fantasy that there is no other way out for these people but a
miracle, De Sica expressed the truth about the infinite cor-
ruption of the existing system more forcefully than would
have been possible through any simplistic, "probable" ending.

There are several other films which I would put in the
same category with *Ordet* and *Miracle in Milan*—films which
attempted to reassess the faith of man and expose the ills of
our time: films such as Chaplin's *Monsieur Verdoux* and
Limelight, Rossellini's *Europe 51*, Bresson's *A Man Escaped*,
Kurosawa's *We Live in Fear*. All these films are parables.
And as in so many literary parables, the truth in these films
is entrusted to the humblest one, or one who is taken either
for a fool, or a clown, or a madman. Such is the simplicity of
truth sometimes, or so strangely does it sound in the ears of
our contemporaries, that it has to be exiled from reason.

Being conditioned to accepting and judging art by the
brilliance of surface alone, we are seldom aware of a deeper
content, or deeper truths, expressed in these films—films
which "reflect the development of the human conscience
within its historical context." The shallow aesthetics of
twentieth-century naturalism cause more sensitive critics (such
as Manny Farber, for instance) to seek refuge in the Thirties
or Forties, in the work of Hawks, Wellman, or Walsh, who
through sheer unpretentiousness incidentally captured more of
the truth about their time than many of our current "realists."

To return to Dreyer: it is through his *consciousness* as an
artist, through his awareness and complete control of his
purpose and his technique, that *Ordet* progresses toward meaning as directly and consistently as, on a different plane,
Bresson's *A Man Escaped*. The very movement of *Ordet*,
slow and thoughtful, conveys the seriousness of these people's
existence. And why is a horse heard whinnying before the
closing of Inger's coffin, as though before a departure? And
who is old Borgen, climbing up and up steps like calvaries

and shouting, helpless, searching? And when he falls upon the old neighbor to fight out his truth—both of them noble and serious old men—doesn't one think of Abraham and the Angel, both blameless, fighting out their truth? And the little girl in white, as for a first communion? And the wake, with the whiteness of the room, and the blackness of death? And the Borgens and their neighbors, walking with lights across the dark rye fields and shouting for Johannes in the night—searching for faith? A purpose? An answer? Or just trembling? Every image of this film is measured and written with meaning, expression. One can interpret them directly, or impose one's own meaning—they still hold. Such is the strength of Dreyer's art.

Ordet—not modern? We have the right to ask that our artists be faithful to the movement of history, that they interpret creatively the various aspects of modern life. Why should we look at the present through the eyes of our fathers? However, from time to time, one has to stop, withdraw into himself, reflect, and try to integrate past, present, and future: return to one's roots. And that is what Dreyer has tried to do. Though in no way a modern poet, Dreyer has so succeeded in evoking the past that he has strengthened the faith of present-day rebels, however few of them remain, in their search for the WORD. When neither bread nor laugh nor life nor water nor cosmos nor wine nor kiss has meaning or content, a poet's voice, the voice of a believer—or a fool's or a madman's for that matter—is a most necessary voice.

Rashomon

Parker Tyler, "Rashomon as Modern Art"

ooooooooooooooooooooooooooooooooooooooooooooooo

Called to international attention with the presentation of
Rashomon at the Venice Film Festival in 1951, director
Akira Kurosawa has been the best known of Japanese film-
makers. *Ikiru* (1952), *Seven Samurai* (1954), *Throne of
Blood* (1957), *The Lower Depths* (1957), *The Hidden
Fortress* (1958), *The Bad Sleep Well* (1960), *Yojimbo* (1961),
Heaven and Hell (1963), and other films have been distributed in Western Europe and the United States. As a director
who writes most of his own scripts, Kurosawa based his
scenario for *Rashomon* on two stories by the popular Japanese writer Ryunosuke Akutagawa, "Rashomon" and "In the
Grove." Kurosawa employs the basic story: a husband and
wife encounter a bandit on a journey through a forest; there
occurs the death of the husband (murder or suicide?) and
the rape of the wife. But instead of accepting Akutagawa's
first-person method of rendering this action four times
through the respective accounts of the wife, the husband
(through a medium), the bandit, and a woodcutter, Kurosawa significantly alters his literary source by adding the
character of the commoner who, sitting sheltered from
the rain, listens to and comments upon the four versions
of the central action as reported to him by the priest and the
woodcutter. Hence the commoner's responses are an added
layer of reality presented to the viewer. In directly presenting
conflicting testimonies, Akutagawa dramatically confronts the

reader with the problem of attempting to determine truth empirically; Kurosawa's incorporation of the commoner makes for greater artifice, enabling him to go beyond recreating Akutagawa's study in philosophical skepticism. The commoner's point of view gives not only structural order to the film but also subtly thickens its already complex, refracted reality. The ending, too, is Kurosawa's invention: as the storytelling and the rain stop, the commoner, stirred by the crying of an abandoned baby, goes to it and greedily takes its clothes. The woodcutter succors the child and departs with it in his arms as the priest, moved by the woodcutter's humane act, watches him recede beyond the gate.

Parker Tyler suggests that the viewer consider the futurist technique of breaking a total, unitary surface into multiple reality as a correlative to the logic of art functioning in *Rashomon*. Hence his discussion of modern painting serves him as an illustrative vehicle for analyzing *Rashomon*, his principal focus in the essay.

———◆———

RASHOMON, THE JAPANESE FILM MASTERPIECE, is a story about a double crime: rape and homicide (or possibly suicide). The time is the eighth century A.D. It is told in retrospect, and in successive layers, by the three participants, the dead warrior (through a mediumistic priestess), his raped wife, and a notorious bandit perhaps responsible for the warrior's death as well as for his wife's violation, and by a woodcutter who alleges himself to have witnessed, accidentally, the whole episode. The quality of the film narrative is so fine that an astonishingly unified effect emerges from the conflicting stories furnished by the three principals and (following the inquest) by the lone witness. The bandit and the woman have separately fled the scene of the crimes, where the woodcutter claims, at first, to have arrived only in time to find the warrior's corpse. Nominally, the film comes under the familiar heading of stories that reconstruct crimes. However, this story does not go much beyond the presentation of each person's testimony.

Rashomon, directed by Akira Kurosawa, 1950 (*RKO*)

The woman claims to have killed her husband in an irresponsible fit of horror after the rape took place; her husband claims to have committed hari-kiri out of grief and humiliation; and bandit claims to have killed him in honorable combat; and the woodcutter confirms the bandit's story while picturing the conduct of all participants quite differently from the ways they respectively describe it. As no trial of either of the living participants is shown, and as no consequent action reveals anything conclusive as to the crime, the decision as to the actual truth of the whole affair falls to the spectator's option. Since technically the woodcutter is the only "objective" witness, he might seem the most reliable of the four testifiers. But his integrity is *not* beyond question; the version by the warrior's ghost has contradicted his version in an important detail—one inadvertently confirmed by the woodcutter's implicit admission (in an incident following the inquest) that he stole a dagger at the scene of the crime. The ghost has testified that he felt "someone" draw from his breast the dagger with which he alleges he committed hari-kiri.

Logically, if one's aim be to establish in theory the "legal" truth of the affair, the only obvious method is to correlate all the admissible facts of the action with the four persons involved in order to determine their relative integrity as individuals—a procedure complicated necessarily not merely by the given criminal status of one participant but by the fact that all but the woodcutter have willingly assumed guilt. A further difficulty, in general, is that nothing of the background of any character is given beyond what can be assumed from his visible behavior and his social status; for example, there is only the merest hint of something unusual in the journey of the warrior and his lady through the forest. Again, even from direct observation, we have to depend a great deal on these persons as seen through the eyes of each other. So, unless one be prejudiced for one sex or another, one social class or another, it seems almost impossible to make a really plausible choice of the truth-teller (if any). Are we to conclude, in this dilemma, that *Rashomon* amounts to no more than a trick piece, a conventional mystery melodrama, left hanging? My answer is *No*. There are several things about the movie which argue it as a unique and conscious art, the opposite of a puzzle; or at least, no more of a puzzle than those modern paintings of which a spectator may be heard to say: "But what is it? What is it supposed to mean?"

Perhaps more than one profane critic has wisecracked of a Picasso, a Dali, or an Ernst, that it demands, *a posteriori*, the method described by the police as "the reconstruction of the crime." My opinion is that the last thing required for the elucidation of *Rashomon*'s mystery is something corresponding to a jury's verdict. Such a judgment, aesthetically speaking, is as inutile for appreciating the substance of this movie as for appreciating the art of Picasso. In *Rashomon*, there is no strategic effort to conceal any more than a modern painter's purpose is to conceal instead of reveal. The basic issue, in art, must always be *what* the creator desires to reveal. Of such a painting as Picasso's *Girl Before Mirror*, it may be said that it contains an "enigma." But this enigma is merely one specific aspect of the whole mystery of being, a particular insight into human consciousness in terms of the individual, and so has that complex poetry of which all profound art partakes. So with the enigma of *Rashomon*. This great Japanese film is a "mystery story" to the extent that existence itself is a mystery as conceived in the deepest psychological and aesthetic senses. As applied to a movie of this class, however, such a theory is certainly unfamiliar and therefore has to be explained.

Chagall with his levitated fantasy-world and childhood-symbols, Picasso with his creative analysis of psychological movements translated into pictorial vision—such painters set forth *nude* mysteries of human experience; each, in the static field of the painting, reveals multiple aspects of a single reality, whether literally or in symbols. *Rashomon*, as a time art, cinema, corresponds with multiple-image painting as a space art. The simplest rendering of time phases in an object within the unilateral space of a single picture is, of course, in futurist painting, such as Balla's famous dog, ambling by the moving skirts of its owner; the dachshund's legs are portrayed multiply with a fanlike, flickering kind of image similar to images as seen in the old-fashioned "bioscope" movie machine. The same dynamic principle was illustrated by Muybridge's original time-photography of a running horse, except that the register there was not instantaneous but successive; at least, the photographer had the cinematic idea of keeping pace with a running horse to show the pendulum-like span of its front and hind legs while its body seemed to stay in the same place (treadmill dynamics). Even in the contemporary movie camera, some movements may be so fast that one gets the sort of blur shown in futurist images. The analogy of *Rashomon* with such procedures of stating physical movement is that, for the single action photographed, a complex action (or "episode") is substituted, and for the single viewpoint toward this action, multiple (and successive) viewpoints. The camera in this movie is actually trained four times on what theoretically is the same episode; if the results are different each time, it is because each time the camera represents the viewpoint of a different person; a viewpoint mainly different, of course, not because of the physical angle (the camera is never meant to substitute for subjective vision) but because of the psychological angle.

"Simultaneous montage" in cinema is the double exposure of two views so that multiple actions occur in a *unilateral space visually* while existing in *separate spaces literally* and possibly —as when a person and his visual recollection are superimposed on the same film-frame—also in separate times. A remarkable aspect of the method of depicting memory in *Rashomon* is its simplicity: each person, squatting in Japanese fashion as he testifies, squarely faces the camera and speaks; then, rather than simultaneous montage, a flashback takes place: the scene shifts wholly to the fatal spot in the forest. The police magistrate is never shown and no questions addressed to the witnesses are heard. When it is the dead man's turn to testify, the priestess performs the required rite, becomes possessed by his spirit, speaks in his voice, and the scene shifts back as in the other cases. Thus we receive the successive versions of the action with little intervention between them and with the minimum of "courtroom action."

Of course, there is a framing story, which retrospectively reveals the inquest itself. The action literally begins at the Rashomon Gate, a great ruin where the woodcutter and the priest, who has previously seen the woman and been present at the inquest, are sheltered during a rainstorm; joined by a tramp, these two gradually reveal everything that has taken place according to the several versions. What is important is the inherent value of the way the technique of the flashback has been variously used. The separate stories are equally straightforward, equally forceful; no matter which version is being related, his own or another's, every participant behaves with the same conviction. As a result (it was certainly this spectator's experience) one is compelled to believe each story implicitly as it unfolds, and oddly none seems to cancel another out. Therefore it would be only from the policeman's viewpoint of wanting to pin guilt on one of the persons that, ultimately, any obligation would be felt to sift the conflicting evidence and render a formal verdict. Despite the incidental category of its form, *Rashomon* as a work of art naturally seems to call for a response having nothing to do with a courtroom.

Of an event less significant, less stark and rudimentary in terms of human behavior, the technical question of "the truth" might prove insistent enough to embarrass one's judgment. The inevitable impulse, at first sight, is to speculate on which of those who claim guilt is really guilty of the warrior's death. But whatever conclusion be tentatively reached, what eventually slips back into the spectator's mind and possesses it, is the traumatic violence of the basic pattern: that violence which is the heart of the enigma. The civilization of this medieval period is turned topsy-turvy by the bandit's strategy, in which he tricks the man, ties him up, and forces him to witness his wife's violation. It is only from this point forwards that the stories differ: the woman's reaction to the bandit's assault, the husband's behavior after being freed from his bonds—everything is disputed by one version or another. But is not the heart of the confusion *within the event itself?* Is this happening not one so frightfully destructive of human poise and ethical custom that it breeds its own ambiguity, and that this ambiguity infects the minds of these people?

All the participants are suffering from shock: the warrior's agonized ghost, his hysterical wife, the bandit, when caught, seized with mad bravado. Unexpectedly—for the paths of the couple and the bandit have crossed purely by accident—three lives have been irretrievably altered after being reduced to the most primitive condition conceivable. Two men (in a manner in which, at best, etiquette has only a vestigial role) have risked death for the possession of a woman. Basically, it is a pattern that was born with the beginnings of mankind. Such an event, in civilized times of high culture, would of itself contain something opaque and even incredible. What matters morally is not how, from moment to moment, the affair was played out by its actors but that it should have been played *at all.* The illicit impulse springing up in the bandit's breast as the lady's long veil blows aside, is so violent that its consequences attack the sense of reality at its moral root. Regardless of what literally took place in the forest's depths that mild summer day, each participant is justified in reconstructing it in a manner to redeem the prestige of the moral sense, which, consciously or not, is a civilized person's most precious possession. It should be emphasized that it is the Japanese people who are involved, and that to them honor is of peculiarly paramount value; even the bandit is quick to seize the opportunity to maintain—truthfully or not—that he behaved like a man of caste rather than an outlaw; he has testified that following the rape (to which, he says, the woman yielded willingly) he untied the husband and worsted him in fair swordplay.

Hence, a psychologically unilateral, indisputable perspective exists in which the tragic episode can be viewed *by the spectator*: a perspective contrary to that in which one of the persons appears technically guilty of the warrior's death. This perspective is simply the catastrophe as a single movement which temporarily annihilated the moral reality on which civilized human consciousness is based. The "legal" or objective reality of the affair (what might be called its *statistics*) is exactly what cannot be recovered because the physical episode, as human action, has been *self-annihilating*. Of course, then, it might be claimed that the woodcutter, not being involved except as a spectator, is a disinterested witness of the episode, and accordingly his story that the three actors in the tragedy really played a grim farce, in which two cowards were the heroes and a shrew the heroine, is the correct version. But the opening scene of the framing story makes it plain that the woodcutter's mind is in a state similar to that of the participants themselves; indeed, he is evidently dismayed and apparently by the fact that all their testimony belies what he proceeds to reveal to the priest and the tramp as "the truth." However, as the shocked witness of such a debacle of the social order—in any case a victory of evil over good—this peasant may have withheld his testimony out of superstitious timidity. If, in fact, he saw all that took place, then the added confusion that the participants contradict each other may raise bewilderment in his simple mind—may even tempt him to exploit his subconscious envy and resentment against his betters by imagining their behavior as disgraceful and ludicrous. It seems within *Rashomon*'s subtle pattern to suggest that even a simple, distinterested witness should be drawn psychologically into the chaos of this incident; after all, there is no proof that he did not invent his own account in competition with the others'. This assumption would lend credit to the conclusion that the real function of each witness's story is to salvage his own sense of reality, however close his version to the event as it took place. Perhaps it would be accurate to add that the facts themselves have no true legal status since each witness is forced to draw on his subjective imagination rather than on his capacity to observe. In this case, each is in the position of the proto-artist, who uses reality only as a crude norm; the sense of invention enters *into* reality. On the other hand, there is the literal truth of the denouement, the climax of the framing story, in which the woodcutter adopts a foundling baby who has been left in the gate's interior. The relation of this incident to the story proper strikes me as the most problematical element of all, if only because the film would have remained intact without it.

Morally, of course, this incident functions as a reinstatement of human values in the sense of good. But the specifically religious view that humanity has hopelessly degraded itself in the forest episode (the view represented by the priest) is more external than essential to the whole conception. The priest thinks in terms equivalent, logically, to the law's terms: truth or falsehood. Since some lying is self-evident, the sin of concealment is added to crime; i.e., concealment of the truth, not of the crime, for all profess crime. Ironically enough, *confession* has become a sin. What seems significant to the whole is the collective nature of the liars: they literally outnumber the truth-teller (whichever he may be). The "sin" involved has gone beyond individual performance and exists objectively as would a natural cataclysm such as a volcanic eruption. That each participant assumes guilt, including the dead man, reveals the comprehensiveness and irresistibility of the disorder. A lie, then, actually becomes the symbol of the operation by which these people mutually regain their moral identities. These identities having been destroyed as though by an objective force beyond anyone's control, any means seems fair to regain them. Since, however, they cannot separate themselves from the sense of *tragedy*, they prefer to be tragedy's heroes—its animating will rather than its passive objects. But why should the three tragedies seem as one?

To revert to our analogy with the visual media of painting and still photography, the plastic reality with which we have to deal in *Rashomon* is multiform rather than uniform. Within one span of time-and-space, reality (the episode in the forest) has been disintegrated. While the witnesses' stories accomplish its reintegration, they do not do so in terms of the *physically unilateral* except in the final aesthetic sense in which the totality of a work exists all at once in a spectator's mind. The analogy is complex, but literally it is with the futuristic image of the walking dog; like this image, the total image of

Rashomon varies only in detail and degree. There is no variation on the background and origin of the tragedy; no contradiction as to the main physical patterns of the rape and the death of the warrior by a blade wound. So the main visual aspect is held firmly, unilaterally, in place. Another image of futurist painting renders the angles of air displacement caused by the nose of a racing auto. Such "displacements" exist in *Rashomon* severally in the respective accounts of a physical action deriving from one main impetus: the desire to possess a woman.

The total psychological space in this movie, because of its complexity, is tendered in literal time as is music. A similar psychological space is rendered *simultaneously* in Picasso's *Girl Before Mirror* by the device of the mirror as well as by the double image of profile-and-full face on the girl. Her moonlike face has a symbolic integralness as different "phases" of the same person; that is, her full face denotes her personality as it confronts the world and her profile her personality as it confronts itself: the mirror image in which the full-face character of her aspect is diminished. To Meyer Schapiro we owe a basic observation as to this painting: it plays specifically on the body-image which each individual has of himself and others, and which is distinct from the anatomical image peculiarly available to photography. The mirror-image in Picasso's work thus asserts a psychological datum parallel with the dominantly subjective testimony of each witness in *Rashomon's* tragedy. The mirror of the movie screen is like the mirror in the painting as telescoped within the image of the total painting; successively, we see people as they think of themselves and as they are to others; for example, at one point during the woman's story, the camera substitutes for the viewpoint of her husband toward whom she lifts a dagger: we see her as conceived by herself but also as she would have been in her husband's eyes. In revealing, with such expressiveness and conviction, what novels have often revealed through first-person narratives or the interior monologue, the film necessarily emphasizes its *visual* significance. The sum of these narratives in *Rashomon* rests on the elements of the tragedy in which all agree: one raped, one was raped, one killed, one was killed. The "variations" are accountable through something which I would place parallel with Schapiro's body-image concept: the *psychic image* that would apply especially to the memory of a past event in which the body-image is charged with maintaining, above all, its moral integrity, its ideal dignity. In a sense, Picasso's girl reconstructs and synthesizes her outer self-division within the depths of the mirror; so in the depths of each person's memory, in *Rashomon*, is recreated the image of what took place far away in the forest as consistent with his ideal image of himself.

In modern times, the human personality—as outstandingly demonstrated in the tragi-comedies of Pirandello—is easily divided against itself. But what makes a technically schizophrenic situation important and dramatically interesting is, paradoxically, the individual's sense of his former or possible unity, for without this sense he would not struggle morally against division: he would be satisfied to be "more than one person." In analytical cubism, we have a pictorial style expressing an ironic situation within the human individual's total physique, including his clothes; we do not perceive, within an individual portrayed by Picasso in this manner, a moral "split" or psychological "confusion"; rather we see the subject's phenomenal appearance portrayed formalistically in terms of its internal or "depth" elements, its overlaid facets, or complex layers of being, which—though presumably not meant to signify a conflict in the personality—correspond logically, nevertheless, to the moral dialectic within all consciousness (subjective/objective, personal/social, and so on). The same logical correspondence is seen even more plainly in the anatomical dialectic of Tchelitchew's recent paintings, where the separate inner systems are seen in labyrinthine relation to the skin-surface. Indeed, man as an internal labyrinth is common to diverse styles of modern painting, all such styles necessarily implying, as human statements, the sometimes bewildering complexity of man's spiritual being. Great beauty is justifiably found in such aesthetic forms, which indirectly symbolize an ultimate mystery: that *human* mystery to which *Rashomon* so eloquently testifies in its own way and which comprises the transition from birth to death, from the organic to the inorganic, which is the individual's necessary material fate.

Against the awareness of his material fate, the individual erects many defenses: art, pleasure, ethics, God, religion, immortality—ideas, sensations, and acts whose continuity in him are preserved by constant cultivation, periodic renewal, unconscious "testimony." These constitute his moral identity in the social order. In them resides the essence of his being, the law of his contentment (such as it be), and his rational ability to function from hour to hour. In the lives of the persons of *Rashomon*, where this objective order prevailed, utter chaos was suddenly injected. Each person was shaken out of himself, became part of that blind flux which joins the intuition of the suspense-before-birth with that of the suspense-before-death and whose name is terror. This was largely because of the tragedy's physical violence, which temporarily vanquished human reason. If we look at the terror of war as depicted in Picasso's *Guernica*, we observe a social cataclysm of which the forest episode in *Rashomon* is a microcosm. Curiously enough, *Guernica* happens to be divided vertically into four main sections, or panels, which Picasso has subtly unified by overlapping certain formal elements. Thus, while the great massacre is of course highly simplified here in visual terms, it is moreover synthesized by means of four stages or views. As wrenched by violence as are the individual forms, they congregate, so to speak, to make order out of confusion. Though Picasso was not recomposing from memory, he might have been; in any case, the drive of art is toward formal order and the individuals in *Rashomon*, as proto-artists, have this same drive. As gradually accumulated, the sum total of *Rashomon* constitutes a *time mural* whose unity lies in the fact that, however different are the imaginations of the four witnesses, whatever harsh vibrations their mutual contradictions set up, the general design (as the film-makers have molded it) remains and dominates the work's final aspect of great beauty and great truth.

Red Desert

Stanley Kauffmann, "The Artist Advances"

○○

Many critics have considered *Red Desert* (1964) to be a static continuation of Antonioni's theme and style in the trilogy—*La Notte*, *L'Avventura*, and *The Eclipse*. The main objections to the film are: lack of movement, triteness of theme, an immobilized, neurotic heroine, and ineffectual male characterizations. In a commanding tone, a voice sensitive to and secure in the knowledge of his subject, Stanley Kauffmann in "The Artist Advances" endeavors to discern the purpose and contextual meaning of the film. In his interpretation the rather "factual" charges against Antonioni, instead, become positive elements. His final statement, the authority for which is the essay itself, is that "There are few living directors who can be compared with him [Antonioni] in level of achievement; there is none who is his peer in shaping the film form itself to the needs of contemporary men."

◆

WITH MICHELANGELO ANTONIONI's *Red Desert*, the art of the film advances. This masterly creator has, in all his films shown here, opened new possibilities. Now, with his first use of color and with other elements, he further enlarges our vision of what a film can be and do.

The story chiefly concerns Giuliana, the young wife of Ugo, an electronics engineer in Ravenna. They have a boy of

Red Desert, directed by Michelangelo Antonioni, 1964 (*Rizzoli*)

four or five. Corrado, another engineer, visits Ugo to recruit skilled workers for a job in South America. Ugo tells him that Giuliana has recently been in an auto accident, was not badly hurt, but is still suffering from shock. (In fact, as we learn, it was a suicide attempt, and the "shock" is her explanation to Ugo of her state of mind.) During Corrado's stay in Ravenna, he visits a shop that Giuliana is going to open, to occupy herself; asks her to accompany him when he drives out to interview a worker; goes to a party in a seaside shack with her and Ugo and friends. All through this, Giuliana is living on her nerve-ends, trying desperately to become "normal," to become *something*. Ugo has to leave for some days on business, and during this time their little boy has a short episode of fancied paralysis. When this passes, Giuliana's disquiet does not pass. She goes out, more or less purposefully to Corrado's hotel. They make love. Later, after they part, she wanders aboard a ship, encounters a Turkish sailor, has a brief, pathetic, disconnected conversation with him, neither one understanding the other. In the last scene she is walking with her little son outside Ugo's factory. The boy asks her why the smoke from a certain chimney is yellow. She says it is a warning that it is poisonous. Doesn't it kill birds? he asks. By now, she says, the birds know all about it and don't fly through it. They walk out of the film, and it ends.

The story is both dry and full, austere and intense. It is a series of incidents with sufficient but minimal connection, not cumulative drama of well-made scenes; yet each of these terse incidents is more than a skin-and-bones gesture (à la Bresson), it is implicative and revealing. Antonioni has always been interested in symbology. His method here is not—as it has been —first, to try to move us in new ways and, second, to have the symbols beneath the emotion resonate within us: it is to hold us, to fascinate us into reading the hieroglyphics he has unearthed, dating from the mid-twentieth century. The figures on these tablets suffer, embrace, reject, but their actions weave a second symbolic language that is the primary meaning and effect.

Or, in another figure, the story is not placed in the usual

dramatic topography of valleys and mountains. It takes place entirely on the heights of character and action; thus the gradations, as in any view above the clouds, are only the relatively slight ones among peaks. Though these gradations are thus more subtle than if one were looking up from far below, they are nevertheless there. But a film that begins and continues at this high altitude makes assumptions between you and itself—about the valleys of character detail and the slopes of plot cumulation. Admittedly the atmosphere of the heights is perhaps a bit chilly, but it stings and clarifies.

The setting of the new industrial town and Giuliana's neurotic state help to illuminate each other. The Ravenna we see is a manufacturing seaport. (All through the film, ships pass in the background.) But by his vistas of factories, inside and out, of new dwellings, of radar installations, even of slag heaps, Antonioni is not making any trite charge of ugliness in the modern world. He is searching out the new life in it, the means of living in it. He has jarred Giuliana into a state of shock to make her hypersensitive—like a clairvoyant of change, of a means to accept life as it is and as it is going to be. In his press conference at the 1964 Venice Festival (where *Red Desert* won the Golden Lion) Antonioni said: "The story was born when I went to Ravenna, which I had not seen for some time. The film was born on the spot and the color was born with it—the industrial ambience of the film." In an interview (with Jean-Luc Godard) in the November 1964 *Cahiers du Cinéma*, he says further:

> My intention . . . was to express the beauty of this world where even the factories can be very beautiful. . . . The line, the curves of the factories and their chimneys are perhaps more beautiful than a line of trees, of which the eye has already seen too much. It is a rich world, lively, useful. For me, I try to say that the sort of neuroticism which one sees in *Red Desert* is entirely a question of adaptability. There are some people who adapt themselves and others who have not yet been able to do so, for they are too tied to structures or rhythms of life which are now bypassed. This is the

case with Giuliana. . . . If I had chosen a normally adaptable woman, there would not have been any drama.

This can be expanded to say, also, that if he had made the film in black and white, the urgency and immediacy of the neuroticism would have been lessened. The color serves several ends. First, quite simply, it is the best use of color I have ever seen in a film, exquisite in itself. It would be a quite wrong emphasis, but one could say the film is worth seeing for its color alone. (And also that there is a buried history of modern painting in it, from the Impressionists through Mondrian to Hopper and Wyeth.) Second, the color underscores the color in the new world, a usually disregarded facet. The age of plastic and mold-injection and die-stamp is an age of heightened colors. Third, he has used color subjectively. Antonioni has said that he had an entire marsh painted a certain shade of gray because that is the way Giuliana and Corrado felt when they looked at it. A small room of the seaside shack, where a lot of sexual teasing and talk goes on, is painted a shade of red, off which, so to speak, the talk can rebound. "It is necessary to intervene in a color film," he says "to take away the usual reality and replace it with the reality of the moment." Yet this subjectivism is gently handled, is complementary, is never carried to musical-comedy lengths. Fourth, color makes the environment a character in the drama. I know of no film in which a greater tension exists between the movement of the story and the places through which it moves.

As the film begins, we hear electronic music; then, over it a woman's voice vocalizing. It is an apt overture. These juxtaposed elements separate, and we hear the *vocalise* again later, in an interpolated idyl. Giuliana is the exponent and victim of these two themes. She is very much herself, a woman in crisis, but she also has something of the abstracted quality of a masque figure. (Those who have noted that Antonioni builds his films around female characters may also note that he has Monica Vitti to build them around. It is one of those happy occurrences in the performing arts when the advent of the right executant evokes the best work of a creator.) A recurrent method used to open a sequence is a shot of a background in slightly blurred diffused focus in which Miss Vitti then appears, very close, in sharp focus. Thus the world is made the scenery of her stage, both in the sense of the author's use and the sense of Giuliana's own neurotic egocentricity. I would concede, however, that both senses are given a bit too much play; something less of Giuliana's gazing out of windows or backing herself into corners would have heightened the impact of both.

The film is susceptible of considerable textural and thematic analysis. Here I can deal with only two moments. The first is a small skillful device. In the opening scene, outside the strike-bound factory, Giuliana, suddenly ravenously hungry, buys a sandwich from a worker who has already taken a bite out of it. Her insistence on buying a sandwich already "begun" is a small arresting gesture, unextravagant, just odd enough to make us wonder about her at once. The episode of the child's paralysis, which turns out to be spurious, is a painful mirror-image of the mother's troubled state. Psychiatrists know that young children apprehend and reflect neurosis in their parents; when a child is disturbed, the physician often asks that the parents (at least the mother) be treated. Suddenly one morning this little boy cannot walk or stand. During this siege, while waiting for the doctor's diagnosis, the mother distracts her son with a story, which we see as she tells it: about a young girl and a lovely, deserted pink beach (the closest we come to a literal substantiation of the film's title). This girl swims in the transparent water in the bright sun, sees birds and rabbits, is alone and happy. One morning she spies a sailing ship, unlike any other that passes by. She swims out to it and finds that, mysteriously, it is unmanned. It turns about and sails away. She swims back to the beach and hears a woman singing (the *vocalise* we heard under the titles of the film). She cannot find the woman. "One mystery is all right, two is too much," says Giuliana. "But who was singing?" asks the boy. Giuliana replies, "Everything. Everyone." The story is finished; and when she returns to his room, a little later, she finds the boy unconcernedly walking about.

The obvious contrast of the idyllic spot with the factory

milieu is certainly not the prime point of the episode. (Anyway, whenever Antonioni approaches an obvious point, he always redeems it with fresh vision.) The episode is a qualified adieu to that girl's world of sailing ships and wilderness and untrammeled freedom: qualified, not because there is the slightest doubt that such a world is almost gone but because it is sheer romanticism to think that such a world was free of mystery, of unanswerable questions. Giuliana says of the ship, "The girl was used to the strangeness of men and she was not surprised." The strangeness of men was and will be—in the natural world, in the machine-monitored world. Thus Giuliana is telling *herself* the story, with that perception of her trouble that neurotics often have rationally as they try to make their way toward health emotionally. In her mind, her best mind, she knows that it is rankly sentimental to think of our times as deterioration.

A personal example: When I walk through the New York neighborhood where I lived as a child and which is now a forbidding canyon of glass-and-steel apartment houses twenty stories high, I am tempted to sigh, until I think that in 2065 men will walk through these streets, then lined with fifty-story buildings, and will yearn for the bygone "human" days of twenty-story buildings.

It is worth noting, for argument, that the Italian press is to some extent anti-Antonioni. Some of their critics seem to resent the fact that he is Italian: as if he does not fit their conception of the Italian character, which is not much different from the travel-poster stereotype. After the Venice premiere a Milanese paper predictably referred to *Red Desert* as *"ancora una volta il 'michelangiolesco' giochetto*—once more the "michelangelesque" little game. (By contrast, and again predictably, some of the French press went to the other extreme and immediately hailed it as an imperishable masterpiece. The film has been a success in Paris.) But if there is anything that this film is not, it is "once more" of anything. The same artist left the same highly personal imprint on it, but it is different both in style and subject from his trilogy.

In style there is small trace in it of the distention of time that was germane to the trilogy, immersion in the extended moment. The handling of scenes is much more theatrically elliptical, and the editing, with rare exceptions, is pared. There are no marked lingerings on scenes, as if the pedal were being held down after the chord was released—a device often, and effectively, used in the trilogy.

As for subject matter, the trilogy was concerned with differing aspects of love as the medium of hope in our world. This film is stripped to naked essence—hope or nonhope unadorned: the prospect of human life in the midst of whirling changes. We live, as we know, in the age of the swiftest transition in history, and all indications are that the speed of change will increase: in everything from household appliances to concepts in philosophy, the whole architecture of thought. Antonioni seems to be saying, without effervescent cheeriness, that what was valuable can be preserved or can be transmuted to a new viability: that the future may contain new, at present inconceivable, values.

His film reaches no grand resolution. The affair with Corrado does not "cure" Giuliana. Her isolated dialogue with the Turkish sailor is not a "come-to-realize" scene. There is no guarantee that she is on the Road to Happiness. But she has finally accepted what has been no secret from her all along: that "what happens to you is your life"; and the very story that she herself tells her son evidences that she has within her a treasury of truth on which she may some day have courage to draw.

There are only three important characters. As Ugo, Carlo Chionetti has the right face and voice; not much more is asked of him. Miss Vitti is, as noted, the perfect Giuliana. She is asked to carry the film and she succeeds. Her vocabulary of uncertainty, in speech and gesture, is rooted in the certainty of her distress, her shame at her distress, her shameless display of it, her anger at the strength of others.

The principal and, to me, only serious flaw in the film is the casting of Richard Harris as Corrado. What he does is suitable enough; he has affecting ease and unexpected gentleness. But (this is a persistent Antonioni habit) what point was there in using a non-Italian who had to be dubbed? (At times rather perceptibly.) In Venice, when Antonioni was asked why he used Harris, he replied wryly that he chose Harris because he was thirty. "In Italy we have many actors of forty, like Gassman and Mastroianni, but we don't have any of thirty." I took this small joke as an oblique statement of regret. I hope I was right and that the practice can be discontinued.

I have now seen *Red Desert* three times, and each succeeding time it has not only seemed lovelier in color, it has had an increased sense of motion forward: in thematic penetration and artistic refinement. But pre-eminent in this sense of forward motion is a conviction that, as in his other recent films, Antonioni is not only making art of a high order, he is finding ways to help keep art itself alive. In these days of chance music, action painting and pop art, aesthetic idiocy in prose and poem, monolithic monomania in architecture, in these days when good artists question by act and statement the necessity for art, Antonioni continues to keep the film fresh and relevant: fresh without inane novelty, relevant without facile nostalgic reference. He has often been accused of being literary; if that is an indictment, he has perhaps been guilty, but here he is more purely cinematic than ever. There are few living directors who can be compared with him in level of achievement; there is none who is his peer in shaping the film form itself to the needs of contemporary men.

The Servant

T. J. Ross, "The Servant as Sex Thriller"

ooooooooooooooooooooooooooooooooooooooooooooooo

T. J. Ross in *"The Servant* as Sex Thriller" claims that sex has supplanted suspense. With our contemporary détente between the subject of sex and moral judgments about it, and with the decline of the crime story as an engrossing narrative vehicle for treating important themes such as "hypocrisy, or self-deception and self-discovery, freedom and responsibility, success and failure, and so on," Mr. Ross argues that "the audience now seeks out those forms in which its perennial questions are set in a sexual context." The great number of films in the late fifties and in the sixties considered artistically and thematically serious that have in them a great deal of sexploitation market has undermined the credibility of the nudie films—has caused many skeptical commentators to question the integrity of the makers of these films and the sincerity of their audiences. Indeed the bullish vigor of the sexploitation market has undermined the credibility of the idea of serious sex films, of—simply—films about life. Mr. Ross analyzes Joseph Losey's *The Servant,* a "sex thriller," as a film intended for a sincere audience that seeks well-made films, sensitive to differences between functional and feigned art.

———◆———

BY NOW "DECADENT" has come to be used as a descriptive term for works whose chills, spills, and suspense mainly derive from their treatment of sex. In this sense, most art films since *La Dolce Vita*, whatever their quality otherwise, have been freely decadent. In the more ambitious films (Fellini's, for example) the decadent line of action develops from, and sums up, an idea on the nature and quality of contemporary experience in general, or, in the most ambitious (Resnais, Bergman) on the "human condition." If nothing else *The Servant* is an ambitious film, comparable in the concentrated and relentless quality of its "vision" to, in particular, the films of Bergman. It offers too as neat a contrast as one could wish to the perspectives on decadence introduced by a continental master like Fellini, who is both sunnier and more aloof in his temperament and art than his northern peers.

Especially in his later films, Fellini has been concerned with the possibility of reformations and reconciliation in the pattern of adult relationships. In contrast, Joseph Losey's films do not celebrate the world as a circus wide open to the skies of possibility, but rather as a Grand Guignol of the damned. The ruthless march of sequence of *The Servant* takes place in a claustrophobic, denatured atmosphere, in a hothouse of regressive instincts, where the presentation of sex serves to reinforce the idea of human relationships as a matter of degradation and entrapment. The lead characters of *La Dolce Vita* or *8½* are conscious of themselves as being in a stage of philosophical, or moral, "anguish" and so concerned to break through their sense of a "common plight" to some larger passion or fresh sense of things; while the characters of *The Servant* are caught up in a personal "torment," in the depths of which they skid along like cumbersome sea creatures, preying on one another as a matter of course.

The title figure of *The Servant* darts into our view with its opening shot. The fox-like alertness and self-composure with which he huffs and puffs his way through a busy corner's traffic is enough to get us set for a character likely to possess the *gestalt* of an "underground man." And Barrett will prove indeed to be something of a dime-store Machiavellian in his zealous application of power politics to personal relationships and in his disdainful sensitiveness to, and readiness to cash in

The Servant, directed by Joseph Losey, 1963 (*The Museum of Modern Art/Film Stills Archive*)

on, stock middle class expectations and responses. In his quick
march through its foreground, Barrett comes across as a man
of the City, toughly unillusioned, indirect in discourse, one
who may be expected to imply more by his manner than by
words. We would expect his whole character to be one
marshalled by the spleen of an overdeveloped sense of vulnerability—a sense not unusual among the anti-heroes of contemporary films and fiction. But what adds most to Barrett's being
a representative contemporary type is his abstractness. He
springs onto the screen full-grown, from no specific past or
place and without any clearly defined impulse or "drive." He
first appears as, literally, the Man on the Street, whom we see
move off the street and into the house of his prospective employer, a house which, too, it is evident from the start, is no
longer anybody's real home, but just a young man of fashion's
pad. Both servant Barrett and master Tony are, as the film
opens, quite equal in being "nowhere."

Yet it is soon clear that Barrett's proper milieu is in fact
among the pads of the *haut monde*, where he proves as much
at ease, and as "knowing," as his employer. It is the latter's
recognition of this which leads to his hiring Barrett after, as
he informs his new man, a disappointing series of interviews
with other candidates.

Tony himself has come down to London from school to
mark time, with the vaguest of job prospects and no inclination toward a career; and the servant, who claims he has
been "in service" for over a decade (which would be the years
of the Great Morale Drift of the fifties), is presently "between
jobs." Servant and master share the same world, the same ambience, in common—and, ultimately, the same knowledge.

From the time he first enters through the front room of the
house to find his way to the owner slumped asleep in an easy
chair out back (the first of several shots throughout the film
which show the servant looming over his master like a smirk-
ing nemesis), through his subsequent intriguings to take advantage of his gentleman's psychic inertness, to his final triumph
when he cavorts with his mistress in the master bedroom,
while the master sprawls dog-like outside the door shut on him,
it is clear that what the servant is after is the gentleman.

Barrett's interest in Tony will combine the abstract passion of analyst to patient, or con man to victim, with intensities of a more personal, more perverse, implication. Unlike the analyst, Barrett's aim is not to free his man but to "get" him, to bring him to that state of collapsed morale and sexual nihilism from which Barrett himself is not free. What Tony comes to know by the end of the film is what Barrett has known from the start of vice, isolation, and terror. The shambles to which Tony is reduced—in the finale, we see him, as we do at the outset, slumped "in a heap" while his servant impassively stands by—represents Barrett's interior condition. In his breakdown Tony is even more "equal" with Barrett than before— the condition of both equating, in the film's terms, with the condition of our modern hell.

Tony's development from initial callow huffiness to breakdown is accompanied by Barrett's change from perky anti-hero, surviving as he may in a brutal milieu, to outright sinister villain exploiting the modern hell with a zany dedication. There is a melodramatic neatness to this. Melodramatic too is the plot in which both are caught up: they meet, grow close, separate after a row, then re-unite, in something of a boy-meets-boy variation on the more traditional formula. The film's symbolic patterns derive chiefly from this reversal of formula; and through the equations offered in its play of images it holds to a movement which is both witty and rigorously objective. The objects and arrangements of the mundane world are shot in such a way as to become images suggestive of the dotings of latent obsessions. *The Servant* gains its best effects in an orgy of nuance, summoning (in a characteristically modernist style) the chills and suspense which may inhere as much to objects and settings as to overt human actions. Objects and settings thus serve as witness to an action concerned with betrayal, disorder, collapse. Effects of this kind depend, in turn, on the received opinion of our day that sublimation will out. On this basis, we have established a set of "stage conventions" as common to us, and as replete with melodramatic possibilities, as the corresponding Elizabethan view on murder.

The over-size mirror, centered on the wall of Tony's

house, for example, with its weirdly ornate and heavy frame, dominates all the decor as the pool of Narcissus; while the chief symbol of Tony's collapse is the staircase of the two-floor dwelling where he and his servant become entombed. Each time Tony climbs the stairs it is to a more diminishing fall—in keeping with the ironic line of action, which develops to Tony's narcissistic regression and consequent withdrawal from action under his servant's influence. When finally he can hardly make it up the stairs to his bedroom at the top, and collapses before its door, behind which his man lords it with the maid, we have an arrangement which tallies in all respects —including its thumping obviousness—with a key closing scene of Bergman's *The Silence*. The lead figure of that film, a high-toned Lesbian, is brought to collapse before a hotel door shut on the lovemaking of her sister and a waiter. Only the relationship of the sisters is affected by this set-to—the waiter representing no more than a gambit in their psychological tug-of-war for dominance and assertion. In like manner Barrett uses his mistress against Tony. The sex tensions and suspense of *The Servant* as consistantly involve the two male leads as those of *The Silence* involve the sisters. In these films it is the silence and space between the leads which determine their hysteria and their fate. In one of the few open air shots of *The Servant*, where the headstones of a cemetery round the corner from the house serve to evoke a sense of rooms from which there can be no departure, or orbits of fate fixed and irreversible, we have a conceit nicely suggestive of the theme and one of both films.

The story of Tony and Barrett is reinforced by a series of vignette treatments of other situations and possibilities in which individuals join in vice or romance, only to be shown as ultimately isolated according to the binding compulsions, the impervious solipsisms, of id or ego. The arrangement of these relationships forms a further symbolic pattern by which the film gains its shape and cumulative force.

The servant himself sets the stage for the first of such relationships. After scoring his initial points of control over his gentleman by winesmanship and devoted upkeep of the premises, he steps up his play by introducing on the scene his "sister"—in fact his mistress—to act as maidservant and as check against the competing influence of Tony's natty and forceful fiancée.

The scene in which Barrett's tart carries out her orders to bring the master to heel is played for chilling effect. In the pall of a murky evening light Tony lurches toward the maid, who sits perched like a veritable "dish" on a corner of his kitchen table. Moments later, over the armrests of a high-backed chair placed facing away from the camera, an improbable medley of arms and legs crop out to wave langorously in the air like tentacles. Animate and inanimate are combined to form the image of some long-faced octopus-like sea beast. From this fall to heterosexual coupling, from the knowledge gained here—and shared with his servant—Tony will be brought step by step to his total collapse in the final sequence. In their subsequent encounters Tony will be shown suffering his maid's assaults as best he can in a macabre benightedness.

In contrast to the loose disarray of the tart, it is the fiancée whose style and story are identified with nature and the natural. She keeps bringing flowers to the house, which Barrett keeps throwing out. The fiancée moves in an aura of stability; hers is the relatively normal world of flowers and open air; and the prerogatives, and dispensations, of power. The continuation of a shared tradition of ancestral portraits hung on the walls of her sweetheart's pad—of barristers, sportsmen, and naval officers—depends on the union between her and Tony. In the scene of his meeting with her parents, the portraits on the wall come to life: for the pair seeking to sound out the young man's prospects sum up in themselves the present state of the Established. Posed in a mausoleum-like house of plaster casts and oppressive draperies, the mother turns out to be a prune-faced platitudinizer; the father, a stock Colonel Blimp.

While the elder couple is thus caricatured in a dismissive way, the camera's treatment of the young lovers takes on an even more sardonic edge. Unlike the tart, the fiancée is rarely appreciated by the camera on her own; she is most closely shot whenever her face and body are juxtaposed against the youth's in the same frame—in which instances both are seen in a way which lessens their differentiation as to sex. Throughout the first half of *The Servant*, as we watch Tony and his girl loll on a rug, or romp through an empty park, or skip heedlessly past gravestones, while knocking themselves out to be carefree, we are gradually struck by the sameness not only of their demeanor but of their dress as well: same jacket, scarves, pants. Their features too are perfectly matched; both are slim-limbed, wilfully wide-mouthed, and haughty in profile, their poise meticulous to the verge of poutiness. With lavish intentness and care, the camera dwells on their features and general swagger. Thus at the same time that the camera offers dispassionate homage to their physical presences, it brings into play at their expense the idea of their romance as essentially narcissistic.

It is on Tony's narcissism, which remains poised and in balance through the first half of the film, that Barrett works. This whole first part of the film, as chic and "tony" as the second is one of "all hell breaking loose," is rounded off by the famous restaurant scene. The scene is controlled by the same idea which controls the orgy-finale of the second half—each part representing different surfaces of the same condition. The diners are shown in pairs, each of whom is revealed to be servant to a situation in which both are bound and punished. A Lesbian couple grouse over their meal, quarrelling inconsolably; a cool professional man and his female companion shaft one another in whispers, their tension-swelled poise as ugly as the drawn features of the Lesbians across the aisle; further down the aisle, two priests gorge themselves while exchanging sex jokes, their portly forms and manner taking on in the process of their enthusiastic feed a curiously sinister air.

And when we later see Tony and Barrett, separately perched at a bar after a falling-out, we understand them to be in the same fix as the diners. Their heedlessness of a third person seated in the space between them reinforces our impression of a scene played to the tense air of a lovers' quarrel: each is distraught at his distance from, and bondage to, the other. Although their parting had followed on Tony's learning of the maid's real identity, neither afterwards takes any more mind of her than of the third man at the bar.

Their subsequent reconciliation is highlighted by a sequence which is the film's most striking evocation of the nature of their relationship. Tidily in keeping with the treatment throughout of psychosexual malaise, the sequence marks that moment of our playboy's regress when he has fallen back to playing the kid's game of hide-go-seek. While he hides excitedly behind a shower curtain, the shadow of a profile is seen floating up the stairway in pursuit. It is distorted beyond life-size or, again, clear definition as to sex. The second's glimpse we are given leaves us guessing, especially since the shadow is jump-cut to after a series of shots devoted to the fiancée's unavailing efforts to win back her man, in the last of which she appears determined to fight fire with fire. The shadow might be hers, or the maid's. A second more reveals it to be the servant's. Ripping the curtain aside, he looms over Tony set to tag him—in a recall of the opening sequence in which he had found his way to, and loomed above, his dozing prey. This time the latter is awake to the point of terror: he huddles back in his tub and shrieks like a child.

After such games, all that remains is the "wild night" finale to celebrate the last stage of Tony's fall to peership with Barrett. In a rigorously composed tableau, we have our last shot of him: sprawled flat on a bed while the most hard-bitten of a crew of viragoes brought on the scene by Barrett hangs over him, her black picture hat encircling her impersonal visage like a black halo. Also present for a final "placing" is the maid herself—the camera now catching her not in her fettlesome charm, but as grim peer of the other women on the scene. It is the same with another waif-like figure who had made a fleeting earlier appearance. Following his quarrel with Barrett, Tony had strolled in a daze through the local railroad station, to find slouched on a bench there (in contrast to the teasing table "dish" earlier pictured) a forlorn demi-whore too peaked even to hustle with much vim. As each eyes the other, the scene fades out. But as one of the gang in the house, this stray figure is no longer the pop-eyed waif but, like the rest of the group, leering, raucous, hard-jawed. In the wind-up, they are all grouped in an image of the preying and the preyed-upon. U or non-U, vulture or wilting prey—no matter —all rub shoulders in an oppressive proximity, for the psychic distances among them are such that each (like the diners of the restaurant scene) must remain in a state of hellish tantalization.

Not excluding the fiancée, who is also brought on for a final bow. In her shock at the scene she walks in on, she almost yields to what seems largely a polite pass on the servant's part; then, with the reserves left her by her tradition, she lashes her antagonist across the face with a steel bracelet. Like his pass, her response is chiefly a matter of form, an incongruous riposte on a field where all the stakes have been won, where the loser has no more left than the style and flourish of her retreat. We last see her outside the house humiliated and baffled, but not much wiser for her involvement in the drama. Like other baffled types in recent films, like the home-fixated mistress of the drifting journalist in *La Dolce Vita;* or the suicidal mistress of the painter in Antonioni's *The Girl Friends,* dismayed over his messy drifting and rages, Tony's girl remains insistently middle class; in the inflexibility of her dream, and code, is her vice. She proves unequal to the scene. As much as her comically treated parents, she is bound to remain an "unaware" type.

All the elements of the film are thus brought together in the finale to get across what the director has to say about the oppressed nature of man, who is seen spinning in his orbit, a satellite isolated in the spaces of his doom.

Losey is a director who never misses a trick that will bear on his meaning; his is not a light touch, no more than is the touch of such sardonically commercial, "cruel," thematically intriguing American directors as Robert Aldrich, Samuel Fuller, or Stanley Kubrick (directors whose work has been especially taken to heart by the French school in film criticism, and those who follow that school's lead here). In their exploitation of *Kitsch* standards and forms for serious, aesthetically interesting use, such directors avoid those tricky

curtseyings to—and occasional elegant circumventions of—
Kitsch sentimentalities lately publicized as "Camp," and go
instead for a brutal, uncompromising assertion.

Films like Fuller's Gothic Western, *Forty Guns*, or *Dr.
Strangelove* or *The Servant* are tautly structured according
to theme. There is little give, or play, or improvisation; evident
instead is a directorial command as firmly in control over
actors' styles as types of setting. Every shot, every gesture, is
as calculated, as "set up" for us, as can be. The risk of course,
is a sometime overscoring into the ludicrous or into flat
staginess. Yet this is the most dynamic style in current
American film-making, the only one with any relationship
to developments in the arts in general over the past half
century. Here is its key difference from Camp, which makes
no pretense to any connection with the style and tone of
avant-garde art, either in its pressure of judgment or in those
creative distortions in form to which pressure in judgment
leads.

Unconcerning and unaffirmative, *The Servant* well succeeds
in projecting a sense of individual experience as a process of
self-enclosure and withdrawal through the traps of being.
And it makes its unendearing point with some force and wit.
It is also sleekly done, with all the production values of the
commercial film, the story-line building to one or two big
scenes, then tapering off to gather steam for another fast
pitch at the close. Not that it has dead spots: by means of
an action both symbolic and suspenseful it manages to exploit
its academic form rather than succumb to it. It is interesting—
or, as used to be said, "absorbing"—on this count alone, for the
"absorbing" in any art is not nowadays easily come by. At the
same time, *The Servant* is advanced in its busy assimilation
(quite in the manner of the New Wave features) of the
techniques, moods, and conventions of modernist writing.
Another likely reason for its general appeal. The growing
audience for art films comes largely from the universities
where, on all levels from freshman to adult education courses
to summer conferences, the conventions of modern art, especially those codified in the twenties, are taken in with the

air one breathes. An audience nurtured on *The Waste Land* or *The Years* will be all set for the latest round of ambiguities and jump-cuts in a Truffaut or Losey. To see the films of the newly arrived directors is to experience, to a degree, old home week in a new setting. As to *The Servant's* remorseless line on Woman, and its insistence on the grotesqueness of the sexual plane of experience—here too are familiar biases to the student of, say, T. S. Eliot or Graham Greene. To recall the heyday of Eliot and Greene is to be reminded too of one telling difference between their emphases and ours. This is most briefly got at by noting that where Eliot's generation gave special time and attention to religion and detective stories our moment's concerted focus has been more on sex and science fiction.

Crime has, of course, long offered a field in which actions ranging in their level of complexity from those of a Vautrin or Raskolnikov to a Raffles could serve to provide not only "thrilling" fare to a cultivated audience but also to isolate and bring into dramatic focus some of the questions most dear to that audience, like hypocrisy, or self-deception and self-discovery, freedom and responsibility, success and failure, and so on. One may briefly suggest that the crime thriller as such has lost its hold on the audience and faded as a form: and all too rapidly suggest as cause the fact that the moral vision divorced from the sex sense is no longer taken seriously, so that the audience now seeks out those forms in which its perennial questions are set in a sexual context. It is film-makers who have been most successful in meeting this demand with a contemporary form. The titles of some recent films—*La Dolce Vita, The Adventure, Odd Obsession, The Five-Day Lover*—taken together seem to be more than a play to the box-office: they point to the form which directors in the decadent line have found suitable for combining taut action with serious inquiry in a non-pornographic, non-cute, non-Camp way; a form which defines itself as a sex thriller. *The Servant*, which is perhaps the most perverse in tone and most controlled in style among recent sex thrillers, is certainly one of the most entertaining in this genre.

The Seventh Seal

Norman N. Holland, "The Seventh Seal:
The Film as Iconography"

ooooooooooooooooooooooooooooooooooooooooooooooo

The Seventh Seal is one of the first of Ingmar Bergman's
films to be distributed in the United States. In the late fifties,
when American audiences believed that a work of art was
least likely to be found at the movies, Bergman films such
as *Wild Strawberries, The Seventh Seal,* and *Virgin Spring*
came as stark revelations that the medium is vital and not
to be judged by the usual fare. The new hope of intelligent
moviegoers was to be further realized with the flow of more
and more Bergman films as well as with the importation of
Fellini, Antonioni, Resnais, Truffaut, Godard, and others. In
the sixties the "Bergman Festival" became a cultural in-
stitution.

Norman N. Holland describes *The Seventh Seal* as a
"medieval film" which celebrates life and emphasizes that
Bergman employs the spirit, symbols, and dramatic devices
of medieval religious drama that celebrated God. Mr.
Holland's discussion of the dramatic significance of motifs
from medieval visual art, such as the figure of Death, and
of the structural and symbolic function of the game of chess
("the central image in the film") ultimately lead to the
illumination of character and meaning. "In short, in *The
Seventh Seal,* as in any great work of art, theme and medium
have become one. . . . He [Bergman] depicts the real world
objectively, with tenderness and joy, but he shows reality
as signifying something beyond itself. And in doing so,

Bergman has established himself as one of the world's great and original directors. He has lifted the film out of mere physical realism and made his audience of chessmen with tricked eyes see in their own moves something beyond the board."

---◆---

ASIDE FROM GIVING US a masterpiece, Ingmar Bergman in *The Seventh Seal* has created a strange and wonderful paradox: a singularly modern medium treated in a singularly unmodern style—a medieval film. It is medieval in the trivial sense of being set in Sweden of the fourteenth century. More important, *The Seventh Seal* is a traditional *Totentanz* in which the allegorical figure of Death, robed in black like a monk, carrying scythe and hour-glass, leads the characters away in a dancing line under the dark, stormy sky. Most important, Bergman shows us, as medieval artists did, an allegorical, iconic reality, in Erich Auerbach's term, a figural reality which can be understood only by seeing that it prefigures something beyond itself. "My intention," Bergman writes in a note to the film, "has been to paint in the same way as the medieval church painter," and lo and behold! he has done just exactly that.

The Seventh Seal deals with a Crusader's quest, not in some faraway Holy Land, but in his own fourteenth-century Sweden. After ten years of holy war, the Crusader has returned home, weary, bitter, and disillusioned. On the shore, the ominous figure of Death steps out of a series of striking dissolves to claim him. The Crusader delays, however; he challenges Death to a game of chess. If the Crusader wins, he escapes Death; so long as the game goes on, he is free to continue his quest for certain knowledge of God and to do one significant act during his lifetime. As Death and the Crusader play at intervals through the film, the knight moves on a pilgrimage through Sweden, the land itself ravaged by the Black Death.

Bergman has in mind some obvious modern parallels to his medieval characters: "Their terror is the plague, Judgment

The Seventh Seal, directed by Ingmar Bergman, 1956 (*Janus*)

Day, the star whose name is Wormwood. Our fear is of another kind but our words are the same. Our question remains." Our plague is intimate, as theirs was, and we too have our soldiers and priests, or as Bergman has called them, "communism and catholicism, two -isms at the sight of which the pure-hearted individualist is obliged to put out all his warning flags." Yet it would unnecessarily limit the universality of Bergman's achievement to call *The Seventh Seal* merely a necroterpsichorean parable for modern times. All men every-where have always lived with death. Bergman is going beyond the *Totentanz,* trying to answer the further question: If death is the only certainty, where is God?

The Crusader's quest gives us the answer, though the knight himself seems never to learn it—or to learn that he has learned it. Accompanied by his positivistic, materialistic squire, a foil to his own abstractly questioning nature, he looks for certainty about God, for "to believe without knowledge is to love someone in the dark who never answers." Yet what the Crusader finds are people who believe in God only as a scourge, the cause of plagues and death, and who respond in kind. Religion for them becomes suppression, cruelty, persecu-tion, the burning of innocent girls as witches, the terrifying realism of the crucifixes in the peasants' churches. In one of the most horrifying scenes ever put on film, Bergman shows us a procession of flagellants: a line of half-naked men lashing one another; monks struggling under the weight of huge crosses or with aching arms holding skulls over their bowed heads; the faces of children who wear crowns of thorns; people walking barefoot or hobbling on their knees; a great gaunt woman whose countenance is sheer blankness; slow tears falling down the cheeks of a lovely young girl who smiles in her ecstasy of masochism. The procession interrupts the gay skit of a group of strolling players and halts while a mad priest screams abuse at the ugliness of his audience, long nose or fat body or goat's face. Glutted with hate, he joyfully proclaims the wrath of God, and the procession resumes its dogged way over the parched, lifeless soil.

Such is religion, Bergman seems to say, to those who see

God as hater of life. Art (as represented by a surly, tippling church painter) becomes the representation of death to gratify the people's lust for fear. Living, as shown in a grotesque scene in an inn, becomes a sardonic "Eat, drink, and be merry." Cinematically, Bergman identifies this side of the ledger by great areas of blackness in the film frame and often by slow, sombre dissolves from shot to shot. Musically, the sound track treats even scenes of merrymaking with the *Dies Irae* theme. In his notes to the film, Bergman tells how:

> As a child I was sometimes allowed to accompany my father when he traveled about to preach in the small country churches. . . . While Father preached away . . . I devoted my interest to the church's mysterious world of low arches, thick walls, the smell of eternity . . . the strangest vegetation of medieval paintings and carved figures on ceiling and walls. There was everything that one's imagination could desire: angels, saints . . . frightening animals. . . . All this was surrounded by a heavenly, earthly, and subterranean landscape of a strange yet familiar beauty. In a wood sat Death, playing chess with the Crusader. Clutching the branch of a tree was a naked man with staring eyes, while down below stood Death, sawing away to his heart's content. Across gentle hills Death led the final dance toward the dark lands.
>
> But in the other arch the Holy Virgin was walking in a rosegarden, supporting the Child's faltering steps, and her hands were those of a peasant woman. . . . I defended myself against the dimly sensed drama that was enacted in the crucifixion picture in the chancel. My mind was stunned by the extreme cruelty and the extreme suffering.

The Seventh Seal finds God for us—or at least another certainty than Death—not in the wormwood-and-gall institutional religion of suffering and crucifixion, but in the simple life of a strolling actor and juggler named Jof (Joseph), his girl-wife Mia (Mary), and their baby. As if to make the parallel to the Holy Family even more clear, Jof plays the cuckold in the troupe's little Pierrot-Columbine skit. Jof is also the artist. He is given to visions, and Bergman shows us one, of "the Holy Virgin . . . supporting the Child's faltering steps." Except for the Crusader, Jof is the only one who can see the allegorical figure of Death. (To the Crusader's materialistic squire, for example, Death appears not as an iconic figure, but as a grisly, rotting corpse.) Jof is a maker of songs whose simple melodies provide the sound track for this side of the religious ledger. Cinematically, Bergman gives us the certainty and holiness of life represented by Jof's family in light, airy frames; quick cuts tend to replace the slow dissolves used for the religion of death.

Yet even innocent Jof can be converted to a thief and a buffoon by the death-forces. In the grotesque comic scene at the inn, he is tortured with flames, forced to jump up and down on the board table in an exhausting imitation of a bear, parodying his own ability to leap beyond the ordinary human. An artist stifled in his art, he responds by becoming a rogue; he steals a bracelet as he makes his getaway.

This grim *reductio ad absurdum* proves, as it were, that death and the religion of death cannot be the only certainty. As a mad young girl about to be burned for a witch tells the Crusader, you find God (or the Devil who implies God) in the eyes of another human being. But the abstractly questioning Crusader says he sees only terror. He seems for a moment to find his certainty of God in a meal of wild strawberries and cream handed him by the gentle Mia, in effect, a communion of life as opposed to the bread and wine consecrated to Death. (Strawberries are associated with the Virgin in some late northern iconography.) The Crusader seems also to find his "one significant act": he performs the service of the knight traditional to medieval art, not the colonizer of the Holy Land, but the protector of the Holy Family. He leads Jof, Mia, and the child through the dark wood. As he plays chess with Death, he sees that the visionary Jof has recognized the Black One, seen his family's danger, and is trying to escape. To help him, the knight busies Death by knocking over the chessmen, incidentally giving Death a chance to cheat and win. By losing the game, the knight gives up his life to let

Jof and Mia escape (in a tumultuous, stormy scene like paintings of the flight to Egypt).

And yet, though the Crusader has pointed the way for the audience, he seems not to have found it for himself. He goes on in his quest for abstract answers. He leads the rest of his now doomed band, a smith, the smith's venereous wife, the squire, and the squire's mute "housekeeper" to his castle. There, in a curiously emotionless scene, the Crusader distantly greets his wife whom he has not seen for ten years, shows her his disillusionment, but says he is not sorry he went on his quest. With the chess game lost and Death near, he knows it is too late for him now to act out the importance of the family himself, but he has learned its worth, though he does not realize its full godly significance. As his wife reads the lurid images of Revelation viii: "And when he had opened the seventh seal," Death, whom they all seem to await, appears. The Crusader asks once more that God prove himself. The mute girl opens her mouth and speaks, "It is finished," the sixth of the seven last words from the Cross. Death gathers them all in, his cloak filling the screen with black.

In short, then, the film answers its question, If Death is the only certainty, where is God? by saying, You find God in life. The opening shots of the film set up the contrast: first a blank empty sky; then the same sky but with a single bird hovering against the wind. Life takes meaning from its opposition to Death, just as Jof and Mia's simple love of life takes meaning from the love of Death around them—or as a chess game takes form in a series of oppositions.

The chess game is the central image of the film. It dictates much of the incidental imagery such as the knight's castle or the "eight brave men" who burn the witch. The playing *(spela)* of chess matches the playing *(spela)* of the strolling troupe. Both are traditional images for the transitoriness of life: Death robs us of our roles; Death jumbles the chessmen back in the box. (The two images are juxtaposed, for example, in *Don Quixote,* II. xii.) The characters themselves and the points of view they represent are played off against one another much like pieces in a game.

There are also some particular correspondences (somewhat confused for an English audience by the Swedish names for the chessmen). The Crusader, distinguished by his cross, is the king of the chess game: when he is lost, all the rest are lost, too. It is the juggler Jof who is the knight (in Swedish, *springare*, the "leaper"). Only these two men have visions that go beyond reality, just as only the king and knight can go beyond the chess board. The juggler-knight (the "leaper") is free at all times to jump out of the two dimensions of the board—Jof's powers as a seer are almost exactly parodied by his tormentors' forcing him to jump up and down on the board table in the grotesquerie at the inn. The only other chessman who can rise off the board during the game is the king, and then only when he is castling, i.e., returning home, like this Crusader. All the pieces or characters, of course, in their own moment of death when they are taken from the board can see beyond it. Yet their visions beyond the physical reality of the board, and the Crusader's, are limited to the allegorical figure of Death; the "leaper" can see not only Death, but also the holy life of the Mother and Child.

In other words, it is the artist who has the vision the Crusader seeks in answers to abstract questions. As the church painter (whose murals prefigure the scenes of the film) says, the artist can conceive God with his senses, giving "not the reality you see, but another kind." Jof the juggler is this kind of artist: he hopes his Christ-like infant will grow up to achieve what he calls "the impossible trick," keeping the juggled ball always in the air, above the board, as it were. And Bergman himself is this kind of artist: he has called himself "a conjurer" working with a "deception of the human eye" which makes still pictures into moving pictures.

In short, in *The Seventh Seal*, as in any great work of art, theme and medium have become one. "Art lost its creative urge," Bergman writes, "the moment it was separated from worship," and, by creating in the iconographic manner of medieval art, Bergman has turned the film back to worshipping (though not God, but life). He depicts the real world objectively, with tenderness and joy, but he shows reality as signifying something beyond itself. And in doing so, Bergman has established himself as one of the world's great and original directors. He has lifted the film out of mere physical realism and made his audience of chessmen with tricked eyes see in their own moves something beyond the board.

Shoot the Piano Player

Roger Greenspun, "Through the Looking Glass"

ooooooooooooooooooooooooooooooooooooooooooooooo

François Truffaut made a blazing entry as a film-maker at
the age of twenty-five with *Les Mistons* in 1957. Then came
The 400 Blows in 1959, *Shoot the Piano Player* in 1960, and
Bride Wore Black, and *Stolen Kisses* have followed.) While
The 400 Blows and *Shoot the Piano Player* have been ac-
Jules and Jim in 1961. (*The Soft Skin, Fahrenheit 451, The*
claimed widely, generally *Jules and Jim* has been considered
his best film. To some extent, the lesser status of *Shoot the
Piano Player* may be the result of two extrinsic factors: (1)
the dazzling techniques Truffaut executed in the film led many
critics to brand it as lacking in substance, as only marvelous
and playful showmanship on the part of Truffaut; and (2)
Jules and Jim, an eloquently romantic film that is centered
on the superb acting performances of Jeanne Moreau, Oskar
Werner, and Henri Serre, came rapidly after it. The complexity of ideas, images, and events and the dislocating,
antitraditional narrative techniques in *Shoot the Piano
Player* place a special burden upon the critic as well as the
audience. "Getting a grip on Charlie," the piano player, as
Mr. Greenspun acknowledges, "is no easy task." "Through
the Looking Glass" is an attempt to explicate the film by
examining the function of the complex of surfaces Truffaut
creates in which black and white imagery abounds along
with many corollary contrasts. Pursuing the implications of
the scene in which Fido drops his milk bomb upon the hood

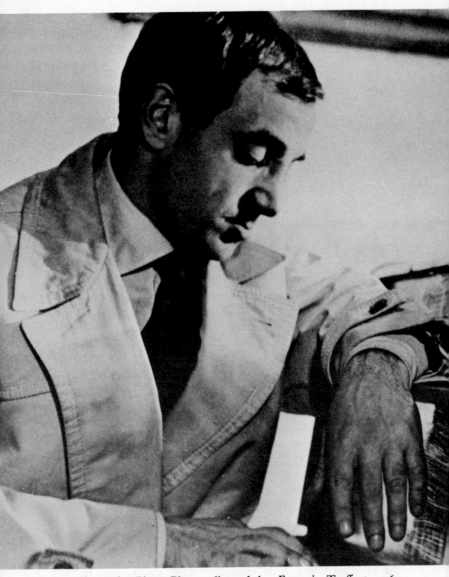

Shoot the Piano Player, directed by François Truffaut, 1960
(*Janus*)

of Ernest and Momo's car, Mr. Greenspun offers the formulation that "white opposes black, but white also makes black;
and white and black are relative not only to one another but
also within themselves. . . . The enabling principle here is
not the moral collapsing of black in white . . . but rather the
fruitful notion of division into opposites itself, a multiplying of distinctions between and within spheres, of which
black and white is only one manifestation. . . ." On the level
of events Mr. Greenspun finds a corresponding proliferation
of meaning paralleling the visual puns: "the catastrophes that
invariably attend Charlie's major withdrawals . . . demonstrate the law that nature abhors a vacuum, at the same time
that they enforce a plunge into the midst of events once
again, restarting the round of activity in which the film
lives." His analysis leads ultimately to important conclusions
that embrace Truffaut's work up to and including *Shoot
the Piano Player*.

———————◆———————

Uneven, mangled, wobbly melodrama about barroom
pianist who gets involved with hoodlums. Satire and spoofs
never quite come off. [Capsule review of *Shoot the Piano
Player* almost any week in *Cue*]

If there is any unifying tone in the film it is an existential
irrelevance, coupled with a shrug from Charles Aznavour,
a masterful actor, which asks, What did you expect?
Existence is a succession of dirty jokes: nothing lasts,
struggle is futile, hope is obscene. (The title *Shoot the
Piano Player* refers to a barroom sign in old Westerns—
"Don't Shoot the Piano Player"—but Truffaut's film might
as easily be called *Why Not Shoot the Piano Player?*)
[Judith Shatnoff in *Film Quarterly*, Spring 1963]

And Truffaut himself is so completely engaged in life
that he pleads for the piano player's right to be left alone,
to live in his withdrawn state, *to be out of it*. Truffaut's
plea is, of course, "Don't shoot the piano player." [Pauline
Kael in *Film Culture* #27]

But Turley banged his hands against his knees. "Why ain't you there?"

"Because I'm here," Eddie said. "I can't be two places at once." [David Goodis, *Down There*]

A RETURN TO *Shoot the Piano Player* now, long after the impact of its initial showing and, I hope, long before its enshrinement as a classic, requires some explanation. *Piano Player* has enjoyed exceptional popular success, bucking Bosley Crowther in the art circuits and at least in New York filtering down to some neighborhood houses; it has excited everybody worth exciting; but among critics it seems to have inspired more enthusiasm for its moods than understanding of its meaning. That it makes some kind of meaning, despite Truffaut's own not very helpful post mortem comment that although a lot goes on in his film there is no theme you can put your finger on,[1] and that such meaning has to do with matters other than whether or not to shoot the piano player, a question obviously designed to be let go begging, is the underlying point to these remarks.

What I have to say will owe something to the most suggestive single commentary on Truffaut I know, Michel Delahaye's fine review of *Jules and Jim* in *Cahiers du Cinéma* #129. *Piano Player* embraces a phenomenology of extraordinary proportions: when a man's inner withdrawal creates a void in nature into which his wife then actually falls, theme and event become effectively indistinguishable, and my notions of how to account for the connections between them derive partly from Delahaye's insights into Truffaut's exploitation of visual-verbal puns and inversions.

I

So much happens in the Truffaut films that it is difficult even for a moment to draw back from their engrossing busyness and fix upon a single image in any one of them for

[1] In an interview analyzing audience reaction in *Cahiers du Cinéma No. 138*. Excerpts are translated in *Film Quarterly*, Fall 1963.

a long close look. But it is a useful thing to do if you wish to isolate a revealing characteristic, and conveniently each of the three features gives us such an image at its very end. One remembers Antoine alone at the water's edge, caught in a still photograph with nowhere further to run, at the end of *The 400 Blows;* or Jules, his back to the camera, striding alone down the path of the cemetery where he has just interred his wife and his best friend; or the noncommittal face of Charlie Koller, almost filling half the screen, appearing at the end of *Shoot the Piano Player* over the same honky-tonk tune with which the film had opened.

The first of these scenes reduces its film to stasis, the second prefigures escape, and the third suggests that everything moves around in a circle to come back pretty much to where it began. The music of Albert's ballad behind the retreating figure of Jules; Charlie's picking up the piano tune once again —by signalling an end to eventful progression both function in a way analogous to Antoine's stopping the movie. And each of the scenes contains a single character, not the suggestive grouping of even two characters in significant relation, so that we are left not with the figurative resolution of a drama but rather with just one figure, a man central to his world (as I think Jules rather than Catherine is for *Jules and Jim*) but bereft of that world's potential for sustaining and varying events. That each of these characters in certain particulars reproduces Antoine, desperately childlike in his need for the motherly attention of the woman who has for some reason been denied him, is thematically interesting for Truffaut's work so far. But perhaps *as* interesting is the final emphasis upon the man himself rather than upon any conclusive configuration to an action. I think it is fair to say that the Truffaut films develop activity rather than an Aristotelian "action," that they are concerned with making things happen rather than with the disposing of events in a dramatic structure, that by their own inner necessity they must at last center upon the actor—he who acts, or causes things to happen— and that they do not so much end as run down, or run on in what is pretty clearly to be mere repetition.

Like *Jules and Jim, Piano Player* includes the telling of many
stories: the normal happy life account of the man with the
flowers, Chico's hard luck story in the café, the central
flashback story of Edouard and Theresa, Theresa's own story
of her shame, the crooks' crazy stories to Charlie and Lena
and later to Fido, the story of the whole clan of the ill-fated
Saroyans—going back generations, Charlie supposes, before
one can discover the root of their curse. And, as in *Jules and
Jim*, such an abundance of narratives seems partly to free the
film as a whole from dependency upon any one story as
basic structure, and to work for the suspension of "narrative,"
among other elements, within some different kind of form.

The problem is to describe the form, and here Michel
Delahaye offers a clue in a few brilliant demonstrations. He
notices, for example, that when Fido drops his milk bomb
upon the hood of Ernest and Momo's car, they are obliged
to turn on the windshield wipers to combat *"l'opacité de
cette blancheur qui risque de faire obstacle à leurs noirs
desseins"* [the opacity of this whiteness which stands in the
way of their black designs]. Thus Delahaye assumes not only
that whiteness darkens, but also that between the *visible*
whiteness of the milk-splattered windshield and the conventional *ideas* of "black designs" there is a viable punning relation. The virtuosity of Delahaye's formulation is immediately
matched and deepened by the movie, for not only are Ernest
and Momo literally rendered dark by the white milk screen
cutting off enough available light to make them no more
than silhouettes, but their own evil "blackness" is within
minutes made bright by their lively talking with Charlie and
Lena in the initial kidnapping. Thus white opposes black,
but white also makes black; and white and black are relative
not only to one another but also within themselves—each
showing a range of highlights and shadows once it is opened to
close inspection. The enabling principle here is not the moral
collapsing of black in white—which shades too readily in the
minds of some critics to a gray acceptance of all conduct—
but rather the fruitful notion of division into opposites itself,
a multiplying of distinctions between and within spheres, of

which black and white is only one manifestation, although a significant one for a film *in* black and white with the piano keyboard as one of its operative images.

Elsewhere I have attempted identifying abstract figures in *Jules and Jim*[2] and I have suggested that for that film, moving broadly through historic time, the circle ultimately is the lively restful figure containing and supporting the abundance of life that everyone has seen somehow as its central value. But *Piano Player* is anti-historical, destroying time in the mirror image of its long flashback, moving in all directions through space, and finding its impetus to movement in the idea of cutting things up—dividing them so as to set part against part in a series of gestures that literally split the screen. *Piano Player* is also full of circles: but notice that each of them, whether in the actual insets of the triple-faced Plyne, Ernest's mother dropping dead, or suave Lars Schmeel ominously fading out between Edouard and Theresa in bed—or in the lyrical slow pan of Lena's room which shares the screen with a stationary shot showing Charlie and Lena kissing beneath an inverted horseshoe[3]—promotes a consciousness of discreet visual elements.

II

The catastrophes that invariably attend Charlie's major withdrawals—according to the principle of multiple relations I have borrowed from Delahaye, by which ideas, things, and images enjoy equality as phenomena—demonstrate the law that nature abhors a vacuum, at the same time that they enforce a plunge into the midst of events once again, restarting the round of activity in which the film lives. Quite simply: Edouard runs out on Theresa after her eloquent admission of emptiness, and her body tumbles into the void he might have filled; Charlie splits from Lena at a crucial

[2]In *Sight and Sound*, Spring 1963.

[3]For the record, there is another bad luck sign, a cracked mirror in the Saroyans' country kitchen. Charlie comes upon it just as his brothers joyfully confirm his membership in the clan.

juncture, and her rush to mend the break ends with her sliding dead down a snowy hillside; even Plyne sinks into the circle of his own crushing embrace after Charlie tries calling it quits.

On the level of human motivation Charlie's fatal attractiveness to women relates to the need everybody in the film seems to feel for somebody else. The easy and real contact made and broken between Chico and the man who helps him at the beginning, Ernest and Momo's need not just to kidnap people but to make friends with them, the brute expression of Plyne's lonely frustration, even the ironic pathos with which Edouard looks for the real pianist in a bedroom mirror—all catch some aspect of a drive towards completion not in self-sufficiency but in personal contact. The amount of self-expression granted Clarisse, Plyne, the brothers, and so many others has more to it than an undeniable delight in character for its own sake; it is also a bid for bridging a gap that always threatens to appear beneath a surface that must be kept full and close if it is not to fail. When Charlie asks Lena for what reason she wants to back him in a return to the concert stage, she answers, not *"pourquoi"* but *"pour qui. Pour moi et pour vous, pour nous deux."*

Charlie's fatal attractiveness has its dark and unique underside as fate—in every woman who advances his career, from the old lady who used to drive him to his piano lessons and away from his brothers, to the mysterious girl with the violin who opens the door to Lars Schmeel's office for him when he is just about to back away—but it is not otherwise so very different from the mutual attractiveness of one for another that permeates the movie, and that finds its typical expression in everyone's telling somebody else part of a life story. Only Charlie clams up, and then people obligingly either tell him his own story (Lena), or make up stories for him (Lars Schmeel), or give him advice on how to improve his story (Schmeel and Plyne). But his own rich life is inward; his deepest dialogues are with himself. In response to Theresa's moving and articulate confession he can only rush out of the room. While he lies in Lena's arms—by the cutting that alternates two time sequences in the course of their love-making—he is in fact already turning away from her while she recounts the history of her attempts to move toward him.

The headlong falls on the way to Charlie that occur in *Piano Player* climax this preoccupation, and equalize planes of expression that in most films have at best no more than a metaphoric relation. Here every gesture takes place in space, or, better, makes the space in which and by which subsequent acts exist. There is no saying that character and situation influence one another; they *are* one another. It is therefore with the authority of image raised to the power of theme, and theme raised to the power of image, that the principle of division vitalizes and ultimately threatens this world. Split into a series of more or less precise oppositions, the strange career of Charlie/Edouard shuttles on, potentially into an infinity of mutually reflecting mirror images.

III

Theresa falls from a very great height. She leaps from the pinnacle to which she has been instrumental in raising her husband (the later parts of their story are largely seen in sequences of walking up and down stairs) both into the void she finds within herself and into the gap he has made in their perfect union, where they were so many things to each other —husband and wife, student and teacher, waitress and customer —in a life game in which, as Schmeel neatly observes, everybody is a winner. Edouard turned Charlie completes her fall, descending down beneath the dark roadway where she dies to the absolute blackness of the cellar he is hidden in after killing Plyne. Together with Lena he ascends again, up into the bright sunlight and snow of the mountains, only to witness another fall beginning his own second descent.

The stories' similarity in spatial outline is completed by various complementary or opposing details: the two impresarios, Plyne and Schmeel, both sure they know what's wrong with Charlie and both after his women; Edouard's desertion of

Theresa because she is sullied, and Charlie's defense of Lena after Plyne brands *her* as sullied; Theresa's loss of identity after Schmeel's attack, and Plyne's insistence that a Lena who speaks foul language is not a woman; a blond waitress in one story and a dark one in the other, but a dark death for the blond and a snowy white one for the brunette; a romantic tale of dedicated love and brilliant success supported by a grimy business deal, and an obscure and sordid life briefly illumined by a recklessly romantic dream.

Two stories, two parts of a life divided up to escape itself, so ingeniously reproducing one another, do more than give the film the air of fatality that persistently dogs Charlie and that finds general expressive outlet in virtually everything from the tough-luck café ballad on up. A major part of their function is realized in the very creation of a pair of reflecting surfaces, which, by their extensive relations to one another, enclose the *Piano Player* world within an apparently hermetic seal of correspondences. Within this enclosure it is hopeless to look for resolution. Charlie necessarily seeks his way through and out, and his famous withdrawal tendencies owe as much to the kind of space he occupies as to any quirk in his own character. Getting a real grip on Charlie is no easy task, as Plyne, Schmeel, Ernest and Momo, and any number of film critics all demonstrate—and as the piano player discovers for himself.

Who *is* Charlie Koller? He is Edouard Saroyan. Who is Edouard Saroyan? A brilliant concert pianist. Is he? Edouard himself asks the question—of the critics, of Hemingway (does he collect my records?), of the janitor, of himself as he stands before a mirror hoping to catch an image of the real thing but seeing only the face that asks the question thrown back at him. Schmeel says that at last he "has" Edouard when he has a portrait painted, the dark figure of a pathetic man against a dark background. But just as Schmeel makes his boast the portrait is totally obscured, not by a deeper darkness but by brilliant flashes of light from news photographers—so that it too becomes a reflecting surface, revealing nothing at all. The problem of identity, the reliable placing

of a man among the things and events of his world, remains
unsolved, but it remains the major problem in the film.

During the sequence with Schmeel and the portrait, Edouard
does something typical: he moves from in front of the photographers' flash bulbs (*they* don't catch him; they catch a pose
imitated from the man in the poster who has ideally conquered timidity) to the darkest recess of Schmeel's office,
which is itself an arrangement in sharp intervals of bright
windows and dark interstices—like the piano keyboard, like
the double life, an alternation of black and white. *All* Charlie/
Edouard's movements are between these extremes. To attempt
making some controlled associations for black and white is to
begin seeing the inclusive mode of *Piano Player*, and, in
determining the potential for characterization of that mode,
to work towards the conditions for life it fosters.

IV

Edouard and Charlie, Theresa and Lena, Schmeel and
Plyne, wealth and poverty, success and failure, light and
darkness—these mirror another, touch, interpenetrate, but
never enter into solution. Simply to look at *Piano Player* is to
exercise a heightened awareness of contrast, beginning with
a single spotlight cutting through a field of black, reaching a
climax in the breathtakingly beautiful ride from Paris to the
mountains—highway lights in the darkness, reflections off the
windshield of Lena's car, brilliant sunlight on a high snowy
landscape—and ending in the screen's strict vertical division
into black and white.

To the extent that the *idea* of black and white hovers over
the film, available for any new improvisation, it engenders
and supports all activity, but actually explains none of it. It
is pattern, and not morality or psychology or anti-psychology,
though it may lend itself to any of these for the time it
takes to complete a gesture or establish an attitude. But this
impartial virtuosity exacts a toll upon the characters whose
lives it activates but whose human responses it does not quite

account for. There is a tension in the film that exceeds the potential of the brilliant determinism I have been describing, and that derives from a feeling but utterly unsentimental understanding of the complexities of lives that are caught in the proliferation of mutually exclusive terms their world offers. Everybody in *Piano Player* is an articulate spokesman for a way of life, but almost everybody understands life as a selection from among absolute commitments. Charlie accepts Clarisse for bed and board but completely rejects her for anything else, Plyne knows exactly what is and what is not a woman, Schmeel divides and conquers—and so on through a range of demonstration that finds in the making of distinctions one of the film's crucial preoccupations. The corollary of so much picking of sides is a special kind of picking apart; the end of sharp distinctions is finally disintegraton. And this is the burden of a speech given a moment before death, Theresa's set confession, structurally at the center of the film, movingly describing a failure in personal integration that many people at one time or another feel but that only she totally articulates.

With perfect instinct, Truffaut has utilized most of the events in David Goodis' miserable novel, merely moving them from New York and Philadelphia to Paris, while rejecting almost all its interpretations of them. The one great exception is Theresa's confession, where he has retained and elaborated upon a body of dialogue that remains isolated as pathos in the novel[4] but meaningfully connects with everything in the film. Theresa describes Schmeel's precisely calculated method of attack, and the change, the loss of the old Theresa, it has made in her. Schmeel has taken her body and discarded her heart; the seduction has been an operation. He has left no visible scar; Schmeel slides out as efficiently as he slides in, and there have been no complications. But in the midst of a gleaming world—white sports car, white apartment, bright lights, shining blond girl—she discovers darkness and filth. A few scenes before, Edouard had looked in the mirror to find himself, and now she reveals that she has looked too—

[4]Pp. 80–82 in the Grove Press Black Cat edition.

but there is no Theresa anywhere, only a used up dirty old rag. Schmeel has come and gone, but for her what she did yesterday is part of what she is today. "Yesterday" is her mirror, and it is different in quality from anybody else's. She looks specifically for an emotional continuity to life, and her way of describing the destruction of that continuity— the dissolution of bright surfaces and an awareness of encroaching night—provides something very like a point of moral reference for the film's methods. Every death in *Piano Player* follows an analogous pattern, but only Theresa's is self-willed, a conscious recognition of the despair that accompanies the pattern, finding between its sharp distinctions the crack that opens to the abyss of total non-being, personal annihilation.

In this complex of surfaces any face is a mask, and every mask presupposes a secret life behind it. Charlie's two secret lives, the one he's leading and the one he's keeping secret, are of course the film's central stories; but other lives and stories have their place. (There are even fleeting suggestions of potential integration—in the late-discovered love and growing family of the stranger who helps Chico up after his collision with a lamppost, the first tumble in the movie and visually, with its dark night and flowers as against morning light and snow, an inverted counterpart of the last; or in the enthusiastic acceptance with which the other Saroyan brothers, great anti-divisionists on principle, welcome back Edouard even with the cops probably on his tail, now that he has killed a man and is one of them.) But when the stories are over and the secret lives have mostly been exposed into obscurity, some faces still remain. As Chico tells Plyne very early, you don't get any information without paying for it; and if one of Charlie's women describes the apprehension of death for her world, the other dies to give it its image—in a terrifying slow dissolve that superimposes the dead face of Lena upon the movie's closing sequence. What we feel at this moment is not so much the pathos of Lena's pointless killing as the authority of death itself. The face that looks back at us from the snow, an inverted image to be sure, conceals no secret at all. What you can see is all there is to it, and that is quite enough. Lena's perfect containment, like Theresa's total emptiness, is a cipher—but one or the other is all there is to discover when the running, fighting, loving, playing, remembering stop.

People have been so busy admiring Truffaut's marvelous inventiveness and vitality that they have ignored the fact that each of his films, beginning with the initiation to manhood through contact with death in *Les Mistons (The Mischiefmakers)*, is finally about the failure, the turning stale, of inventiveness and vitality. The three features seal this point by turning their child-man protagonists into emblems of life possibilities exhausted; and especially in *Piano Player* the emblem is fully, schematically developed. A wide screen divided down the middle into white and black, the line of the piano top across the bottom, Charlie's impassive face against the dark—the resources of film itself, the terms of this film's life, the man positioned to one side, and the machine for banging out the tune spanning both sides, holding the world together, keeping things going for the time being.

The Silence

F. Anthony Macklin, "Dark Pilgrim:
The Vision of Ingmar Bergman in The Silence"

ooo ɔo ɔoooooooooooooooooooooooooooooooooooooooooo

The Silence, coming seven years after *The Seventh Seal*,
often has been viewed as a thematic and stylistic point of
departure for Ingmar Bergman. In many ways *The Silence*
is different from the earlier films, including the first two of
the trilogy to which it belongs, *Through a Glass Darkly*
and *Winter Light*. In *The Silence* Bergman creates a relatively static film. Plot development is displaced for an order
that gains coherence through the totality of somewhat discrete images and actions; there is a quasi-narration which in
its turns depicts the ineffable agonies of characters. Also, the
film is characterized by a heaviness of atmosphere and a relentless absence of modulation. And, while Bergman has
made films that are densely filled with the past lives of his
characters, the characters' relation to other times and places
is only sparsely hinted at in *The Silence*. However, few
critics have explored the possibility of interpreting the film
in the perspective of the continuity of Bergman's art. Taking
Wild Strawberries as a point of comparison, a film that seems
as totally different from *The Silence* as any of Bergman's
films, F. A. Macklin argues that Bergman "does not careen
from the path of his previous vision" and explores the ways
in which "*The Silence* stays on the same road of life, but it
has different pilgrims."

◆

The Silence, directed by Ingmar Bergman, 1963 (*Janus*)

ONE OF BERGMAN'S most optimistic and satisfying films is *Wild Strawberries* (1957), but it contains more parallels with *The Silence* (1963) than any other of Bergman's work. Though seemingly vastly different, the two films complement each other. Both take place on trips that change their characters irrevocably.

Wild Strawberries is the story of Isak Borg, a seventy-eight-year-old man of medicine who is cold and unfulfilled. As the film begins he relates a nightmare that portrays his sterility. In his dream he is walking alone when he sees a clock without hands. He looks at his watch, and it is handless. He spies a man and goes up behind him and touches him, but the man disintegrates into a heap of clothes and a flow of black blood. Then a carriage comes by; the wheel comes off and narrowly misses the old man. A coffin falls off the carriage, and as Isak Borg goes near he sees his own body in the coffin. As the body tries to pull him in, he wakes up.

Awakened early by this chilling nightmare, the old man decides to drive to the town where he is to receive an award for fifty years in medicine. Marianne, his daughter-in-law, who is visiting him, decides to go with him to see her husband, Evald, with whom she is not getting along. As they begin the trip, Marianne reveals to the old man that she thinks he is selfish and insincere, and that she does not like him.

On the way, the old man stops at the house of his childhood and wanders among the strawberries. He dreams of the past and of his sweetheart who married his younger, more romantic, brother instead of him. He remembers the family and its life.

As Isak and Marianne continue their trip they pick up three youths whom they call the "children," a poetic guitar-playing minister-to-be, a nihilistic doctor-to-be, and a vivacious girl devoted to the carpe diem life. Their passengers alternately bicker and rejoice. As they go farther, they are forced by an accident to pick up a man and wife, two hateful people who viciously attack each other. Sara stops the car and banishes them. As the woman leaves she asks forgiveness.

When Dr. Borg stops at a gas station he is remembered, in a soft moment, by the proprietors as a good man. But, in his heart he is cold and guilt-ridden, for he has realized he has wasted his life.

He stops at his mother's house. She is ninety-six years old and has outlived her children except for the doctor himself. She too is old and bitter.

As Marianne drives on, the old doctor sleeps and dreams another revealing dream. He is outside a door, and he impales his hand on a nail sticking out of the door jamb. Then he is admitted into the house by a man who leads him into a classroom with students watching from the arena seats. He is given three tests, all of which he fails. First, he looks into a microscope, but all he can see is the reflection of his own eye, staring back in terrible ego. He is told to read words from the blackboard, which contain a doctor's first moral. He cannot read them. They say, "to ask forgiveness." Finally, he examines a woman and pronounces her dead at which she recoils in mocking laughter. In his dream, Dr. Borg has lost all his craft; he has nothing. He then dreams that he sees his wife commiting adultery as she actually had, a memory that has haunted him. He has nothing but guilt.

The doctor wakes up and finds the car has stopped. While the "children" are out gathering flowers to honor the old professor, Marianne confesses that she had told Evald that she is pregnant and that she was going to have the child even though her husband—a copy of his father—does not want the responsibility of having a child, the responsibility of living. The doctor asks why she is telling him, and she responds that the visit to his mother had frightened her. She sees her husband also falling into sterile coldness. Then the gay youths return and bestow the flowers upon the doctor, and the journey continues.

They arrive in the city, and Dr. Borg receives his prize. Afterward, as he lies in bed, the doctor calls Evald to him. Evald admits that he needs his wife and is giving in to her. Marianne enters and hugs the old man, and he says he loves her and she says she loves him.

The "children" sing a farewell song beneath his window

and scamper away. Dr. Borg goes back to bed with a vision of his youth. He has been vitalized by really seeing those around him for the first time; he can die in peace.

The Silence (1964) is also a story of the road. Two sisters, Ester and Anna and the young boy, Johan, son of Anna, are traveling home by train. It is stiflingly hot, and the older sister is ill and vomiting. It eventually becomes clear that she is dying. The little boy plays unhappily by himself in the passageway outside the compartments. Inside, a tension is apparent between the two sisters.

They all get off the train and go to an old baroque hotel in a strange, foreign town. Anna, the younger sister, washes and splashes cologne on herself and her son, and then they lie down and sleep while Ester drinks in the other room.

Johan awakes and journeys throughout the halls of the hotel with his cap pistol. He pretends to shoot the workman fixing the chandelier lights. He comes across a group of dwarfs who payfully dress him in a girl's dress until their leader enters and halts the play. Johan also shoots the old manager who eats sausage and shows him pictures from his youth while he strokes him gently. The boy hides the pictures under the rug. Johan also spends his time by urinating in the hallway.

Meanwhile, Anna wakes up, and ignoring the staring eyes of her sister who is a Lesbian, she goes out to a café and then to a show where she witnesses two people in violent sex in another seat. She flees.

When she returns to the hotel she is greeted by Ester who has spent the day in solitary suffering. Ester has been drinking and has masturbated. She faces Anna and demands to know what she has been doing. Anna tells her that she has been making love in the back of a church with a man she picked up.

Ester pleads with Anna not to leave again and tries to kiss her, but Anna leaves and goes to meet her new lover in the hall. They make love in her bed as Johan listens outside the door.

Johan tells Ester, who confronts Anna; they argue as the

man waits. The next morning Anna and Johan go to breakfast. Back in the hotel room Ester is struck by attacks of suffocation; she dreads a strangling death.

When Anna and Johan return, Anna viciously tells Ester they are leaving her. Johan throws himself into the arms of Ester who lies in bed.

As the boy and his mother travel home in their compartment on the train, Anna throws open the window and stands in the whipping rain. Johan holds a piece of paper, his inheritance from Ester. Ester was a translator, and he had asked her to give him a list of words in a foreign language. Anna grabs the piece of paper, but seeing it is just foreign words, throws it back. For the boy, however, they possess a glimmer. Written on the paper are the words "heart" and "hand." Johan looks at his mother bitterly. His world has no dreams.

In a summary of plot, the parallels between the ultimately idyllic *Wild Strawberries* and the vicious, ugly *The Silence* are probably not apparent. However, there are a great many similarities. Dr. Borg and Sara in *Wild Strawberries* and Ester and Johan in *The Silence* bring revelation to one another. Both pictures end with death near. Both end in awareness.

Time is an obsession with Bergman. It dominates both films. *Wild Straberries* opens with the image of time. In his stark nightmare, which sets the tone of his life, Dr. Borg sees the clock with no hands and his watch without hands. He has nothing. The past is dead, and nothing lives in the present. He touches the man who collapses into a bundle of clothes; he cannot communicate in any human way. His own body tries to drag him into the coffin. Only his own heartbeat booms. The dream shows the death of time, of meaning.

The watch without hands appears again when Dr. Borg is visiting his ancient mother. She gives him his father's handless watch. Again the emptiness is expressed. His mother complains that her room is cold, but it is cold because she herself is cold and lacks human warmth. Bergman uses time and temperature to show moral value.

When the "children" give Dr. Borg the flowers, it marks a change. The doctor looks at his watch—it has hands—and he says they'd better go on because it is getting late. It is late for him, but not too late.

At the conclusion of *Wild Strawberries*, the old house-keeper winds the clock beside Dr. Borg's bed; it is ticking with life.

In *The Silence* time also dominates. All the characters wear watches. Johan and the old manager carefully check their watches: they are both keeping time. But the ticking of time becomes horribly ironic as Anna looks out the window after sex. She has used, and abused, time. And, time, running out, haunts Ester as it haunted Isak Borg. For her, time is draining away like the raindrops.

In the world of Ingmar Bergman, to exist is to suffer. But if the harsh ticking of life is shown by Bergman, he also employs a group of characters in his films who hold life's vitality and are vivacious and boisterous. In *Wild Strawberries* the "children" possesses this affecting joyousness. In *The Silence*, however, the bright characters are dwarfs, warped men. Everything has become abused in *The Silence*. There are numerous sex symbols. Sex is abused. Ester, who is a Lesbian, masturbates; Anna, who approaches nymphomania, fornicates in the back of a church; and even Johan in his own limited way, urinates in the hall of the hotel. The adultery of Borg's wife in *Wild Strawberries* has become the total abuse of the characters in *The Silence*. The boy, Johan, is effeminate and Oedipal. The cap pistol which he shoots at the man who is changing the chandelier lights, the dwarfs, and the old manager is a sex symbol. The dwarfs dress Johan in girl's clothing. Sex, and humanity itself, is awry. Another symbol is the tank that rumbles into the street at night and mutely symbolizes the brutality, the menace of sex. While this symbol remains impotent and distant for Ester, the guns do fire a salute to Dr. Borg after his award in *Wild Strawberries*. Again, the same basic symbol in both films: one silent, the other exploding. Both seem ironic. Neither character has had a satisfactory, complete sexual relationship.

If sex is a source of man's misery and frustration according to Bergman, he draws the greatest conflict from his Puritan

background. It is the struggle between the intellect and feeling,
the mind and the heart. Both *Wild Strawberries* and *The
Silence* are primarily concerned with this. Dr. Borg in *Wild
Strawberries* and Ester in *The Silence* are the scientists, clinical
and aloof. The old man and the older sister are caught up in
sterile detachment, the cold extreme of the intellect. Yet Dr.
Borg finally communicates with Marianne, and Ester communicates with Johan. Marianne throws her arms about Borg,
and Johan throws his arms about Ester. Both Dr. Borg and
Ester are lying in bed when they receive those gestures of love.
Love is not dead in Bergman's world.

In both films there are sensual extremes in conflict with the
coldness of the intellect. Isak Borg in *Wild Strawberries* is
thrown over by his fiancée for his younger, more exciting
brother, and his wife commits adultery realizing that he will
"forgive" her in his cold way. The contrast is even greater in
The Silence. Against the icy control of Ester is the extreme
heat of feeling of Anna. She glories in bathing herself and
sensually splashes water on her breasts. She is physical, emotional, but her only intellectual expression is the adjective
"nice." Even Bach's music to her is "nice," nothing more.
Again, irony is apparent in the fact that the artist Bach's name
and her son's are the same—Johan.

In the face of frustration and despair, Bergman's characters
search for communication. It comes in the form of confession.
In *Wild Strawberries* Sara confesses her fears to Dr. Borg, and
near the end of the film Evald comes into his father's room,
pulls a chair alongside his father's bed, and sits as though he
were a confessor. Evald and Isak come as close to communication as they can, and Evald admits his need for his wife.

In *The Silence* Ester also feels need of confession as death approaches. She confesses to the old manager of the hotel that
she has not married because she hates the rotten smell of man's
semen. Instead, she has developed "attitudes," but these have
failed and she is left in terrible loneliness.

Confession is not the only religious element in *Wild Strawberries* and *The Silence*. There is also the symbol of crucifixion
in both films. Both Dr. Borg and Ester are "crucified." In the

doctor's dream, he impales his hand on a nail before entering the building and failing the three tests. In *The Silence*, Ester hangs on the head bar of the bed as on a cross and suffers an attack of choking as death draws near. Both crucifixion scenes precede ascension to knowledge of self.

Bergman is writing in a Puritan tradition, much as Nathaniel Hawthorne did in this country. The intellectual isolation and cold hatred of man is the curse of Isak and Ester as it was the curse of Hawthorne's Goodman Brown, Ethan Brand, and Roger Chillingworth. Ingmar Bergman is modern man, an artist struggling with modern horrors, uncertainties, and paradoxes. He, as perhaps no other modern artist has been able to do, has created evil and despair that are explicit and actual instead of the shadows for which other moderns have settled. Bergman goes further; his evil lives. There is a horror to it that has seldom, if ever, been expressed in the film, or in literature for that matter.

Wild Strawberries and *The Silence*, respectively, present us with age and youth, the past and the future. For Isak there is redemption from a bitter existence; for Johan there is the beginning of bitterness. But the boy possesses a clue to the truth the old man has found; he has in Ester's words that which some day may save him. In the emptiness around him, he has known love by the hand and the heart of a wretched woman who is dying in total loneliness. Ingmar Bergman asks man to listen to the expression of Marianne and Ester, of life itself, and to remember it as the comunication of love from the rim of hell, from the depth of suffering.

With *The Silence*, Ingmar Bergman completed his trilogy of disgust. (*Through a Glass Darkly* and *Winter Light* are the first and second parts.) With this shocking and stunning film Bergman does not career from the path of his previous vision. *The Silence* stays on the same road of life, but it has different pilgrims.

La Strada

Edouard de Laurot, "La Strada—A Poem on Saintly Folly"

ooooooooooooooooooooooooooooooooooooooooooooooooo

La Strada, made very rapidly on a very small budget, came after *Variety Lights* (1950), *The White Sheik* (1952), and *I Vitelloni* (1953), films that antedate Federico Fellini's international reputation. Some critics hold these films of the early period to constitute his best work. Others feel that in all his films Fellini is a great artist but that his themes and characterizations carry a taint of incredibility. The story of *La Strada,* the fateful relationship between the brutal Zampano and the selfless Gelsomina, has been described by G. B. Cavallaro as "the fantastic history of a sad honeyman with a posthumous declaration of love." Edouard de Laurot analyzes the complex of artistic elements that make up Fellini's lyric style which is used "in praise of saintly folly, where madness is a blessing and poverty a virtue." He maintains that in the world of *La Strada* "there is no need—and no place, even— for man to create his own meaning through action of his free will, by imposing human significance upon things." And he concludes that "while a great work of art cannot be created out of slight substance, an exquisite one can."

———————◆———————

FROM EVERY STYLE, however individual, concrete procedures, techniques and principles can be detached, defined, and put into the common store of our knowledge of filmmaking. The highest function of film criticism should be to combine aesthetic evaluation with technical analysis.

ANALYSIS OF STYLE

Synopsis of Action

The structure of the main action in *La Strada* is simple and loose enough, and, as we shall see, intentionally so. Gelsomina, a lunary simpleton girl is sold for 10,000 lira by her destitute mother to an obtuse and brutal itinerant stunt-man, Zampano. They travel—and sleep—in Zampano's moto-trailer, stopping at towns along the road (La Strada) where he monotonously performs the only act he knows well: the breaking of an iron chain with the muscles of his athletic chest. He teaches her some paltry clowning acts with the impassive cruelty of a dog-trainer. Yet it is not this mistreatment that hurts her most, but an oppressive sense of being useful to no one. Her reiterated attempts to communicate to Zampano the candid wonder of her experiences in discovering the world crash against the apathy of a rock. She rebels, feebly, and is repeatedly subdued by Zampano. When winter sets in, they seek shelter with a roadside circus. There they meet Matto ("the Fool") a whimsical acrobat who, by his taunts, provokes the humorless Zampano into drawing a knife at him. Zampano is incarcerated for one night—a night of freedom for Gelsomina, during which she learns from Matto that she too can be "useful to someone." She now confidently awaits Zampano's recognition of her existence as a person but is, again, rebuffed. Later on, Zampano comes upon Matto on a lonely highway and beats him in a fury of revenge. Matto dies of the wounds. Zampano, camouflaging the unintentional murder as an automobile accident, flees. Haunted by his conscience and by Gelsomina's plaintive call for "Matto," he abandons her on a plateau in the mountains, under the winter sky. Years pass before he discovers that she died in a seaside town. Stricken by the consciousness of his

La Strada, directed by Federico Fellini, 1954 (*Brandon*)

ignominy and loneliness, he crumbles down on a beach at night and cries.

A Poem Film

It is a blending of Fellini's past as man, writer and director that we find in the conception and execution of *La Strada*. Although his work is as yet entirely unknown to American audiences, Fellini has been engaged in film-making for over ten years. In his youth, he traveled with a troupe of itinerant variety showmen, worked as a script cartoonist and, later, wrote comical film scenarios for Macario and Fabrizi. After the liberation of Rome, he collaborated with Roberto Rossellini as script writer on *Rome—Open City, Paisan, Francesco Giullare di Dio, The Miracle* (in which he played the part of St. Joseph); and with Alberto Lattuada on *The Mill on the Po*. *La Strada*—the fourth of the five films he directed and wrote himself—is his most personal, most autobiographical and, perhaps also, his most expiatory film. Yet in creating it he did not so much seek to transpose literally onto the screen a few pages from a *journal intime* as he tried to recapture the elusive hesitations and evanescent raptures of the soul that no diary, however intimate, can register; to re-create not the happenings themselves, but the faint essences they emanate. Such a subject lends itself easily to a trivially nostalgic treatment; but Fellini avoided facility and created a film that conquered the hearts of international audiences and, what is most significant, astounded many a film-maker by the sustained originality of its intensely lyrical style.

Viewed from the standpoint of cinematic aesthetics, *La Strada*, already on the level of the script and in its subsequent development, can be defined as a neo-surrealistic poem film. This classification is useful, for it helps us separate, define and organize the complex elements and procedures that are specific to Fellini's style. Its main characteristics are: a tragicality, unpredictability instead of suspense, ambiguity between reality and fantasy, thematic and visual ellipses, idiosyncratic acting, symbolism of characterization and visuals, affective overtones.

The Adventitious

Although different in many respects from films traditionally recognized as neo-realistic, *La Strada* is related to neo-realism in that it is not a filmic version of a dramatic plot. Drama in the classic sense is dominated by the concept of Necessity, either external or internal, in that scenes, as well as characters, are part of a rigid plot, each scene giving birth, like a chrysalis, to the next one. In a story like *La Strada*, this causality is eliminated and replaced by a succession of episodes added one onto the other in accordance with the novelistic formula of an arbitrary accumulation of events. It is from this absence of a dramatic structure that the film derives one of its most important characteristics: a sense of unpredictability and spontaneity. But the structure is not only episodic; it is also loose or open—receptive to the intrusion of adventitious elements and happenings. Often, too, it is precisely these happenings that become "pretexts" for carrying the action forward. Thus, for example, entirely gratuitous from the point of the *main* action is the scene during the country wedding when Gelsomina is asked to cheer up an apathetic sick boy, confined to bed in a dark, grotesquely furnished room. It is, as it were, a "loop" in the linear development of the narrative. After this interlude, she returns to the situation (her dependence on Zampano) from which she had been furtively snatched away. The scene, however, has a *thematic* function: it is part of Gelsomina's wondrous discovery of the world, and it displays her unquestioning generosity in bringing joy to anyone she meets in her wanderings. We find another type of the "adventitious" in a scene where three uniformed musicians playing trumpets appear as if out of nowhere, silhouetted against the sky, marching in Indian file beside a lonely country road. The *first* effect is surrealistic for, later on, we make the link, realizing that they were the harbingers of the circus to which they enticed Gelsomina. In this case, then, an extraneous event was not a "loop" but a point of departure for a new developmnt in the story. Let us now look closer at the "surrealistic" element. Zampano has met a whore in a tavern and is taking her for a ride in his moto-trailer:

> GELSOMINA: Shall I get in?
> ZAMPANO: You wait here. (The moto-trailer leaves.)
> GELSOMINA (*M.S.*): But where are you going?
> DISSOLVE. STREET. NIGHT.
> *L. S.* Gelsomina sitting on steps A lonely horse passes.
> DISSOLVE.

There is nothing unusual about such a transition (here, condensing the passage of time while Gelsomina is waiting)—except for the gaunt, lonely horse. Its sudden appearance is poignantly incongruous, poetic, semi-fantastic, but the laws of nature have not been violated, this actually *could* have happened; the horse was not flying! Like Kafka, Fellini builds the fantastic with detailed fragments of the most undeniable reality, but unlike Kafka, he does not allow fantasy to infract the real, even allegorically. His "surrealism" is one of suggestion, of overtone: it is not shown, but rather, emanates from situations to be ultimately resorbed in reality. It is also, as if intentionally, denied by the rigorously naturalistic handling of scenes of violence—fights, escapes, drunken brawls, etc., and by the consciously planned alternation of buffooning and serious scenes.

Ambiguity; Ellipsis; Thematic Composition

This fluidity between the real and the poetically real, the commonplace and the magical is further enhanced by the *ambiguity* which Fellini sustains, on many levels, throughout the film. For example, the protagonists are unobtrusively removed from their context in life, deracinated. We barely notice, or take as mere jokes, Zampano's characteristically gruff and evasive answers to Gelsomina (in the tavern):

GELSOMINA: Where do you come from?
ZAMPANO: From my part of the country.
GELSOMINA: Where were you born?
ZAMPANO: In my father's house. (Calls out) Waiter!

All we can deduce from Gelsomina's background, as shown in the film, is that she is poor; of Matto's provenance we know only that he is "a gypsy's son." The same equivocality is maintained in the characterization: we see Gelsomina and Matto alternately in and out of the stylized make-up. Gelsomina's age is not unequivocally presented (a teen-ager? an adolescent? a young woman?) nor Matto's homo- or heterosexuality; for hints at the latter are counterbalanced by other allusions equally establishing. Behind Matto's mannered chuckle and his buffoonery, there is more than the ruse and cunning of circus people; and through his ballet-like bearing and resilient gait, his everyday self merges with his incarnation as a funambulesque seraph. Despite this deliberate ambivalence, the characters are not vaguely presented; they retain, or acquire thereby, the uniqueness of their identity. Yet, without ceasing to be persons, they become symbols of themselves, detached, exalted into living myths, and, in an apparent contradiction, they seem more *convincing* than true.

Fellini makes frequent use of ellipsis. The first type is what I shall call a "feint." For example:

(Gelsomina has just arrived in a strange town. She is seen standing with a woman against the background of a circus trailer that blocks off the horizon.)
GELSOMINA: Oh! Where are we?
THE CIRCUS OWNER'S WIFE: In Rome. St. Paul's cathedral is over there. (She points off frame.)

And Rome too remains "off frame" until the end of the film. The next shot is not the predictable "Long shot: Distant view of Rome with St. Paul's Cathedral to left" or something similar, but "ZAMPANO AND CIRCUS MANAGER UNDER THE TENT." This is a feint; our attention is directed to an object or idea which is surreptitiously elided, and our imagination is thus invited to work.

But we also find ellipsis in a broader sense throughout the film. Fellini protects himself, through selection of locations and framing, against the intrusion of elements in the ambient reality that would disturb one of his dominant themes: a semi-fantastic life on the margin of society. In fact, in contradiction to the title *La Strada*, the action takes place not "in the street," or "on the road," but more exactly, on the road*side*. Most of the visual texture of the film consists of the backgrounds to Zampano's and Gelsomina's nomadic existence—vacant lots, *terrains vagues*, peripheries of towns, and that desolate no-man's-land, with its dunes enveloped in vapory spray, that runs along the littoral between the highway and the sea—enhancing the feeling of melancholy, solitude and alienation. Whenever, sporadically, Fellini makes contact with life other than that of his protagonists, it is, again, *"para-*shot"—touched at a low angle of incidence. The country wedding scene takes place, significantly, on the roadside too, but more than that, the anonymous wedding party itself is only seen fleetingly, glimpsed at the edge, or else condensed into symbols. One recalls the woman who, having prepared the food and served the guests, eats standing up "like a horse." The streets in front of the police station when Gelsomina awaits Zampano's release are cleared of pedestrians and traffic. Only the tall, modern apartment houses suggest that we are in a large city.

Yet if throughout the film such "thematic framing" is consciously and carefully sustained, the camera work is never marked by an attempt at producing arresting compositions. The photography is restrained; for the most part, the lighting is diffuse and subdued. Aside from a few scenes, gray daylight or dusk light are used. Fellini does not seek striking light "reliefs" or contrasts. Knowing that art consists in concealing art, he allows photography to be absorbed in content. In some scenes, however, the texture of the frames and the quality of the lighting become more evidently symbolic—part of the theme itself. The carefree, aerial Matto is killed in broad sunlight; after that, in a succession of quick dissolves, leafless branches of Lombardy poplars, hazy mountain vistas, shot under a murky sky, *become* Zampano's flight from his own conscience, and Gelsomina's grief. But Fellini does not only select suggestive texture: he creates it. Zampano's moto-trailer, a vehicle wholly original in design, a funeral and fantasque hybrid of hearse and truck, becomes Gelsomina's home, convent and, like Zampano, himself, her destiny.

The Person as Character

The poetic and non-dramatic conception of *La Strada* is also reflected in the way Fellini created his characters and directed his actors. Aside from the concept of Necessity, classic drama implies at least a degree of rationality, conflict of conscious wills and self-recognition. Gelsomina, Matto and Zampano are not subjugated to a plot that is "character in action;" they are not only individuals, they are, first and foremost, *persons*. At every moment of the film, we feel that they can, unpredictably and spontaneously, turn against the unfolding situations, while in a drama, they would be afforded only a choice within predetermined alternatives. Gelsomina's roaming afield, her enchanted choreography of discovery is as much—or more—a part of *La Strada*'s action as the murder of Matto. At times, when we are under the film's spell, we do not know whether she will come back to the established situation, or whether the story will follow her. But in directing them as actors, Fellini gave his protagonists more than external freedom; he gave them the right to create the parts they interpret out of the most intimate depths of their selves. Masina's, it seems, is one with Gelsomina's role: her most secret idiosyncrasies and secretive gestures revealing her as a person from the inside, as she feels herself in her subjectivity. It is an interior monologue externalized in actions and movements, freed from subjugation to the *one* action of a plot. Gelsomina, with her spurts of velleitary rebellion, her abortive departures, her ritualistic communion with the elements, her sudden outbursts of anarchic hatred (when she wants "to burn all, all") could be reduced to characters we have seen on the screen before. But the Gelsomina of Giulietta Masina, with the wonderment and pathos of her exophthalmic face, her plaintive whining, her innate *commedia dell'arte*, her childlike grimaces, is irreplaceable. More than acting, it is an act of confession without which the meaning and motivation of her "prescribed" actions could not be disclosed. It is thanks to this fusion of actor and person that these grimaces and whimpers, these externalized confessions are not mere form; for they do not, as words in prose, point to objects other than themselves; but, like words in poetry, *they themselves* become objects, *become content.*

Affective Continuity

Let us now examine how Fellini maintains continuity of action in a film essentially episodic in structure and often ambiguous in treatment.

> *COUNTRY ROAD.* Gelsomina following three musicians, in step with the music. *DISSOLVE.*
> *SCENE IN A SMALL TOWN. A PROCESSION IS PASSING. DUSK. VOICES SINGING LITURGIC MUSIC.*
> *L.S.* Details of the procession: crucifix, holy images, saints, a priest blessing the crowd.
> *M.S.* Gelsomina in the crowd, her eyes wide open in beatific admiration of the religious insignia.
> *L.S. ENTIRE PIAZZA.*
> *L.S. INTERIOR OF CHURCH. CHURCH BELLS. DISSOLVE.*
> *EXTERIOR. NIGHT.* Man on Rope. Piazza in town at night.
> *RAIN OF APPLAUSE.*
> C.U. ANNOUNCER (through loudspeaker): In a moment Matto will perform the most dangerous of his stunts. Walking 40 metres above the ground, he will eat a dish of spaghetti. . . .

In the film, the final shots of the Procession scene, the (one) shot of the church interior, and the Piazza scene at night contain rows and festoons of electric bulbs, such as are used in Italy to decorate towns on festive occasions. This is an almost conventional visual link. Yet there is another link, this one invisible and not heard (music goes out at end of church shot), but felt. Through this transition from Church to Circus, we are introduced to one of the underlying themes of the film: man's fundamental need for metaphysical expression passes from religion to art. For it is here that Gelsomina sees for the first time the winged Angel-Acrobat, Matto, suspended against constellations of artificial stars. The transition, then, is obtained on two levels at the same time: the straightforward visual continuity and the *thematic* continuity evolved through a sustenance of *affective* overtones. Significantly, in his use of music, Fellini avoids facile effects commonly employed for such links.

CRITIQUE OF CONTENT

In its internal consistency, *La Strada* is more than a remarkable example of personal style. We may then ask: What is Fellini's image of the world we live in, his conception of man and the ethic he advances? Men are separated by astral distances and do not realize their unity in the human condition. Obstinately and gropingly they quest for understanding and belonging: everyone needs someone. This is the meaning of the last shot of the film where Zampano, having repeated *"Ho bisogno di nessuno,"* is finally struck down by a cosmic terror and realizes, in his anguish, man's solitude in the face of Eternity.

The motives for Gelsomina's conversion to a faith in her usefulness are more explicitly formulated. During her "night of freedom" Matto uses the parable of the stone: "All in this world serves some purpose . . . even this little stone."

GELSOMINA: Why?

MATTO: Because if this stone is useless, then everything is, even the stars.

GELSOMINA: What is it useful for?

MATTO: I don't know. If I knew, I would be God. He knows everything.

This is Fellini's explanation of human destiny. Undeniably, man's highest quest is to give meaning to his existence in the world. But neither pure matter (here, a pebble) nor man as a pure existent have being, or else this quest, expressed through man's conscious action, would be superfluous. In Fellini's Pantheism, however, the meaning of things and people is preexistent to man's conscious actions; it is offered from above, metaphysically, by a spiritual agent. Meaning precedes existence. Therefore, there is no need—and no place, even—for man to create his own meaning through action of his free will, by imposing human significances upon things.

But a more strictly theistic conception of the world and man is to be found in the scene at the convent where the theme of vagabond life is given a metaphysical justification:

THE NUN: We change convents every two years, so as not to forget the most important thing: God. We travel, both of us. I follow my Husband, and you, yours.

GELSOMINA: Each her own.

Fellini's attempt to secularize the concept of God as Gelsomina's husband results in a fatalistic mysticism: we all have to be useful to "someone," follow a personal god, even if it is a Zampano.

Aside from metaphysical doctrine, we also find in *La Strada* Catholic mythology: the Franciscan world inhabited by saints, beggars and simpletons, the weak and the oppressed who alone possess the secret of happiness and salvation—a world antipodal to that where "wealth is a sign of God's grace" and salvation is sought through efficiency. The Angel-Fool, the Poverella-Gelsomina, the sinner but, as Gelsomina calls him, "poveraccio" Zampano, are all loved and excused in this lyric in praise of saintly folly, where madness is a blessing and poverty a virtue. Merged with these Christian doctrines will be found also purely pagan mythological elements, expressed through complex symbolism. The sea as Eternity, Time, Infinity, from which Gelsomina departs and to which she returns to die. Zampano washes his face in the purifying water, his first contact with Eternity. Everyone has his guiding fire—or should have. Gelsomina speaks of fire sparkles; Matto dies in flames;

and Zampano cannot start a campfire on the plateau. Time as Death is symbolized in Matto's watch in which he reads the end of his life.

The temptation to create myths is known to all artists. But to believe in myths is to believe in the immutability of human nature, to believe that man is in the hands of ineluctable destinies. Beyond its poetic appeal, the secret of the "ineffably touching" quality in *La Strada* can be summed up by a phrase of Descartes: "All our failings come from the fact that we were once children." *La Strada*'s philosophy is for those who have secretly remained children; for those too who, not having been previously exposed to the mithridatic effects of "angelism," will be quietly drugged by its magic. Just as the primitive and essentially infantile world of mythology is left behind by a mature and rational man, the ideas and ethic of *La Strada* have long been transcended by humanity's development. The simplistic morality advanced by Fellini as a remedy for man's alienation from others and from the world is impotent in the face of the problems of modern society. Today we are aware of other dimensions; we know that men live circumscribed by concrete situations, subjected to economic and social realities that limit and hamper them in their attempt to reach their fellow men. These realities can no more be denied in the name of a mystique of spontaneous spiritual brotherhood than they can be removed with the help of attitudes inspired by a revived medievalism.

Whether we should accept *La Strada*'s message is a matter of taste—and depth. But while a great work of art cannot be created out of slight substance, an exquisite one can. Fellini has given the screen a poem of bitter and tender beauty. Between the triumphant chant of Man in the revolutionary epic and the morbid howling of egos in the psychological drama, Gelsomina will be heard intoning the plaint of a soul and offering up an inarticulate plea for mercy.

This Sporting Life

Robert Vas, "Arrival and Departure"

○○

In England in the late fifties and early sixties the "Angry Young Men" wrote novels about the working-class culture of the welfare state that became the material of the wave of "New Realism" directors who were intent upon revitalizing British cinema as well as society. The novels of John Braine (*Room at the Top,* 1957), Alan Sillitoe (*Saturday Night and Sunday Morning,* 1958, and *The Loneliness of the Long Distance Runner,* 1959), and David Storey (*This Sporting Life,* 1960) are works of social protest portraying heroes in conflict with a spiritually vacuous postwar British society. These particular novels were made into films by Jack Clayton, Karel Reisz, Tony Richardson, and Lindsay Anderson, respectively. The ideological and artistic similarities between the novelists and the directors are close and, in both groups, the English tradition in art of social focus and narrative mode is strongly present.

Many critics have felt that the limitations of the films of these directors is that they present characters more noticeable for the propaganda significance of their destinies than for their reality as individuals whose problems and fate transcend conditions of class struggle. While *This Sporting Life* has fallen victim to the general charge, and while it contains weaknesses few have denied, Robert Vas argues that it is a film of substantial merit. He admits its shortcomings but also sees it as a superior achievement within the context of

This Sporting Life, directed by Lindsay Anderson, 1963 (*The Museum of Modern Art/Film Stills Archive*)

the movement principally because Frank Machin, the protagonist, is "steered toward tragedy," not in the direction of adroit protest against social environment. He finds that it marks a departure in the development of recent British cinema in that "We approach the story through the interior drama, and soon realize that in fact the interior drama is the story. The result is a thick texture, carrying the complexity of life itself, defying us to give a straight answer to the question of what the film is finally about." Mr. Vas defends the many fine aspects of Lindsay Anderson's directorial work, yet agrees with most critics in finding Anderson lapsing into inconsistencies of psychological point of view. An example of the defense of Anderson against the opinion of most critics is Mr. Vas's evaluation of the "spider scene" as artistically sound. He considers it functional in the motif of Machin expressing himself with his fists.

———————◆———————

THE COMPARISON ALMOST OBTRUDES itself: on an early February day in 1956 the terrible mechanical laughter in *O Dreamland* resounded from the South Bank like a trademark of protest for a generation; and on another February day, exactly seven years later, this anger, now given a deeper intensity of expression, found its way to the commercial respectability of the West End. It took seven years of admirable strategic manoeuvring to achieve this transition. In Italy the same kind of process took only a year or two; in France and Poland whole schools have emerged and dissolved since 1956. And now, when we in Britain seem finally to have an audience, producers, actors and writers for this new realism, the appearance of the first really major work is necessarily an arrival as much as a departure. It builds on the achievements of the last seven years, unifies patterns and points towards directions still unenvisaged.

Paradoxically, in *This Sporting Life* Lindsay Anderson is the first to free himself from what seven years ago he was the first to aim at: the direct attack, the deliberate harnessing of poetry to propaganda, which came then as a shot in the arm but which has gradually been left behind by the complexity of life itself, so that it now seems a constricting rather than a liberating attitude. Here Anderson demonstrates that his social consciousness is not, and never really was, a programme: it is the *sine qua non* of the existence of his world. He doesn't need to pull out and dwell on all those now fashionable aspects of English life—the North, the rainy Sunday, the tired face of the Establishment. His world simply exists within this context. Freed from the anxious guidance of a reporter/sociologist director, the characters are encouraged to discover their own feelings as they go along. I cannot recall any British film (perhaps since Jennings) which has thrown itself so courageously and with such hungry intensity into the complicated texture, interaction and social background of human feelings, and which sorts them out in such an exciting process of artistic discovery. In our cinema, where emotions are so often confused with emotionalism, this film never has to underline that it has feelings. It is, simply and naturally, a film of the senses.

It is precisely this adult responsibility which distinguishes *This Sporting Life* from the flustered inconsistencies of, say, the later Woodfall productions. A new kind of subject, especially a socially conscious one aimed at a new audience, must surely demand an added responsibility from the artist. Yet how often in recent years has the British scene been exploited instead of explored, its depressing aspect prettified to make it all seem even more miserable? How often have subjects been taken up and almost simultaneously dropped, as the artist from his new ivory tower gives us his high-angle shot on the Average Man down below? Thoughts and feelings may have been there on the screen—but how often have they survived the next week's general release? How often have they really had the power to disturb?

This Sporting Life begins like a rugger match itself: at once the whole field springs to action. A sudden, subjective shot, like the mysterious pavilion in *Hiroshima, Mon Amour*, perplexes like a first-minute goal, but gradually fits into the pattern of a subjective flashback technique which dominates the

first third of the picture. Formally this is the most complicated and diffuse section; and I will not attempt, as many
reviewers did, to approach the essence of the film by way of
this technique. I think it should be handled rather as an introduction, an exposition, which establishes the methods of the
film and the background to it.

The technique may seem a bit confusing and even alienating.
Some flashback scenes (the dance-hall and the subsequent
fight; Machin's appearance at the amateur singing contest; all
the scenes involving Johnson) may strike a lower level. But in
general this device seems the best possible way to establish
atmosphere, characters and relationships simultaneously. The
first brutal blow on the field where "loudspeakers blare the
'Entrance of the Gladiators,'" or the dressing-room with its
"smells of dry dust and sweat, carbolic, a tang of leather and
polish," fertilises the heavy soil in which tragedy can later
strike root. The rugger playing in itself is never more than an
active background to the story, a fitting battlefield for the
drama. We are introduced to the close hierarchy of the team
and to the wider social hierarchy of the industrial town; to the
industrialists, Weaver, for whom his players are his own
personal stable, and his tired rival Slomer, whose "old and
famous Rolls is parked in the tradesman's drive" when he
goes to Weaver's Christmas party. We are given the fullest
possible background to Frank Machin's story, his unscrupulous
advance to rugby league stardom, but only glimpses of Mrs.
Hammond, the widow he lodges with and grows to love. Yet
when we reach the heart of the picture, the story of their
relationship, we suddenly realise that everything has in fact
been prepared for this central section. It is as though the
concentrated tragedy of *Romeo and Juliet* had grown from the
fragmentary technique of, say, *Antony and Cleopatra*.

But the flashbacks serve a more important purpose than that
of a mere structural device. The critic who dismissed this
technique as "old hack, grown weary in Hollywood service"
and "the most lucid memories ever evoked at a dentist's, under
gas" is betraying his own failure to interpret beyond what is
actually on the screen. If the scenes had occurred in a

sophisticated French film, no doubt, it would have been a case of deliberate *mise en scène*. But in Britain's industrial North . . . ? In fact, the sudden, subjective glimpses at the beginning, counterpointed by the tough realism of the setting, stir up our interest in the character and encourage us to look out for his *interior* drama. Our continuity will obviously be a loose one, drawing the "molecules" of the hero's thoughts and emotions into a slowly thickening texture. Everything that happens is going to be seen from his point of view.

Just how consistently this interior quality is present throughout the film (although in different forms) emerges clearly from one scene—in fact the weakest in the entire work—when it is *not* present. This is the evening out at the restaurant, where Machin behaves as he never really would—at least, not at that stage of the story. (In the novel, this scene occurs much earlier.) Here the subjective view is abandoned, and the film takes the standpoint of a detached onlooker. In most British films this would be the natural point of view; but in the context it comes as a puzzling break in the unity of the whole. We must have been *with* Machin if it strikes us so strongly that we are now outside him.

There is, perhaps, yet another break—and this is where the role played by the flashback technique becomes somewhat impure. We were encouraged at the outset to adapt ourselves to an interior style which was consistently carried through until about the middle of the picture. Then, roughly after the Christmas party scene, the subjective narrative rightly changes into a more straightforward one, concentrating on the complex relationship between Frank and Mrs. Hammond. But once this change in style has occurred one may feel that the film itself has only *used* the more formal method of subjectivity, rather like a useful gimmick which can be dropped once it has done its job. Only in the last twenty minutes or so, with the visionary rugby scene in the mud, is the subjective technique taken up again, to fulfil the drama it has introduced.

At its best, however, the "portrait of a man" blends with the "story of a man": interior and at the same time narrative cinema. Among the personal "molecules" of Frank's story there are plenty of useful reference points for the story to hang on to: the £1,000 cheque; the excursion; the Christmas party. Action and psychological portrait start and attack together, one being used in order to help the other. We approach the story through the interior drama, and soon realise that in fact the interior drama *is* the story. The result is a thick texture, carrying the complexity of life itself, defying us to give a straight answer to the question of what the film is finally about.

We may approach *This Sporting Life* as a study in human behaviour or, as its creators prefer to call it, in temperament. It certainly offers a key to Frank Machin, the aggressive ex-miner, the glorious gladiator under the grey sky of Wakefield. A helpless giant, always moving, always chewing, to women a "Tarzan," "tiger," "cat" or "performing ape," Machin is imprisoned by his size and strength and demands that his own and others' feelings live up to them. But the world, at least the only woman he needs, "cannot accommodate this sheer greatness." "I was a hero," he says in the novel, "and I was crazy because she seemed the only person in the world who wouldn't admit it." His is the typical fate of tragic heroes who strive to achieve something worthwhile but go about it the wrong way, and cannot help getting into a mess which they are then unable to explain. His real purpose is a frantic search for his own identity. His character may bear a literary, almost intellectual charge in its tragic emphasis, but his best means of expression are his bare fists.

The blow of the fist comes like a visual motif in this film (the novel uses different means), in which emotions and behaviour find their expression in physical terms. It is the blow received during the match which sets off the complicated machinery of subjective remembrance. At the Mecca dance, Machin expresses his helpless jealousy of the footballers through a gratuitous punch. It is a punch which helps him to earn his place in the team. When Mrs. Hammond shows no interest in the £1,000, his response is a blow on the table. Later, he hits her in the cemetery: "I couldn't think why she should say all this, and the shortest way of stopping it I found was to hit her." Force urges the final conflict to its culmination: again a physical outburst. And perhaps this desperate feast for the fist gives a meaning and motive to that crushing of a spider above Mrs. Hammond's death-bed, which comes, in its context, as a sudden disconcerting re-capture of the direct, subjective methods of the opening. This, then, is a culminating blow: a classical hero would consummate his grief in a monologue, but Frank Machin speaks with his fist.

The film-makers' aim was to avoid sociological generalisa-tions, to present a character who is larger than life and for that reason better fitted to stand for a wider, more hazardous poetic truth. "Tragedy is concerned with what is unique," writes Anderson. Archie Rice, the Entertainer, Colin Smith, the Long Distance Runner, and the original Arthur Seaton of Sillitoe's novel were all unique, larger than life, within their own terms even tragic characters—yet in the films they were not steered towards tragedy. Nor would the original Arthur Machin of David Storey's novel himself reach this height without the emphases of the film's method. True, certain aspects appear to be inferior if one must make comparisons with the book. There Machin's character exists against a livelier background of his affairs with other women, his friend-ship with Maurice and Judith, his relations with his parents. The written text does more justice to Johnson's character; to the game itself; to Machin's downfall as a member of the team and his gradual re-emergence. Generally, the author's first person singular identification with the hero is more shaded in the novel than in the film, which demands a different and more direct kind of identification from its authors. Here everything takes a compressed and dramatically heightened form. The Machin actually visible on the screen will be much bigger than in the pages of the book; so his behaviour and Mrs. Hammond's reaction assume additional size, a further edge of intensity.

It is Mrs. Hammond's character (seen in contrast with his, and yet from his point of view) which fully brings out the scope of the film. Her strange and silently suffering nobility, her dignified misery, her full-time self-destruction, would make her a perfect Chekhovian character, if her suppression of self were not at the same time so perversely stupid and unnatural. She is a fragile little woman who made bombs during the war, was happy and beautiful in her youthful independence, then staked everything on a single card and lost herself in a marriage which she probably made hell for her husband. When she is left alone, a widow with two small children, she falls into the ready-made role of martyr. "She didn't want to be seen. Her life . . . had been taken up with making herself as small, as negligible as possible. So small she didn't exist. That was her aim. And it was exactly opposite to mine. I wanted the real Mrs. Hammond to come popping out."

The relationship begins to take shape amidst the early flashbacks, and especially in the excursion scene, the only one in which she loosens up a bit. This simple episode, lasting only a few minutes, is a world in itself, full of its creators' search for the essence of their story. The giant dwarfed by the natural surroundings; the quick close-up of Mrs. Hammond against the skeleton ruins of Markham Abbey; Mrs. Hammond catching the white ball against her black coat with innocent, childish surprise; and the unselfconscious games of the children, playing as though released from a prison of whose existence they had been unaware. The texture of the relationship is established by the time it takes over the dominant role in the film and turns it towards tragedy. She is unable to give him the response he demands—"You're so big," she says, "you're so stupid, you don't give me a chance." Although she becomes his mistress she cannot let her feelings go along with it. By then we cannot even judge which does most harm: his aggressive demands or her unnatural renunciation of life. Instead of the best the relationship brings out the worst in both of them. The sense of approaching tragedy is heightened by his inability to put his feelings into words; by the fact that his only way of expression, the physical, is exactly the one by which he alienates her. The *huis clos* feeling of their inability to communicate brings with it the explosion: the violent, final break.

It is at this moment of his "tragic guilt" that the account of the relationship reverts to Frank's personal story, and the picture gains a frightening, almost abstract charge. In the visionary rugby scene the film begins to gather in its own harvest; and this marks the beginning of what is perhaps the most powerful and unashamedly emotional half-hour in the record of British cinema. Here, living up to the size and power of its hero, *This Sporting Life* achieves that universality of tragedy which has so far eluded the new British directors. Here pain *is* called pain, and the feeling is one of liberation. . . .

There is a shot earlier on in the picture which summarises its creators' attitudes: it shows Mrs. Hammond sitting before the fire, talking to Machin about her late husband. First we see her head from behind; her sleek blonde hair in an idealised and youthful romantic vision. Then she suddenly turns into profile, revealing a roughly shaped nose, hollow cheeks, hard features. Here is a pathetic amalgam of the robust and tender, eruptive and suppressed, demanding and accepting—and out of these many contrasts emerges something of the quality of contemporary Britain, the mixture of aggression and withdrawal, anger and passivity.

To some extent this duality was also present in *Saturday Night and Sunday Morning* or *Look Back in Anger*, though not with such a demanding emotional conviction. The main protest here is not, as one critic holds, a consciously social one: "gladiatorial slaves and suave, unscrupulous tycoons." It lies rather in the heat of the emotions, in an outcry against "not taking things too seriously," being ashamed to feel. To ask for "coolness" and detachment" (as did another critic) from a film which intends to be and is "hot" seems a very English miscalculation. And through this heat is communicated, in the words of its author, "the whole tragedy of living, of being alive" today, in Britain, in the world. A laconic tragedy, if you like, which begins with the hero breaking his front teeth and ends with him, alone and unhappy, taking out his false teeth before another match.

To reach this point, Lindsay Anderson had to get rid of a certain kind of facile romanticism which mingles with the genuinely humane in *Every Day Except Christmas*. He emerges as a talent with strong reserves, able to encompass the small psychological glimpses as well as the overall emotional sweep: the exposition of Mrs. Hammond's character; the self-contained entity of a simple shot in which Machin's hand puts the cheque on the table and her hand, instead of reaching out for it, flicks up the handle of her sewing-machine; recognition of physical sensations, like the cold water sprinkled over Machin when he stands in the shower; the use of overlapping sound, handled here with the split-second accuracy that bears the stamp of an artist. There are, of course, a number of scenes which remain below the level of the whole: the dinner; the strip club; the Mecca dance; the card game in the bus; the scene in the Weavers' room at the Christmas party; the doss-house (an untimely return to straight observation at this moment in the film); and perhaps all the scenes involving Johnson, whose character seemed to me too studio-born, by comparison with the novel, to evoke the inexplicable strangeness surrounding him and his mysterious disappearance from the story. The film doesn't do justice, either, to the two children. Their parts are never really developed, perhaps rightly since the film hardly needs them. But then why take them up and then finish them off in such a disturbing and unresolved way with the shot in the hospital corridor?

Although the film knows very well what is is doing, there is no "exciting" cinematic vision here. Anderson and his cameraman use the best of that traditional feature language which serves as the basis for the work. Collectors may by the way recognise possible homages—to Humphrey Jennings ("One Man Went to Mow") and even perhaps to Joan Crawford (Mrs. Weaver). All in all, it is not so much a *film d'auteur* as, rather, a film *with* an author.

And with a close team. This is a genuine piece of creative collaboration, not only from Reisz, Anderson and Storey but from every department. Richard Harris seems to build up the character before our eyes, offering different emotional and physical variations on the key theme of "big." Rachel Roberts is one of those rare actresses who can give dignity even to the smallest part, can combine without effort the down-to-earth and the rarefied. Their scenes together, in the shabby, closed room of the house in Fairfax Street, with her dead husband's boots on the hearth, are perhaps the perfect equivalent of a D. H. Lawrence cinema. Colin Blakely's Maurice and Anne Cunningham's Judith seem to be intruders from the lighter world of *Saturday Night and Sunday Morning*, though this may have been deliberately done to emphasise Frank's isolation. Arthur Lowe as Slomer seems a less harsh and more complete performance than Alan Badel's effective Weaver. In her few scenes, Vanda Godsell's smilingly frustrated Mrs. Weaver confidently asserts the lady's own right to use her husband's stable. The economical score by Roberto Gerhard affords a masterly contrast to the giant hero, unostentatiously adding that extra dimension which film music stands for. Denys Coop's camerawork, more deliberate and professionally firm than in *A Kind of Loving*, takes an equal share in the total creative experience of discovery.

With all this there comes an even happier discovery. Can it really be true that a British film, made within the commercial framework, can show such courage in expressing feeling, and such genuine responsibility towards the feelings it expresses? Well, here it is: it has been done. A film which in its outlook on life and people is so very British also achieves a kind of universality. It is an exploratory work, and this involves numerous falterings, mistakes, impurities in style and content. But it is an arrival as much as a departure; a breakthrough perhaps to a more demanding audience, and more courage in production; a password to the unashamed expression of emotion. The main thing is that it is with us. Let's not try to classify it: just be proud of it and never, never take it for granted.

Throne of Blood

J. *Blumenthal*, "Throne of Blood"

ooooooooooooooooooooooooooooooooooooooooooooooooo

The Japanese film-maker Akira Kurosawa's *Throne of Blood*, an adaptation of *Macbeth*, has been regarded as the most successful filmic treatment of Shakespeare. Yet it does not contain Shakespeare's language. Many attempts at adapting Shakespeare's plays have failed as a result of misapplying stage gestures, speech delivery, and theatrical settings in film; the medium of film demands greater naturalism and approximates reality without the exaggeration of theatrical speech and movements. In his essay Mr. Blumenthal seeks to demonstrate that Kurosawa succeeds in capturing the spirit of Shakespeare's *Macbeth* by finding visual equivalent in the physical world for the states of mind Shakespeare renders verbally. Also, he discusses another instance of interesting cinematic Shakespeare, Sir Lawrence Olivier's *Henry V*. Although he recognizes Olivier's attainment, nonetheless he finds the film *Henry V*, unlike *Throne of Blood*, to be essentially a product of theater. He argues that making *Macbeth* a cinematic experience comes from Kurosawa's genius for making nature eloquent, from "his ability to imbue a place with such deep moral meaning that the place often seems to take charge and structure the narration on its own." And further on he advances the view that Washizu (Macbeth) as a characterization "is rather the spirit of Macbeth distilled to almost pure materiality."

Throne of Blood, directed by Akira Kurosawa, 1957 (*Brandon*)

AKIRA KUROSAWA's *Throne of Blood* (1957) is the only work, to my knowledge, that has ever completely succeeded in transforming a play of Shakespeare's into a film. What is important about this is that the film is a masterpiece in its own right, and the first of its kind. Up to now, Shakespeare adaptations for the screen have been perpetrated (this is the only word for it) mainly by those whose first love is the theatre. Maybe this is the way it has to be. Maybe *Throne of Blood* is an aberration, and truly gifted film-makers will always try to liberate themselves from the dreaded literary media so that they can concentrate on culling their own experience for film material. I guess it is even possible to argue that Shakespeare adaptations for the screen should be left to artists such as Olivier, so that they can bring the great soliloquies and reconstructions of the Globe Theatre to the provinces; for this, too, is an important function of the film. But then, who is to say where film-makers such as Kurosawa (as opposed to men of the theatre) should seek inspiration—especially when they succeed in turning out great films?

As easy as it may be to film a play, it is quite another thing to make a film out of one. Orson Welles, who has shown a genius for both media, is a good case in point. He has tried making films out of two of Shakespeare's plays and has failed—miserably with *Macbeth*, gracefully with *Othello*—both times. His *Othello*, beautiful as it is, fails because most of its cinematic flourishes are gratuitous. His toying with the medium remains toying for all its mastery. Welles is too often guilty of serving up chunks of pure Shakespeare that have been sugar-coated with an unusual camera angle or composition, or nicely sliced up by a bold cut. Although this is all very fascinating to look at, the experience of looking is empty at the centre. It is film as hobby, or ornament, but not as expression.[1] No matter from what angle one photographs it, or the number of cute little pieces into which one cuts it, the material in its original form (the play, the in-

[1]The image of Iago caged and being returned to the castle, with which Welles frames the action of the film, and the brilliant sequence in the sewers, are among the exceptions to this.

dividual scene with dialogue intact) remains essentially what it was. In such cases the filming is a more or less gratuitous decoration of the subject and not what it must be: an inevitable articulation of it.

THE FOREST

This takes us to *Throne of Blood*. At the same time, it takes us to Kurosawa's profound commitment to creating meaning by the manipulation of material reality. No doubt this is for him just as much an involuntary response to experience as it is a commitment; but whatever its sources, the form it takes in this film is revealing. To begin with, Kurosawa is doing much more here than simply letting us see the things that Shakespeare's characters describe, and the places where the action is set. This time-honoured but very limited device for filming plays is far from his only resource.[2] The point is that Kurosawa actually thinks by manipulating material reality. Birnam Wood, for example, which has only a few lines of vague description devoted to it in the play, becomes in Kurosawa's hands a physical presence that is potent enough to embody the film's very complex network of themes. The forest in *Throne of Blood* was born with Kurosawa's conception of the film. It is not the result of a makeshift adaptation, nor is it even a fancy visualisation of the play. It is rather an offspring of the metamorphosis from play to film, and it is to a great degree responsible for charging *Throne of Blood* with an inner principle of motion, for making it an autonomous work of art.

It might help to look at the problem from Kurosawa's point of view. He feels deeply sympathetic to the theme of *Macbeth* and is moved to make a film out of it. The play is about a noble and highly ambitious warrior faced with the dire task of gaining control over his own vivid but treacherous

[2]As it is, for example, for Max Reinhardt (*A Midsummer Night's Dream*, 1935), whose enchanted forest inhabited by real people, and whose cardboard castle, merely underscore the intractability of his material.

imagination. He needs to prove himself to himself and can do so only by acting out his most horrible visions, wholly embracing whatever evil he encounters in his own soul. Self-control and self-destruction soon become identical, and this is the tragedy. As Kurosawa must have seen it, the crucial problem was to find a natural means of externalising, of objectifying, Macbeth's thoughts. By "natural" I mean that the object chosen had to appear to exist in the real world just as Macbeth did, living and growing there. For it is not enough that Macbeth's thoughts can be photographed; photographing them must bring them to life.

Birnam Wood, a marginal symbol from the original work, was perfect for the part. Even in the play, it is only when the forest defies the laws of nature (just as Macbeth subverts the moral order) that Macbeth's fate becomes explicit and he realises that the kind of self-control he sought was suicidal. In the film, however, the forest is more than a marginal objective correlative of the theme. It is both the battleground where the conflict rages and the very incitement to conflict. If this sounds like a fair description of what is called the "world" of a work of art, we are on the point. For this is precisely the role that the forest plays. It is the life at the centre of the film, what we always look for but seldom find in film versions of anyone's plays.

A sizeable portion of *Throne of Blood* is devoted to the terrifying spectacle of Washizu (Macbeth) waging war on the forest. In an extended sequence near the beginning he and Miki (Banquo) thunder through a dense, murky forest on horses no less frightened than they. (The forest is referred to as "The Labyrinth" and much is made, here and later in the film, of the difficulty of finding one's way out of it.) Washizu is clearly the leader: *he* will find a way out, for he cannot bear the sense of dread and helplessness he feels before the blind paths, the unidentifiable shrieks and moans, the thunder, lightning, and fog. He starts at what he thinks an evil spirit, unsheathes his sword, and letting out a blood-curdling cry, half defiant and half hysterical, he plunges into the dark with Miki following him. The reality of this forest is overwhelming.

It breathes, and sweats, and twitches, and speaks in the unknown tongue. It is easily as powerful a presence as Washizu himself; and this is exactly what it must be, since for Washizu this first encounter with the forest is nothing less than a headlong plunge into the self.

In this sequence Washizu and Miki are on their way to Forest Castle, where their lord is waiting to reward them for leading the victorious battle against the rebel forces. Control of this castle soon becomes Washizu's obsession, and already he is struck by the thought that one would be truly invulnerable if he could control the forest, which is the only means of access to the castle. In a moment the crazed horses burst through the underbrush on to a small clearing that glows with bones, a chalk-white, sexless, ageless demon sits spinning a loom and chanting the prophecies that eventually drive Washizu on to the ultimate dare. "I must paint the forest with blood!" he will cry. The forest is Washizu's mind. As his ambitions reveal, it is no longer controlled by his lord. His lord is therefore vulnerable, but no more so than the doomed Washizu, whose position is ironically similar.

Kurosawa has at least this much in common with most other great film-makers: his ability to imbue a place with such deep moral meaning that the place often seems to take charge and structure the narrative on its own. I am not suggesting that the place equals the film. It is simply necessary that the place come alive and help shape the film. If it generates no conflict, if it does not partake of the reality of the characters' experiences, place remains meaningless. And if the place is meaningless, so is the film. A very painful example of this failing is the painted-backdrop universe of Olivier's *Henry V*. It is as if a novelist had tried to preserve *The Ring of the Niebelungen* by objectively reporting all the action, characters, dialogue, and scenery exactly as they appear on the stage. And then concluded his lark with a request that we actually read his work.

In *Throne of Blood*, however, place becomes an autonomous reality. The horses gallop through the forest and Kurosawa, always behind a maze of gnarled trunks and barren branches, gallops with them.[3] The whole—the men and their horses, the composition of the frame, the narrative, and the theme itself—is galvanised by the hellish milieu. This applies equally to the interiors, whose simple theatricality constitutes a world within that of the all-encompassing forest. Behind the flimsy walls man makes to seal himself off from an amoral nature, there is a lucid, quiet geometry that is assaulted throughout the film and, in the end, shattered. Toward the end, before the forest moves, a futile war council between Washizu and his captains is thrown into confusion by a flock of squealing bats which suddenly comes flapping into the hall from the forest. Washizu understands only too well what this means. He screams for his horse (*à la* Richard III) and rides for the last time to that unholy clearing seeking the assurances he could not obtain from others. The forest, which is the objectification of Washizu's mind, both controls and contains the action of the film.

Finally, there are the tumultuous comings and goings of the men and their horses which function so importantly as the narrative link between castle and forest. They enable the director to tell his story with great economy and force and deserve a little section to themselves.

THE HORSES

I am reminded here of those two sleepy creatures who might conceivably have served as the drunken chamberlains but were forced instead to labour as mounts for Macbeth and Banquo at the beginning of Welles's film on the subject. Not that Welles should have made Kurosawa's film, but we do have some right to expect that a flair for phantasmagoria will show up in more than flashy editing and pretentiously symbolic sets—in the life surrounding the characters, for example.

[3]Kurosawa's imitators have succeeded in making a cliché of this image, but that is their problem.

ROSS
And Duncan's horses—a thing most strange and certain—
Beauteous, and swift, the minions of their race,
Turned wild in nature, broke their stalls, flung out,
Contending 'gainst obedience, as they would
Make war with mankind.

OLD MAN
'Tis said, they eat each other.

I grant that the old man's footnote would present problems.
Ross's description, though, is the work of an excellent scenarist,
and one whose talent Kurosawa did not fail to notice. From
a lingering shot of Washizu and his wife retiring as the
chaos loosed by the murder seems finally to have subsided,
there is a jolting cut to the next morning, and we see the
king's horses "contending 'gainst obedience," much as Duncan's
did. The entire castle is aroused again as the horses, in their
frantic rush to flee the thing they have sensed, stampede
through a row of huge banners which flap resoundingly as
they are dragged off towards the forest.

The sequence is typically Kurosawa in the calculated
violence of its execution. All the action is shot from a worm's-
eye view and up close; a few rapid-fire shots of the rebellious
steeds and the stunned, helpless men and we move on immediately to the film's loose counterpart of Macduff, Noriashu,
who is making off under cover of the excitement to warn
Miki of his suspicions. The narrative takes an important step
forward and nothing is left hanging. The brief turmoil here
is anything but a decorative cinematic effect. We already
know from the forest sequence at the beginning that Kurosawa
is modelling his world on that of Shakespeare. The whole of
nature is sensitive to moral traumas in this type of world, and
the moral traumas themselves are often of such magnitude as
to unhinge the whole of nature. Kurosawa's great gift is that
he has the power as a film-maker to make us experience this
world. If he had tried to abstract from the process the thing
that Shakespeare, working as a dramatist, did—if he had

given us a reaction to the event instead of the event itself—
everything would have been lost. We would have neither
play nor film.

Let me give another telling example, one for which
Kurosawa did not have Shakespeare's potential genius as a
scenarist to serve as inspiration. (Isn't this, by the way, at the
heart of the matter? That Kurosawa relies on Shakespeare
only as a scenarist whose vision is consonant with his own,
and never as a maker of pentameters?) Miki decides, because
of the prophecies, to throw in his lot with Washizu even
though he is certain of Washizu's guilt.[4] He is now a guest at
Washizu's new residence, Forest Castle. The sequence opens
in Washizu's chamber, with Lady Washizu playing the role of
evil counsellor. She does not trust Miki and knows that
Washizu doesn't either, so she gives voice to what he desires
yet dreads even to think of: another murder. We cut immediately from Washizu's speechless, petrified face to the
courtyard, where Miki's horse, normally gentle, seems to be
going mad. It is charging around the courtyard and refuses
to let the groom saddle it. Miki's son interprets this as a bad
omen and pleads with his father not to ride forth that after-
noon but to stay for the banquet and tend to his affairs the
next morning. Miki laughs this off as childishness, but no
sooner does he move to saddle the horse himself than we
cut to a shot of the courtyard taken from the ramparts of
the castle. It is night, and still, and the courtyard, far away
and off in the lower lefthand corner of the frame, is deserted.
Miki's men are seated up here in a circle discussing in hushed
tones the strange turn of events during the last few days.
Suddenly they fall silent. They hear something in the distance.
It becomes louder and finally identifies itself as the sound of
a galloping horse. The shot is held a moment longer, just
long enough for Miki's beautiful white stallion to come
racing into the courtyard, riderless. The cut is to Washizu
at the banquet. Washizu, of course, is paying no attention

[4]The changes in the plot will be dealt with at greater length in the
next section.

to the entertainment or his guests; he cannot stop gaping at the one empty seat in the hall.

This passage, which lasts no more than three or four minutes, is film narrative at its most eloquent. Kurosawa edits with an unerring instinct for clipping each action at its climax so that it will reverberate throughout the whole, and movement and placement within the frame are always obliquely at the service of the story. But the sequence is also noteworthy because it allows us to catch Kurosawa in the act of narrating what Shakespeare dramatised, and in doing so it reveals how greatly film narrative depends on the material components of the world being depicted.

Kurosawa builds the entire sequence around the reactions of Miki's horse. The movements of this short-circuited creature are responsible for all the characteristic ellipses in the narrative; they say everything that has to be said until Washizu's own body and face take over again at the banquet. At the same time, they necessitate doing away with much of the play. The elaborate preparations with the murderers, and even the murder itself (presumably excellent cinematic material), are discarded. Kurosawa has no use for even the murder because the world he is creating already contains its own narrative potential. It is a world of morally sensitised objects (the forest, the horses, the bodies and faces of the characters) which throughout the film lead a life of their own. And in their autonomy they demand that the film-maker adhere to their logic. If the film-maker is really making a film, and not just filming a play, he is only too willing to accede.

All appearances to the contrary, I am not arguing for the horse-opera notion of film aesthetics. Silver, too, neighs when there is trouble in the air, but who hasn't had the urge to strike him mute? One does not need horses, or chases, or even the unleashing of stupendous natural forces whose mass can be hurled across the screen, in order to make filmic films. One thing that is indispensable, though, is the ability to convince the spectator that the surfaces of body, face, and place, bristle with nerve-ends, and that the synapses between the three generate the meaning and control the structure of the film.[5] Kurosawa does this again and again in *Throne of Blood*. I hope it is clear that what he does bears no relation to such things as Olivier's desperate attempt at the end of *Henry V* to add a dash of "cinema" to the recipe in the form of an equine extravaganza.

THE CHARACTERS

Probably the most radical result of this transformation from play to film is the total absence from the latter of Shakespeare's diction. That Kurosawa's characters in *Throne of Blood* speak Japanese is only half the point. The other and more important half is that they speak only when they can't communicate in any other way, and then in language that is terse, unadorned, brutally functional. As far as one can tell from the subtitles, Shakespeare's poetry is gone—not just translated and trimmed, but gone.[6] In our discussion of the forest and the horses we saw some of the things that take its place. There it was best to concentrate on the fundamental similarity of the problems facing Macbeth and Washizu. But the film's scrupulous avoidance of Shakespeare's verse is closely related to some equally fundamental differences in plot and characterisation. These differences deserve attention because they take us deeper into the question of how character is developed in a film, and they may even provide some basis for a speculation on what types of character, if any, are most suitable to the medium.

LADY MACBETH

I have given suck, and know
How tender 'tis to love the babe that milks me—

[5]This sounds very much like Kracauer's definition of what a film should be (see his *Theory of Film*), but his notion of film as "the redemption of physical reality," dependent as it is on what he calls the "stream of life," would leave little room for *Throne of Blood*. He would probably have severe reservations about its tight plot and medieval setting.

[6]In what I suppose is an attempt to be faithful to Shakespeare, a recent Russian film version of *Othello* went so far as to use English-speaking actors. This kind of piety is not one of Kurosawa's virtues.

I would while it was smiling in my face
Have plucked my nipple from his boneless gums,
And dashed the brains out, had I so sworn as you
                              Have done to this.

Such is the chilling eloquence that Shakespeare uses to build the character of Lady Macbeth. Lady Washizu, however, is denied this mode of self-expression. She is endowed instead with a purely physical power, one that reaches far beyond (although it includes) the immediately visible gesture. A short time before the action of the film opens, she conceives Washizu's child. This pregnancy becomes the pitchfork with which she goads her husband into carrying out his evil intentions, and she needs few words to exploit her advantage. The child, who was to have been the ultimate beneficiary of the plot to kill the king and Miki, becomes with Lady Washizu's miscarriage one of its victims, and by the same token an incarnation of the plot itself. After Washizu gains control of Forest Castle, Lady Washizu acts out this perverse fertility rite by dancing, insane with joy, in the room where the king was murdered. But the pressures of approaching failure soon bring on the miscarriage, which in turn precipitates Lady Washizu's nervous breakdown. (The cause of Lady Washizu's madness is one of Kurosawa's most brilliant additions to the story.) In the mad scene she simply huddles in the middle of her empty chamber, scrubbing her hands and whimpering. We neither see nor hear of her again.

Earlier I mentioned the hero's vivid but treacherous imagination. Yet one would be hardpressed to find much evidence of a vivid imagination in what he says. What we are given is a barrage of gapes, grunts, shrieks, and snorts; and the taunt motions of a trapped but still powerful animal. Washizu cannot articulate his nightmarish visions, but there is no doubt that he has them. Some of this we encountered in his reaction to the forest. There is more. When Miki's ghost appears to him at the banquet—that it does appear is also germane to the question at hand—he staggers all the way across the hall and back, the spasmodic thudding of his feet threatening at any moment to splinter the thin wooden floor. The delicate Japanese architecture is used throughout as a sounding board for the man's tremendous violence. He crashes into the wall, gasping for breath, his eyes half out of their sockets. The banquet soon ends and one of the murderers reports that Miki's son has escaped. The stricken Washizu kills him on the spot without saying a word; he screams, flings the sword away, and reels out of the room. We are meant to feel here that the powers of the forest are assaulting the fragile order of interiors that are not really interiors at all, but merely veneer, flimsy defences against the bestiality within. Although the faculty of speech eludes him, this is what Washizu feels (and expresses) with every bone in his body.

We are never allowed to forget the hero's primitive physicality. When Washizu finally glimpses the forest moving, he shudders and crouches in a corner of the ramparts unable to believe his eyes. With great effort he musters the courage to try to embolden his men. Pacing the rampart like a caged lion, he roars down into the terrified crowd. (The camera is placed well beneath him here and pans unsteadily back and forth, imitating his nervous motion.) But his men have had enough. The forest has moved and this creature's doom screams at them with his every gesture, no matter how brazen. They draw their bows and turn them on their master, denying him the honour of dying, as Macbeth did, with "harness on his back." The result is gruesome, for it is some time before Washizu, howling and writhing, with dozens of arrows stuck in him, is caught in the neck.[7] He falls (in slow motion) into the courtyard and his body, which seems as if it will never stop bouncing, raises huge clouds of dust. The entire army backs off, fearing that the demon may not have been completely exorcised. It has, though, and when the body finally comes to rest, the film ends.

[7]Kurosawa had real arrows shot at the actor here. As Anderson and Richie point out in *The Japanese Film*, "His interest was not in using the real thing simply because it was real but that the effect on film was greatest when real arrows were really aimed at Mifune." The same might be said of the forest.

It seems to me that the main consequence of these various transformations is that the grotesque *rapprochement* between the human and animal kingdoms common to both works is more complete in *Throne of Blood* than in *Macbeth*. Essentially the same thing happens to both heroes, but this could not have been expressed filmically unless Macbeth were transformed into a more instinctive, more physical, creature; one for whom the moral dimension of behaviour exists but seldom crosses the threshold of conceptualisation into verbal poetry, or into philosophy. Washizu is no less sensitive than Macbeth, and no less moral. But because there is no place in the film (in any film, for that matter) for Shakespeare's poetry, he must of course be less of a poet, and less of a philosopher, and perhaps not quite the classical tragic hero that Macbeth is in the play.

Even at the news of the miscarriage and at the sight of his deranged wife, even in his attempt at the end to rally his men, meanings for him remain locked in their physiological symptoms. Given Macbeth's eloquence, Washizu might have succeeded in dying more nobly, with "harness on his back." But this is to confuse the two characters. For Washizu's character is controlled in this important respect by the requirements of the medium. His men turn on him because his body and face, awesome as they are in this final attempt to command, cannot conceal his awareness of his imminent destruction. Washizu is simply not articulate enough to mediate, in the lofty manner of the classical tragic hero, between his perceptions and his gestures. If he were, he would not present the powerful film image that he does.[8] It is fitting that Kurosawa should exploit this by placing him on the ramparts in full view of everyone and at the mercy of those to whom he cannot help but reveal himself.

All this is not to say that Washizu cannot think. The point

[8]Even the sophisticated, terribly self-conscious characters in Antonioni's films are usually at a loss for words to express their plight (when they aren't too weary to do so). This verbal lethargy and frustration are important sources of the often tremendous impact of these figures as film images.

is that he thinks in another medium. When Macbeth hears of his wife's death he delivers the famous speech beginning "Tomorrow, and tomorrow, and tomorrow. . . ." Washizu, looking into his wife's chamber, sees part of the result of his folly huddled in the centre of the room; his whole being sags and he moves off heavily to his own chamber. We follow him there. He enters the room and lets his limp body drop to the floor. "Fool!" he cries. "Fool!" These are the only words he speaks. Occupying the frame with his seated figure, however, are two other objects: his sword, and the throne. Kurosawa holds this eloquent shot for a long time. It is as good an indication as any that Washizu is not a brutish man incapable of reflection. He is rather the spirit of Macbeth distilled to almost pure materiality. Lady Washizu is the spirit of Lady Macbeth distilled in the same fashion. These distillations are the lifeblood of the film. Without them a meaningful and moving narrative would have been impossible.[9]

As for the lesser characters, they receive much the same kind of treatment. Macduff (Noriashu) is an interesting example because in the process he loses not only his eloquence but also his glorious role as avenger. Although he is presumably among the forces attacking Forest Castle at the end, after he ineffectually warns Miki of his suspicions we never see him again. One result of this is that the effects of the central action on the body politic are not dwelt upon as they are in *Macbeth*. We may be thankful for the absence of all the tedious business between Macduff and the mealy-mouthed Malcolm, but we do demand that the social implications of the tragedy, which are integral, find some expression in the film. And this they find not in subtle political machinations, but in the monstrous betrayal that Washizu's men are

---

[9]If this statement seems too strong, have a look at Judith Anderson's Lady Macbeth in George Schaefer's film version of the play. Shakespeare's diction was meant to be rendered theatrically—it cannot be rendered well any other way—and at this Miss Anderson is expert. On the screen, however, her excellent theatrical performance becomes operatic and therefore ludicrous. The film-maker who tries to preserve a theatrical experience ends up sacrificing the best virtues of both media.

forced to perform at the end. This is indeed a primal social situation. It can be seen (without stretching the point, I believe) as a re-enactment of the ritual replacement of the old king. In this the film seems even closer to the Dionysian roots of tragedy than the play; and seems also to descend, in its own way, just as deeply into the darker side of human nature and relationships. In his search for the surfaces he needed as a film-maker, Kurosawa had to chip some of the crust of civilisation off the drama. Macduff (and Malcolm) were part of that crust.

A final question arises. Are there certain types of character that are not really fit for film narrative? Let me venture into these deep waters with the speculation that no film-maker could help but grossly distort or over-simplify a character such as Hamlet's. I am not talking here about the problems that Olivier encountered in trying to preserve a theatrical performance of the role, but about those that would be involved in trying to create the character filmically. And the problem is not Hamlet's complexity, for Macbeth, too, is a very complex character and Kurosawa was able to re-create him filmically by means of a distillation that neither distorted nor simplified the fundamental meaning of his experience. Hamlet would be untranslatable because of the verbality of his experience. One can be verbal without one's experience being so. Macbeth, who is at bottom a man of action, is also a great poet, and therefore a good example of this. The verbal experience is typical of those who never wholly enter their experience, those who can only act at acting. It is typical of the theatrical, role-playing personality, which is *par excellence* Hamlet's. Macbeth, on the other hand, always lives his experiences, and thereby provides Kurosawa with the irreducible core of raw, unquestioned reality that is the first premise of most great films.

Polonius asks Hamlet what he is reading. "Words, words, words," Hamlet answers. A pun of this calibre should be able to withstand the strain of one more meaning. I submit it as a description of exactly the kind of self-conscious verbal construct that is the basic form of Hamlet's own character and experience. It is the theatre that has always nourished this sensibility and it seems therefore destined to remain outside the mainstream of film-making.[10]

[10]In his recent book, *Metatheater*, Lionel Abel convincingly traces the modern theatrical sensibility ("life seen as a dream, the world as a stage") back to *Hamlet*. This sensibility has had very little influence on the great film-makers.

Ugetsu Monogatari

Eric Rhode, "Ugetsu Monogatari"

oooooooooooooooooooooooooooooooooooooooooooooooo

In presenting conflicts of universal range and human depth, director Kenji Mizoguchi's art transcends locale and setting and relates cogently to the condition of contemporary man. Like *Rashomon*, *Ugetsu Monogatari* (1953) belongs categorically to the postwar Japanese genre of medieval adventure films, a type that has its commercial Hollywood counterpart in the Western; the sword is the chief prop of the former, the six-shooter of the latter. Many of the period films offer high adventure and escape into a remote, eerie world of exceptionally demonic villains and heroes exerting great physical prowess and cunning. But *Ugetsu*, like other superior period-type films to reach the West, is infused with profound moral vision. Eric Rhode sees Mizoguchi's artistic success in the ability to balance and hold in equipose the real and fantastic worlds: *Ugetsu* "preserves a surface of ordinary everyday happenings whilst at the same time creating a childhood world of animistic fears, so that the predicaments of the characters are plausible both in naturalistic terms and in terms of the rich, more obscure movements of the mind." And his essay reinforces the claim of Anderson and Richie in *The Japanese Film: Art and Industry* (1959) that Mizoguchi's *Ugetsu Monogatari* is "one of the director's best films and one of the most perfect movies in the history of Japanese cinema."

KENJI MIZOGUCHI IS GENERALLY recognised as one of the masters of the cinema. In France he is a prize pet in the *Cahiers* menagerie. Over here his *Ugetsu Monogatari* took fourth place (with *Greed*) in the *Sight and Sound* critics' poll. At the same time only one of Mizoguchi's films has been distributed commercially in this country: *Street of Shame*. Not unpredictably, this sensitive study of geisha life was billed as a second feature to a nudist travelogue and played for a roaring six months. Now, six years after Mizoguchi's death, we may be allowed a more serious opportunity to appraise his talent since *Ugetsu*, one of the last and possibly the greatest of his eighty-eight films, is finally being shown commercially in London.

This *Ugetsu* is an essay in the uncanny: an unearthly fable, uncanny because it revives in us those childhood fears aroused by a wind whistling in the chimney-piece or doors creaking in the night. Throughout it, as in a dream, we find ourselves in a mysterious, fabulous country of rivers wreathed in mists, drab dry villages, parched plains, and ghost-haunted castles. Nothing is what it seems. The geography of this country is of no map; it shifts and changes as do the ghosts in the castle. And there is no peace. A terrible unease possesses the land. Muffled gunfire troubles the air. At any moment we might expect the ground to open beneath our feet and the mountains to spout fire. Such daimios as the Lords Shibata and Nobunaga —"that hideous beast"—are unknown powers, seldom seen but always about us in the presence of their myrmidons— those spitting samurai, brigands and pirates, who pillage land and sea, rape women and sack villages.

At the centre (or is it the periphery?) of this nightmarish world rides a sanctuary of apparent calm. In one of a cluster of hovels live two potters, Genjuro and Tobei. Though their existence is hard and poverty-stricken, they are not without the comforts of family life. Genjuro adores his perfect wife Miyagi and his child; Tobei has arrived at a working relationship with his less perfect Ohama. This stability is reassured by their few possessions, the rice and flour which sustain them and the wheel and clay which provide them with a pittance

Ugetsu Monogatari, directed by Kenji Mizoguchi, 1953 (*Janus*)

of gold. Yet this stability, as we soon realise, is illusory, for the natural order on which it is based has been disturbed. Miyagi, the perfect wife, sees clearly how war has changed the spirit of man by arousing in him a desire for a different life; and she pleads with her husband to accept his lot and try to find happiness through his work. In effect, Miyagi here states the theme of the film: that human wishes are illusory and inevitably lead to disaster. As the story demonstrates, all the characters save for her yearn for what they naturally should not have, and all of them achieve their ambitions at far too heavy a cost.

Marauders descend upon the hovels and with relish begin to sack them. And so the potters and their families take flight, leaving behind of necessity a kiln of baking pots. Nothing is certain: the possessions which gave them confidence are as insecure as the spirit of man, and as easily broken. In a sequence of great beauty, Mizoguchi shows us the flight of the refugees from the ruined village. As always, his effects are simple and original: a static long shot of villagers streaming from right to left through high reeds gives way to a diagonal tracking shot of their squatting in a declivity—a transition which may sound obvious, but which only a master director could bring off as breathtakingly as it is done here. The satisfied marauders leave the village, and the potters creep back: to their delight, they find their kiln undamaged.

This episode is best described as an exposition; for by establishing the general insecurity, the disorder of nature within and without the soul, it does no more than foreshadow the plot, which now begins. The potters, frightened by the thought that the kiln might all too easily have been destroyed, determine to market their wares as soon as possible. And yet, with barbarians lurking behind every bush and tree, how are they to make their way to the city? Discovering a small pirogue, they decide to travel by water, and so push out onto the lake. The journey is eery; the lake is so dark, misty and forbidding that the traveler might take it for Lethe, the river of death. Not unexpectedly, when a prow glides up through the mist, the potters assume it to be a phantom ship and its

sole slumped passenger to be a ghost. This irony is a typical
misunderstanding in a film where nothing is what it seems.
For the passenger in fact is all too human and has been
mortally wounded by pirates; and, before their boats swing
apart, he woefully warns the potters of the dangers of the
lake. Genjuro rightly sees this omen as evil. He lands his
wife and child on the bank and then proceeds with Tobei and
Ohama to the market. What he does not realize is that the
omen is a warning against the separation of families and not
against the threat of pirates.

As in a Jacobean play, the action now splits into plot and
subplot, in each of which the two potters take separate parts
as protagonists. Both plots are variations on the main theme
and parallel each other in numerous ways. Broadly speaking,
they both describe how a man may be seduced by an ideal of
perfection, how he cheats to realise it, and how, as he discovers
the falsity of the ideal, he must pay a heavy price for having
been both ambitious and dishonest. In the subplot, for instance,
war has aroused in Tobei an obsessive desire to become a
samurai, to follow the formal life of a warrior. In the city
he is able to achieve this, for by the sale of pots he makes
sufficient gold to buy himself a suit of samurai armour. Luck
is with him: by chance he is the only witness to the decapita-
tion of a war-lord. Stealing the dead man's head, and somewhat
pusillanimously stabbing the executioner in the back, Tobei
then trots off to a rival war-lord and offers him the severed
head. This is a witty move. Tobei is at once proclaimed a
hero and appointed captain to a troop. Thus, a trifle shabbily
perhaps, his ambition is realised. The price he has to pay
for this is that his deserted wife is left a prey to other samurai.
Staggering across a plain she is accosted by four oafs who
drag her into a conveniently empty palace and rape her.

Mizoguchi shows here by a visual parallel—the scene in
which gold is scattered over the raped Ohama mimes the
scene in which Tobei is paid for his service—how both
husband and wife have been degraded by the husband's ambition. And there are other, more abstract parallels. Throughout
Ugetsu the effects of war and money are shown as similar

and disastrous, though Mizoguchi never explains in what way this is so. Later, in a moment of great anguish, Ohama, who has become a prostitute, meets Tobei accidentally in a geisha house and asks him to buy her service. By the prows of two beached pirogues they act out a reconciliation: Tobei admits, a trifle implausibly I think, his folly and the two of them return to their hovel, hoping as Ohama says that "our sufferings were not in vain."

This robust subplot is woven into the more delicate texture of the main plot, which, superficially, has quite a different story. While selling his wares in the market-place, Genjuro is approached by two women. One is a beauty, the crane-like Lady Wakasa, the other a senile nurse-attendant, who asks Genjuro to deliver a large number of his goods to the Wakasa residence. Genjuro, attracted by the Lady, willingly agrees. At her magnificent castle, the hopelessness of their desires becomes plain: as much as he wishes to possess the perfection of the lady, she wishes to learn the secrets of his art. Both these desires are impossible and are, in a sense, intimations of danger. Yet Genjuro is so enchanted by the world he has entered that he does not realise how sinister it is. This atmosphere of doom is skillfully built up by Mizoguchi as the Lady Wakasa sings to the potter:

> *The best of silks, of choicest hue*
> *May change and fade away,*
> *As would my life, Beloved One,*
> *If thou shouldst prove untrue. . . .*

As she sings the camera pans rapidly around the room, and from a dark samurai mask comes a low coarse laugh. The nurse hastily explains away this strange noise by telling Genjuro that it is made by the Lady's dead father, who is showing, in a fashion, his approval of her lover. Whereupon the Lady asks Genjuro to marry her; and he, without admitting that he is married already, happily concurs.

The love scenes that follow are as stylised as a Hokusai print. First: a rock-pool and the lovers slide towards each other through curlicues of steam. Then: a lawn, and far away from us on a white silk carpet the lovers chase each other, their stiff robes twirling about them. A close-up of their restless faces against the sky is followed by another long shot of the lawn and the lovers embracing. Yet, while this frolic is going on, Genjuro is still paying for his idyll. His wife, returning home from the lake, is laid upon by brigands and murdered for the sake of a few crusts of bread. And disillusionment is at hand: a priest tells him that since Lady Wakasa is a ghost, he will be dragged through the gates of the dead if he does not give her up. A confrontation takes place. The nurse-attendant admits that the Lady is not real, as none of them are. She is the ghost of a girl who died young and who has returned to the world to find the love she was denied. Genjuro, having suppressed a pang of pity, takes up a sword and in a strange and almost balletic sequence drives the ghosts out of the castle. In doing this, he accidentally falls and knocks himself out. On returning to consciousness, he finds the castle has become a charred ruin, and has been so for years. Apparently he has already entered the world of the dead. "The best of silks fade away," sings a remembered voice. Perfection is unattainable and all is a dream.

So Genjuro returns at dusk to his family and asks for a forgiveness which is freely given. Yet he still lives in illusion. The next morning he is told by neighbors that his wife is dead and that it must have been a ghost who welcomed him back. The two plots now unite again, as Genjuro and Tobei return sadly to work. All is not lost, however, for one of the main points of the film is that man must learn how illusion is a part of reality. As he works at his pots, Genjuro hears the voice of his dead wife, telling him that she will always be with him, that her memory will be his inspiration. And so, with these words, piety has been restored and the theme has fulfilled itself. As Genjuro's child lays flowers on its mother's grave, Mizoguchi cranes up his camera so that we see, in a distant field, two men tilling the soil. With this, as it were, inverted cadence, the master brings his film to a close.

In the West we are inclined to be defensive about the

supranatural. Although from the spate of films dealing with vampires and outer space it is clear that we have an appetite for it, no one finds this appetite reputable. Our characteristic response to works of this kind is ambivalent: as much as we may enjoy them and call ourselves addicts, we still have feelings of mild guilt and speak about them as if we were victims of some fashionable vice. For the same reason, the intention of the people who make these films is as ambivalent as our response; their treatment of the supranatural tends to be both spoofing and ponderous. The genre, in fact, is the most difficult in the business, and it is hard to think of any top-line director in the West (Franju perhaps excepted) who would think of risking his reputation by trying to work within it. If by chance one of them were tempted to do so, I very much doubt whether he would treat his subject with anything like Mizoguchi's seriousness.

Why is this? It is not as though we were short of material. In English literature alone, the legends of Malory, or *The Lord of the Rings*, or *Sir Gawayne and the Grene Knight*, to give a few examples, all have latent cinematic ideas. Why are producers inhibited in taking them up as projects? The reason, I think—and this is why they are so awkward in their handling of the genre—has to do with the way they view reality. "Reality, as conceived of by us, is whatever is external and hard, gross, unpleasant," wrote Lionel Trilling regretfully in *The Liberal Imagination*. Though this censure may no longer be true of the best novels being written now, this limited conception of reality still seems omnipresent in the cinema and conditions the structure of most films. Consider, for instance, the techniques employed to create character. For the most part, such techniques are simple, schematic, and in no way take into account the inner world of the individual. And yet, until we understand this inner world, the actions of human beings are barely comprehensible. For the phantasies, of which this inner world consists, are the primary content of unconscious mental processes and condition the behaviour of even the most "normal" person.

This is probably what Ibsen meant when he wrote: "Life

is a contest between the phantoms of the mind"—a remark which, I think, goes a long way towards explaining why Ibsen's realism has so much substance, and why the tensions between his characters have such depth. Against this richness, the realism of many so-called realistic films appears thin, for the very reason that these films do not take seriously enough into account the phantoms of the mind. Since phantasy is an essential part of the total world, we crave, however vicariously, to make up for its loss. And so, if we cannot have a full-blooded realism, we can at least supplement our normal fare with a relish of vampires and flying saucers. Mizoguchi, however, does not appear to be inhibited by such an impoverished realism. The conventions he uses—of the fable—allow him to create both a world of actuality, in which such urgent problems as the fear of war and the lack of money are made vivid and true, and a world in which the phantoms of the mind are given full play. In doing so, he reminds us indeed that these two worlds are interdependent.

Ugetsu, as I have said, is an essay on the uncanny: that is, it preserves a surface of ordinary everyday happenings whilst at the same time creating a childhood world of animistic fears, so that the predicaments of the characters are plausible both in naturalistic terms and in terms of the rich, more obscure movements of the mind. This dualism is both established and sustained by the conservatism of Miyagi. For when she asks her husband to accept his lot and to disregard the itch of ambition, she does in effect voice the theme on which the conventions of the film are based. Life is for her, as for Edmund Burke, a covenant between the dead, the living and the unborn; our duty therefore is not to rebel against the parental images, but to accept tradition and honour the dead.

Within the context of this theme the convention of the ghosts becomes plausible, for they represent the manner in which the past, with all its phantom memories, desires and histories, plays a vital part in the present and gives it meaning. Whether or not we find this conservatism repugnant, we must admit that it allows Mizoguchi the chance to realise vividly a number of humanist truths about the nature of inspiration, the interplay of motive and ideal, and the importance of piety ("a reverence for life"). Significantly, one of the finest of humanist films, Ichikawa's *The Burmese Harp*, is a fable with a theme identical to this. The paradox may well be that liberal humanism can only work under these conservative conditions.

Not surprisingly, the realism of *Ugetsu* is close to the realism of Greek drama. And this is not fortuitous. In his film Mizoguchi depends on the Noh theatre, both for his type of plot and for the style in which he composes his images. And the Noh theatre, as Ezra Pound pointed out, has similarities with both the Greek and the Shakespearian drama; for all of them are developments of the miracle play. *Ugetsu* is Shakespearian in the function of its images (Mizoguchi uses the symbol of war in much the same way as Shakespeare uses the symbol of storm), and in its double plot; and Grecian in that its ghosts play the same part as do the gods in Greek mythology, and that its unity is built up around a single moral conviction. Moreover, I believe that Mizoguchi would have agreed with Aristotle that a work of art should imitate the movements of the mind and not an ordering of facts; for it is in this sense, above all, that his realism is classical.

Umberto D.

Vernon Young, "Umberto D.: Vittorio De Sica's 'Super'-naturalism"

○○

With the virtual absence of the financing that makes possible studio productions, the postwar film-makers in Italy turned to the streets to create an intensified realism out of the natural settings of urban life. The illusion of reality that is conveyed by the documentary film finds its nearest approximation in the work of Roberto Rossellini, Vittorio De Sica and others in feature films such as *Open City*, *Shoeshine Boy*, and *Bicycle Thief*.

Most discussions of De Sica's films, particularly of *Bicycle Thief*, praise simply his humanity and observe his fidelity to the naturalistic ideals of the neorealist cinema. Other than admissions that he is able to get remarkable results from nonprofessional actors, usually little is said about his art. De Sica's is an art that appears artless. His beguiling simplicity which tenaciously resists explanation is difficult to confront in crticism. Yet Vernon Young gets behind the veil of artistic innocence and analyzes De Sica's purposeful but unobtrusive combinations of sound and images that build into motifs and eloquent rhythms. The thrust of his argument is that in *Umberto D.* De Sica displays a deft, calculated art and his evidence is unsettling to anyone determined to adhere to stock notions of neorealism.

———◆———

SOCIOLOGICAL FILM CRITICISM IS forever mistaken because it is forever misled—on humanitarian principles or by self-righteous-ness or from color-blindness—into confusing ends with means. Asserting that importance lies in subject matter, it fails to recognize that no subject is important until awakened by art; assuming (to give its charity the benefit of the doubt) that love is greater than art, it fails to acknowledge that the art *is* the love. Vittorio De Sica's new film, *Umberto D.* (new here—it was released four years ago) provides a characteristic opportunity for confused judgment. To praise the film for its human appeal is as needless and as miserly as to praise a beautiful woman for her conspicuous virtue.

Umberto Domenico Ferrari or Umberto D., as he prefers to call himself, is a retired civil-service clerk living on an inadequate pension and, as the film opens, facing eviction from a furnished room which, ghastly as it may be, is the only place he can call home. His sole companion is a mongrel dog, Flick. To maintain their precious, if contracting, haven (the landlady has taken to sub-renting his room to transient lovers while he is out), the old man joins other aged pensioners in a demonstration (unsuccessful) for higher allotments, sells his gold watch and his dictionary, tries to beg but is unable to support the shameful resolution, engages in frustrated transactions for boarding the dog or giving it away, and finally attempts suicide by standing in front of an oncoming train with the dog in his arms. Flick, in panic, escapes, and Umberto D., trying to recapture him, saves himself. The film closes on the old man trying to regain the dog's trust in a deserted park, with an occasional train speeding by.

So rehearsed, the film may easily be construed as an artless and unbuttered slice of life, a testimony of "naturalism": ostensibly a method of expressing reality without inhibition, without overtones and as far as possible without style. Nothing could be further from the case. Like *Shoeshine* or *Bicycle Thief*, and with justification even more subtle, De Sica's *Umberto D.*—a masterpiece of compassion which he has dedicated to his father—might be termed *super*naturalism if this compound had not been preempted for another kind of experience entirely. The fidelity of De Sica's attention to the plight of the man Umberto, realistic in its living details, is

Umberto D., directed by Vittorio De Sica, 1952 (*Edward Harrison*)

enriched by a host of modulations working under and through the story line, so delicately registered as to be imperceptible save to that second awareness evoked from most spectators without their being able to define it. Cinematically created, these modulations are not arresting, since they accumulate from thematic relationships in the scenario. De Sica's use of the camera is clear-eyed, rather than ingenuous. As in his other naturalist films, his cinematographer (in this case G. R. Aldo, the same who was bewitched, with De Sica, into assisting David Selznick's Florentine hoax, *Indiscretion of an American Wife*) is not called upon to exhibit striking angles or movement; De Sica's compositions rarely startle one by their ingenuity. *What* he forcuses on at a given point is more significant than the *way* he focuses. The way is never neglected, it simply isn't exploited; for it is to De Sica's purpose to move with un-elliptical life as closely as he dares without vitiating motion-picture technique altogether. To subordinate the essentially cinematic as he does is itself a technique of ineffable skill; and to efface his signature as a director from the style of a film argues a modest purity of aim.

In *Bicycle Thief*, De Sica developed the film's rhythm by a *pas de deux* of man and boy in their scouting expedition through the city, the boy nervously anxious to keep in time with his father's mood and intention. The adjustments of temper and of tempo, the resolution, the haste, anger and embarrassment, the flanking movements, the frustrations and periodic losses of direction: these constituted a form of situational ballet which gave the film its lyricism. There is no such springy movement in *Umberto D.;* the quality of its forms is established otherwise.

The possessive theme is time; its epiphanies are sounded in a scale of variations. Before even the credits have appeared on the screen, the bells of early Mass ring out as the pensioners gather in the street. After they have been dispersed by the carabinieri, Umberto D. offers his watch for sale to an acquaintance, murmuring his own pride in its workmanship with an imitative "tick-tock, tick-tock." As this scene is

succeeded by one at a restaurant, where he resumes his attempt to sell the watch, the background noises of dishes and
spoons seem to take up the clicking pulsations of time.
Thereafter a tap dripping, footsteps, voices saying goodnight
below Umberto's window, his alarm clock, the musical score
itself and bells of one kind or another maintain this rhythm
and reminder of the irrevocable. When, at the deepest moment
of his despair, after he has failed to beg or borrow, Umberto
D. returns to his room—already breached and dismantled for
the landlady's new domestic arrangements—the clock ticks
more loudly; it is virtually the only sound we hear besides
the old man's breathing. . . . Intent now on self-destruction,
he inquires first about boarding the dog. The haggling of the
couple with whom he tries to deal, conducted in that ful-
minating rhythm of the back-street Roman, is intercut with a
ferociously barking mastiff—the voice of all the world that
opposes Umberto's need. He turns away, with Flick still
unprovided for, and his retreat is mocked by a housewife who
has flipped a carpet over her windowsill, which she then
beats at a measured, doom-like pace. Time piles up. A beggar
chants plaintively, "Signora! I have two children. . . . Signor!
I have two children." As a well-dressed woman ignores his
appeal, he repeats the plaint like a warning, between savagely
clamped teeth, "SIGNORA! I HAVE TWO CHILDREN!" . . . Streetcar
and railroad-crossing bells rattle and jangle. Umberto D. makes
his futile attempt at self-extinction and is left with his problem
as the train catapults by.

Sound, which is time, is always extraneous to Umberto D.
It impinges; it does not involve him. The clatter of social life
is beyond the fringes of his consciousness; he hears it but it
isn't speaking to him. Maria, the landlady's adolescent servant-
girl from the country, is ever ready to respond as far as her
own preoccupation will allow, but she is pregnant (by whom
she is not sure) and fearful that the landlady will find out
and discharge her. With eyes misleadingly alive, she seems
forever on the verge of communication with the old pensioner,
only to escape into her private world of ignorance and fright.

And Umberto D., on his side, is as incapable of saying the words that would unite them in their misery. (Beyond an ineffectual reprimand to one of Maria's "seducers," he operates within the circumference of his own pain.) As he lies in his bed, sweating, anxious, sick and alone, the landlady, her friends and her preposterous suitor sing pompous operatic choruses in the sitting-room. Music, badinage, whispers and coarse laughter announce, without reassurance, the life of others.

Visually the narration is equally cogent, taking in without appearing to emphasize the incongruities, the excrescences, the implacabilities of life at a level of civilization where the meretricious and the ugly are accepted or suffered, where in fact the vitality of a people cut off, by a superimposed culture, from its native modes, expresses itself by choice through a corrupt aesthetic. At the house of Umberto D.'s landlady the camera, with flat-lighted neutrality, exposes the importunate vulgarity of middle-class Italian decor: the mock-Imperial wallpaper, the cut-glass, the lambrequins like shrouds, the fringed table-scarves and (most horrible item of all!) a lamp in the form of a Grecian nymph, with naked light-bulbs sprouting from it. (The stilted terrors of the family photograph album.) There are some remarkable instances in this film of De Sica's sparing use of a background object as *direct* symbol. The old man's coat hanging lifelessly on a gigantic stand which looks like a monstrous underwater growth is analogous to the social situation in which man is an unbraced, drowning remnant in the ruins of a cheaply florid dream of empire—and when Umberto D. returns to his room the last time, a shot of the hallway gives prominence to a stuffed falcon among the bric-a-brac. The most impressive *vis-à-vis* is depicted in the painful scene of Umberto D.'s tentative rehearsal of begging (during which he tries using Flick to cover him until the humiliation of being encountered by someone he knows forces him to the pretense of teaching the dog a new trick). An overpowering classical column, cracked at the base, is the backdrop for this joyless act.

De Sica's balance between the lifelike and the cinematic is tenuous; if he had actors less responsive to the naked untheatricality he is commonly after, his muted formalism might suffer from the risks he takes. But he can afford to dwell at length on the faces and motions of Umberto D. and Maria precisely because Carlo Battisti and Maria Pia Casilio are sentiently, gravely, inside life. (Neither is a "professional." Where, but in Italy, can one find so much unconscious histrionic talent?!). Few directors could manage, without losing their hold on the continuity, the beautiful cadence in this film where the coming of day is enacted through the actions of Maria as she gets out of bed. The scene is wordless, leisured and almost unbearably intimate. There is little in it that could not be performed on a stage, but in its brief duration and its breathing nearness, in the particular placing of the camera for each view of the pregnant girl struggling to experience joy which gives way to fear and then to a daydream indifference, it is a marvel of movie timing and perspective.

Maria, while subordinate to Umberto D., is by an inspired implication complementary. Neglected youth and discarded old age. The girl and her involuntary burden-to-be; the man and his voluntarily assumed burden, Flick: girl and man subservient to the loud concerns of society, exemplified by the middle-aged landlady who is handsome in a brassy way, venal, pseudo-respectable and heartless—living in a world of opera, ormolu and broken-down technology. In *Shoeshine* the horse was a symbol, if you like, of the unattainable, a dream of power and freedom. The bicycle in *Bicycle Thief* was an occupational necessity which became a projection of the man's self-respect. Flick, neither ideal nor economic necessity, may be felt as representing the last thing a man will surrender: it is the love in the man, Umberto.

When De Sica and Cesare Zavattini (who wrote the story from which, with De Sica, the screenplay was shaped) avoided the easier termination, of suicide accomplished, by ending the film on an inconclusive (which is not to say indecisive) note— Umberto D. and the dog gamboling under the cedars—we can be sure they were saying very clearly: Life sometimes leaves you nothing but love, and in your deprivation and anguish you cannot bear to support even such a burden. But this is your only identity and until the day you die you must not put aside the little humanity left to you. . . . Umberto D. tries to entrust the dog to another; he tries to give it away; he tries to destroy it. In the end he is still, as our idiom says, "stuck with it."

Birth quickens in the unclaimed Maria; the venal landlady marries a fool; Umberto is homeless but keeps his pet. De Sica's films in the naturalist vein have been accusations of the fascist aftermath; they take their place with the most profound cinematic achievements by sounding vibrations in a dimension larger than the political. . . . When Umberto D. twirls down the path under the trees with the jumping dog, we recall not only the other De Sica "conclusions"—Pasquale, in *Shoeshine*, facing a lifetime of expiation; the frustrated "bicycle thief" and his son renewing the life-circuit by joining hands; the poor, of *Miracle in Milan*, flying away on their brooms to an unlikely heaven—but also perhaps Baptiste, in *Les Enfants du Paradis*, striving against the tide of revellers cutting him off from Truth, the woodchopper in *Rashomon*, undaunted by fearful disclosures of moral ambiguity, deciding to adopt the abandoned baby—and Chaplin disappearing into a California horizon (the *first* time!).

The Virgin Spring

William S. Pechter, "The Ballad and the Source"

ooooooooooooooooooooooooooooooooooooooooooooooo

Ingmar Bergman's *The Virgin Spring* (1959) is a cinematic version of a folk ballad. Film-makers have learned about adapting a play or novel from previous film-makers, from the very tradition of adaptation in movies; such opportunity for profiting from the experience of others is not to be enjoyed if one chooses a ballad as the source of a film. To do so is especially challenging, not only because one is left largely to his individual talent but also—and more significantly—because the ballad, the briefest kind of narrative, is thin in its physicality and, furthermore, is mysteriously remote from the present. The imagination must play with what few words there are. These factors do not bode well for the possibility of transforming ballad material into a medium as immediate and as immersed in physical reality as film. In "The Ballad and the Source" William S. Pechter offers general commentary on *The Virgin Spring* with particular concentration on the differences between the ballad and Bergman's film. His evaluative insights into the relative success of Bergman and the implications of the differences between the ballad and the film are balanced and illuminating.

———◆———

IN A SENSE, it hardly matters what one says about *The Virgin Spring*, or about Bergman. No matter; the latest Bergman is upon us, and, predictably, the college kids will once again be queuing up, along with all those other species of intellectual, academic and nonacademic, full and part-time, that surface at the art theaters for the ritual Saturday night. The time is now; Bergmania rules the waves; even the French New Wave is somewhat overwhelmed by its momentum. Not to know the work of Ingmar Bergman is to be ignorant of much that is most impressive in the contemporary film; yet to know only Bergman is to be, in another way, equally ignorant. And too many people who watch other and better films still *see* only Bergman's.

Nevertheless, *The Virgin Spring* should be seen. It, and, indeed, all of Bergman's work has earned for itself a place in the history of all that is serious and ambitious, seriously ambitious, in the cinema. Compared to Bergman, men far more talented—Renoir, for example—are made to look merely frivolous: a man talking of God, and a man staging a cancan. And stamped upon this seriousness is always the mark of Bergman's own, unmistakable preoccupations. A young girl, riding through the medieval forest on her way to Mass with a gift for the Holy Virgin, is brutally assaulted and slain by three vicious herdsmen; the girl's father avenges her by taking the three murderers' lives, then prays to God for forgiveness of his act, and vows to build a church; and, on the spot where the girl was slain, a spring gushes forth from the earth: a miracle. From whom else but Bergman could such a film derive? Dreyer, perhaps; but the difference is in the details, such as Bergman's ubiquitous, earthy servant types, in this case a beggar, with their characteristic philosophical reflections: ". . . human beings. They tremble and worry like a leaf in the storm—because they know, and because they don't know." All is mystery, all is depth.

The Virgin Spring opens abruptly on a startling image. A dark, slatternly girl is blowing on a smouldering hearth; suddenly, the smoking embers burst into flame. No premonitory swooping gulls, creaking coaches, or slanting coffins; we open *in medias res*, starkly, mundanely in the thick of things. Gone is the complex visual texture that has marked

The Virgin Spring, directed by Ingmar Bergman, 1959 (*The Museum of Modern Art/Film Stills Archive*)

Bergman's recent work; instead, all is now deliberate simplicity. The family figures move with apparent artlessness about their plain, rough rooms; they sit at the table in a row, resembling, in their lack of perspective and adornment, some primitive Last Supper. As Vernon Young has noted [*Film Quarterly,* Summer, 1960], it is camera placement rather than camera movement which characterizes Bergman's style. It is this fact which enables Arthur Knight to write with awe of one of Bergman's films that "there are long dialogue sequences daringly played from a single camera position." It is only in the uncompromising context of a Bergman film that such deliberate stasis could be described as "daring." In *The Virgin Spring*, it is only by a difficult effort that one realizes there is a camera there at all.

All this is to the good, for simplicity is prerequisite to the success of such a film. The source of *The Virgin Spring* is a folk ballad of seventy-two brief lines of concentrated power and beauty. In a preface to her published screenplay for the film, Ulla Isaksson has described some of the difficulties involved in translating the ballad into a film.

"Insofar as possible, the film tries to retain the original story of the song, its simultaneously cruel and beautiful visual nature, the relentless insight into human life, and the Christian message. But in print the song takes only three pages and leaves out every kind of personal characterization and psychological motivation. The film must, in quite another way, make this story of young Karin and her parents realistic, comprehensible, coherent, convincing in psychology and milieu. However, it did not seem possible to reproduce with entire realism the norms and attitudes of such a distant time, and expect modern men to understand them. The crucial task was to find as much common ground as possible and to build the film on that, so that the song might be both preserved and communicated. Certain additions to the story were therefore essential."

Some of what has been added to the original ballad, particularly in the way of nuance and emphasis, is extraordinarily fine: as the mournful cry of the cuckoo when the herdsmen first catch sight of the girl in the forest, and the mother's slight, involuntary move backwards when one of the murderers, having shown her the dead girl's garment in an effort to sell it, moves forward to touch it; the mother's senseless attempt to prevent from being touched what has already been defiled provides what is perhaps the truest dramatic movement in the film. One can also admire the sophistication with which Bergman treats the clash of paganism and Christianity, a theme which he has introduced into the film. In the terms of the film, both beliefs are granted equal reality, and their conflict is made not one between truth and superstition but rather between an equally potent good and evil, in which Odin's curses have all the efficacy of God's miracles.

And yet all the film's intelligence and sophistication seems finally less shatteringly profound than the irreducible simplicity of the ballad. In the film, the miracle occurs only after the father, having revenged himself, begs God's forgiveness and vows to build a church; in the ballad, the spring appears immediately upon the girl's death; all else is subsequent. Contained in this rearrangement of the event is all the difference between a world conceived in terms of total faith, and one of subtle meanings and symbolic justices; in short, all the difference in the world.

In expanding his source, Bergman has lost the crystalline simplicity of the ballad, and not gained anything to equal it. In Bergman's film, the miracle comes as a poetic apotheosis, an emblem of goodness; in the ballad, it is simply *there*, God working full time, without glosses for his audience, his inscrutable works to perform.

But, for Bergman, a world without explanations is finally unendurable, however much he may flagellate his rationalism with the lash of faith. Bergman has written, "To me, religious problems are continuously alive. I never cease to concern myself with them; it goes on every hour of every day. Yet this does not take place on the emotional level, but on an intellectual one. Religious emotion, religious sentimentality is something I got rid of long ago. . . ." In *The Virgin Spring*, against every natural inclination of his temperament, Bergman has attempted to give us a miracle play, pushing himself deliberately onward into an alien religiosity. But it is really no less credible that a real spring should miraculously burst forth from the real ground than that such should happen in a film of Bergman's. If there is a lesson in *The Virgin Spring*, it is that the one thing which sophistication cannot will is true simplicity.

Viridiana

Andrew Sarris, "The Devil and the Nun: Viridiana"

○○

With over twenty-five films in forty years, Luis Bunuel
has come to be regarded as the one-man Spanish film industry. In the twenties he collaborated with Salvador Dali
on the surrealist film *Un Chien Andalou (An Andalusian
Dog)*, and was recognized as a committed member of the
surrealist movement in art. In retrospect, however, it is
clear that Bunuel is inherently surrealistic in the direction of
his art and intensely Spanish in his temperament and experience. An early training by Jesuits and a childhood in
a devout Catholic family seeded his career of steadfast
rebellion not only against the religious but also against the
secular order of society. Long after the surrealist movement
waned, Bunuel's deepest visions remained surrealistic—an
irrational and sometimes demented mix of spirituality and
animality. Bizarre dovetailing of mystical and sexual experience in a violent and brutal world leads to numerous
portrayals of a depraved humanity. Bunuel has said that the
novice in *Viridiana* gives proof of her humanity. Andrew
Sarris finds that with this film "For the first time in his
career, Bunuel ends his action in an existential enclosure in
which hell, in Sartre's phrase, is other people." Subsequent
to his analysis of *Viridiana*, in making observations about
Bunuel's career and fortunes, Mr. Sarris explores the thematic
and philosophical implications of Bunuel's characteristic use
of the camera: "His camera has always viewed his char-

acters from a middle distance, too close for cosmic groupings and too far away for self-identification."

———————◆———————

WHEN LUIS BUNUEL'S *Viridiana* finally materialized in the dreary twilight of the 1961 Cannes Film Festival, many of those present were surprised to discover not merely a great film but, indeed, a really good movie. Some of the more modern critics still rotating around the Resnais-Antonioni axis were a bit suspicious of Bunuel's archaic technique, and the Festival Jury hedged its bets by jointly honouring Bunuel's rousing entertainment in *Viridiana* and Henri Colpi's tedious coupling of amnesia and ambiguity in *Une Aussi Longue Absence*. For once, the international box-office barometer has more accurately recorded the relative merits of the two works. Of course, every film is liked and disliked both for right and wrong reasons, and *Viridiana* is particularly susceptible to partisan critiques. Bunuel's personal triumph has been used to chastise everything from *Marienbad* to the Vatican, with the predictable counterreactions. However, when one attempts to place Bunuel in apposition or opposition to other directors, his remarkable isolation becomes apparent. On the most obvious level of identification, he is the only great Spanish-language director, and his career is one of the most bizarre in film history.

For a long time before *Viridiana*, Bunuel had been treated as a victim of the world's repressions and inhibitions, variously represented by French censorship, Spanish fascism, Hollywood commercialism and Mexican mediocrity. The Bunuel cult, at least in the Anglo-Saxon countries, had become an exercise less in cinema than in metacinema, that is, the study of cinema which might have or should have evolved under the proper social conditions. This cult assumed the mannerisms of privileged scholarship by exploiting the director's underground reputation as the creator of *Un Chien Andalou* (1928) and *L'Age d'Or* (1930), banned works carrying the cultural prestige of surrealism but generally unavailable to the lay public. Bunuel himself was gradually fossilized in the swamp

Viridiana, directed by Luis Bunuel, 1961 *(Kingsley International)*

of his legend by the reluctance of his defenders to confront the uneven quality of his career as a whole. Consequently, many of us at Cannes had to readjust to a new conception of Bunuel as a master instead of a martyr. Realizing that he had become a creature of festivals and film societies, and that his efforts held no interest for the distributors with the big cigars, most of us were quite willing to go along with the Bunuel claque in awarding him another sympathy prize, as for *The Young One*. Then, almost miraculously, the old surrealist crossed everyone up with a resounding commercial success.

Viridiana has a plot which is almost too lurid to synopsize even in these enlightened times. The heroine is summoned from a convent by her uncle, Don Jaime, an old Spanish *hidalgo* living on a neglected estate (Spain?) in obsessive mourning for his dead wife (the Republic?). The novice arrives on the thirtieth anniversary of Don Jaime's marriage. Viridiana's resemblance to the *hidalgo's* wife introduces the theme of substitution so dear to Hitchcock, but Bunuel is less concerned with the illusion of the substitution than with the sexual drives aroused by it. Failing to persuade his niece to marry him, Don Jaime orders a compliant maid to drug her. He carries her upstairs to the accompaniment of *The Messiah*, while Bunuel intensifies the outrageous eroticism of the situation by photographing the choreography of abduction through the prying eyes of the maid's little girl. Almost inexplicably, Don Jaime desists from his attempted rape. The morning after, in progressive stages of desperation, he tells his outraged niece that she has been violated, then denies the violation, outraging her even more with his mendacity, and after watching her departure, hangs himself. Viridiana returns to atone for her guilt, and the second movement of the film begins with the maid's little girl skipping with the rope that has been the instrument of the *hidalgo's* deliverance.

The incestuous texture of the film is maintained with the entrance of the novice's virile cousin, Jorge, a pragmatist of the most ruthless kind. He discards his mistress to pursue Viridiana more efficiently, but willingly seduces the adoring maid in the interim. While Jorge is patching up the estate in slapdash Spanish fashion, Viridiana is pursuing the Franciscan ethic by adopting the most revolting beggars in the area. Bunuel intercuts the Angelus recited by Viridiana and her scabrous flock with detail shots of Jorge's rebuilding. Bunuel's despair for Spain leads him to dismiss reform as a possibility; Jorge is moved by humane feelings to purchase a dog which is chained under a cart and forced to trot along at a horse's pace. No sooner is the "liberal" purchase consummated, than another dog comes trotting by under another cart going in the opposite direction, reversing the pattern of futility on the same Spanish road. The demolition of Viridiana's principles is reserved for the film's remarkable climax.

The beggars' orgy is set up dramatically by the departure of Viridiana, Jorge, the maid and her little girl on business in the town. For the first time the beggars move into the house itself, and assault every sacred feeling of property that any audience could be presumed to possess. Wine and food smear fancy tapestries, antique furniture is smashed, ornate dishes and glasses are broken. But unlike their colleagues in depravity from *La Dolce Vita*, the beggars enjoy themselves, and suddenly with *The Messiah* blaring on the gramophone, the screen reverberates with a hymn to liberation. These vile creatures (and Bunuel leaves no doubt of their vileness, their cruelty, even their mean hypocrisy), these blind, halt, leprous, syphilitic dregs become gloriously human.

When Viridiana and Jorge return, they are assaulted, and Viridiana's slowly vanishing purity is saved only when her cousin bribes one of the beggars to murder the would-be rapist. Deciding that two lives are too high a price to pay for her chastity Viridiana casts her cross and her crown of thorns into the flames, and prepares to surrender to Jorge. The production's government supervisor, who must have been dozing until this point, finally intervened. Viridiana and Jorge must not be left alone in a room after this, he ordered. Bunuel dutifully complied with a *ménage-à-trois* ending in which Jorge, Viridiana and the maid play cards together in the long Spanish evening while the camera recedes on the hellish tableau to the accompaniment of some appropriate American juke box slop.

How Bunuel managed to realize *Viridiana* at all under the supervision of the Spanish censor may never be fully explained. The intangibles of national prestige may have played a part. Also, the myopic vision of the bureaucratic mind may not have fully grasped the almost magical transformation of images into ideas between shooting and screening. It would be naive to think that Bunuel was without guile in this undertaking. The deviousness of his subsequent interviews was worthy of Hitchcock, and there is enough ambiguity in the film itself to confound the most perverse critics. For example, there seems to be some controversy about the fate of the beleaguered heroine. To put it bluntly, is Viridiana, the chaste novice in the film, actually raped by the syphilitic beggar who murders her first attacker? If so, does she then renounce her vows of chastity as the result of a D. H. Lawrence awakening? The argument for this interpretation depends upon the time gap assumed in the editing of the action. The fact that Bunuel compels normally fastidious critics to ponder such lurid questions reflects the dark humour of his conceptions. And it is this dark humour which rescues Bunuel from the absurdities of Ichikawa.

Whether or not Bunuel has circumvented the censor with suggestive elisions, the plot of *Viridiana* gives one pause. The modern cinema, such as it is presumed to be, is supposed to have supplanted plot with mood. Then suddenly, Bunuel bursts in like a resurrected Victorian novelist steeped in violent depravity and unashamedly flourishing the most obvious symbols. The spectacle of a contemporary director cutting away metaphorically from a brutal seduction to a cat pouncing on a mouse jolts the critic who has finally adjusted to the languorous introspection of an Antonioni. Then, too, the flagrant display of eroticism, sadism and fetishism reveals the director's personality with the embarrassing Krafft-Ebing frankness one recalls in the films of Stroheim and Lang. Bunuel may have been more shocking in the past, but never before have his shock effects seemed so much the warp and woof of his philosophy. *Un Chien Andalou* and *L'Age d'Or* have their moments, of course, but audiences are usually cushioned for "avant-garde" cinema where anything goes. *Las Hurdes (Land Without Bread)* and *Los Olvidados* mask details of horror with a socially conscious narration. Even though it is hard to imagine any other director conceiving of a mountain goat falling off a mountain or a legless beggar being rolled down a hill, the spectator can console himself with the thought that this is not the best of all possible worlds, and that the next election or the next revolution may improve conditions. There is no such consolation in *Viridiana*, Bunuel's despairing allegory of the Spanish condition. For the first time in his career, Bunuel ends his action in an existential enclosure in which hell, in Sartre's phrase, is other people.

If every director must be assigned a political station, Bunuel is unmistakably a man of the left. He actively supported the Spanish Republic against Franco's insurgents, and he has been highly critical of the Establishments in Mexico, America and France. A story is told about Bunuel, perhaps apocryphal but still relevant. It seems that Jean Epstein, with whom Bunuel began his career in 1926, once offered his Spanish assistant an opportunity to work with Abel Gance. Bunuel reportedly refused because of what he considered Gance's fascist leanings. Epstein, a Gallic product of apolitical *amitié*, was outraged, but Bunuel stood his ground. Later, Bunuel had a falling out with Salvador Dali over the sacrilegious treatment of *L'Age d'Or*.

The point is that Bunuel has been more intransigent over the years than most of his colleagues, and he has had more than his share of problems, but where one sometimes suspects the temptation of martyrdom in a Stroheim or a Welles, one is struck mainly by Bunuel's tenacity. During the long drought between 1932 and 1947 without any directorial opportunities, he remained on the fringes of the industry in New York and Hollywood. Despite several cancelled projects in Mexico and France since 1947, he has managed to direct twenty films, about half of which are meaningful projections of his ideas and personality. Even in a potboiler like *Susana*, released in 1950, the year of *Los Olvidados*, there are one or two passages which foreshadow *Viridiana*.

There is a danger in attaching an explicitly political moral to Bunuel's career. For a director of the left, Bunuel has evidenced almost no interest in the mechanics of reform or revolution. The superimposed narrations in *Land Without Bread* and *Los Olvidados* suggest amelioration, but the images of the films operate autonomously in terms of a fatalistic Spanish temperament. Even in his Mexican films, there is no trace of the theory of progress through technology, and one could never imagine his making a tractor film behind the Iron Curtain. He has never concerned himself with the mystiques of peasant and worker; nor has he dramatized the injustices of economic exploitation in any detail. As the late André Bazin observed, Bunuel lacks the Manichean tendencies of a propagandist. As cruel as his world may be, its characters are never divided into villains and victims. His obsession with mental and physical deformities generally deprives his plots of any sociological plausibility. Even his handling of the racial issue in *Robinson Crusoe* and *The Young One* is too perverse to serve as a respectably liberal blueprint.

Ado Kyrou's recently published book on Bunuel sheds some new light on the paradoxes of the director's personality. Particularly interesting is some of the director's own film criticism in the late twenties, when, like many critics today, he tried to establish polar relationships. Where Truffaut has invented the Lumière-Delluc and Sagan-Queneau games, Bunuel pioneered in the Keaton-Jannings game. Bunuel preferred Keaton, with all the hostility to German expressionism such a preference implies. He frankly admired the American cinema for its empty-headed grace and rhythm, qualities which he attributed to a Jungian sense of racial instinct. Conversely, he understood his own limitations, and his perceptive humility is still one of his greatest virtues. Bunuel is not and never has been a stylist of the first rank. He would have been lost in the Hollywood shuffle on commissioned projects even though he functioned creditably and efficiently on impossible Mexican assignments. To Bunuel, the cinema is just a vehicle for his ideas. Once these ideas have taken the appropriately plastic form, he shoots very quickly, and any additional values are either incidental or accidental. One of his Mexican producers has reported that Bunuel seems bored by the actual shooting of a film.

Even though one may treat Dali's accusations of atheism as malicious slander to get Bunuel fired from the Museum of Modern Art in New York, Bunuel's films are clearly not intended to win friends and influence people for the Church. As a director who began his career by throwing live priests and dead jackasses out the window, and then compounding his sacrilege by confusing Christ with the Marquis de Sade, he has been almost exclusively identified in terms of these and subsequent impieties. By titillating anticlerical audiences with glimpses of forbidden frankness, Bunuel has found it difficult to convey the full dimensions of his metaphysical rebellion. As soon as he introduces the theme of sexual liberation into the argument, the latent puritanism of the organized left reacts against the degeneration of protest into anarchy. Yet even Bunuel's anarchy is unusually individualistic. Where Vigo is concerned with the disavowal and destruction of social institutions, Bunuel invokes the biological anarchy of nature to reconstruct humanity. Bunuel finds it quite natural for the protagonist of *El* to notice the legs of a pretty girl while he is washing a priest's feet for a Catholic ceremony. Bunuel's defiance of the Church for excluding nature from the altar thus takes on a mystical quality. The pleasure Bunuel takes in the beggars' orgy in *Viridiana* is almost indistinguishable from the religious ecstasy of self-denial one finds in Bresson. It is perhaps appropriate that Bunuel lacks Bresson's sensibility while Bresson lacks Bunuel's force.

The odd circumstances of Bunuel's career preclude an analysis of periods and stylistic progression. More than most other directors of comparable stature, the man is inseparable from his art. His camera has always viewed his characters from a middle distance, too close for cosmic groupings and too far away for self-identification. Normally, this would make his films cold and his point of view detached, but by focusing on the abnormality of life, Bunuel forces his audience to accept man unconditionally. When we look at the monstrous long enough and hard enough, we realize, in Truffaut's phrase, that there are no monsters. The drawback to Bunuel's choice of distance is that he creates horror without terror, and pity without catharsis. In short, he lacks the sense of tragedy his ideas demand.

How a director who seems so disconcertingly obvious can turn out to be so complex is one of the mysteries of the cinema. For example, it seems too symmetrically ironic to synchronize a beggars' orgy with Handel's *Messiah*. However, Bunuel has never been a champion of background music. He simply does not care enough about his score to seek something more subtle. Yet, his indifference to details that cleverer directors have mastered only reminds us that ingenuity is no substitute for genius. Bunuel's blend of the real and the surreal, the grotesque and the erotic, the scabrous and the sublime, never quite fits into any critical theory. The triumph of *Viridiana* leaves us just about where we were before, but henceforth we shall have to allow Bunuel to tailor his own strait-jacket.

Woman in the Dunes

Dennis Giles, "The Tao in Woman in the Dunes"

oooooooooooooooooooooooooooooooooooooooooooooooo

Woman in the Dunes (1964) is a Japanese film that has appealed to Western audiences as a poetic and profoundly moving, though ambiguous, parable of the elemental reality of man's relation to the natural universe. It is the story of a man held captive with a woman at the bottom of a sandpit. Director Hiroshi Teshigahara has said that he sought "to create a microcosm of existence in which there would be two heroes, a man and a woman, isolated from the rest of the world, but into which there would be introduced a third character—the sand." The lyrical, absorbing beauty of the images and sounds of the film and the isolation of the setting from the everyday world leave viewers with the feeling that they have observed a world of phantasmagorial experience, but also with the awareness that they have confronted universal truth. Few, however, have responded to it in terms of a formal, philosophical frame of reference. In "The Tao in *Woman in the Dunes*" Dennis Giles interprets the film as a dramatization of ancient taoist principles: "The film seems to be a taoist Bible explaining how salvation can be achieved."

———◆———

WOMAN IN THE DUNES *(Suna No Onna)*, directed by Hiroshi Teshigahara and adapted by Kobe Abe from his own novel, seems most readily accessible as an expression of an ancient

Chinese philosophy known as taoism. The ancient Chinese symbol of tao consists of   road,   head of a leader,   foot (follower). Tao is the path, the process, the way that a man follows, that all things follow. When a man follows this path he is said to be "in the tao," or in the natural order of things. The tao can be called the path of least resistance. To be in harmony with, not in rebellion against, the fundamental laws of the universe is the first step on the road to tao. Tao, like water, takes the low-ground. Water has become, perhaps, the most popular taoist symbol. The symbolic value of water is also one of the most striking elements in *Woman in the Dunes*. The low-ground to which the tao flows is usually a valley or a pit. Since water flows into these natural depressions, the valley becomes the real as well as the symbolic "dwelling place of the tao." The yielding nature of water is a feminine characteristic, and concave surfaces are also female in nature. Thus the valley, the pit, and the tao are all feminine. The yielding nature of water is called the "Mysterious Female." "It is there within us all the while; draw upon it as you will, it never runs dry." The valleys are nearer to tao than the hills; and in the whole of creation it is the negative, passive, female element alone that has access to tao, which can only be mirrored "in a still pool." Stillness (ho p'ing) and nonaction (wu-wei) are necessary in order to be in the tao. Only by remaining passive, receptive, and yielding can the tao assert itself in the mind.

When we first meet the entomologist guest in *Woman in the Dunes*, he is trudging over dry, un-taolike *hills* of sand. When he rests, a stillness settles over the landscape. Then the entomologist receives a hallucination (or an inspiration) of a woman—the taoist element first asserts itself. As is its character, this tao-female image yields to the harder, more concrete images of the village men, the hairy creatures who are the entomologist's guides and betrayers. It is only natural that they should betray, according to the taoist interpretation, because they are masculine. Being masculine they are not in the tao and are thus false in character. Anything that is non-tao is not true because only the tao is true reality. All

Woman in the Dunes, directed by Hiroshi Teshigahara, 1964
(*Contemporary*)

other phenomena are deceptive. The tao never initiates, but grows out of itself like a child grows in a woman—like the child grows inside of the lonely widow in the picture (Kyoko Kishida). Although the entomologist is masculine, there is still hope for him. The actor, Eiji Okada, possesses a passive kind of handsomeness, the same blandness he possessed as the architect of *Hiroshima Mon Amour*. Within this blandness lies the potential for taoist nonaction to assert itself. Furthermore, the entomologist is an insect collector. Insects follow the tao because they don't think. Their actions are spontaneous; and the essence of the tao is spontaneity. However, the essence of entomology, of all science, is classification and logical order. The tao is not reached by logical thought, but by intuition. Thus the entomologist cannot climb out of the pit by scientifically using the natural slope of the sand. When he finally escapes by scientific means, his flight leads only to a pit of quicksand. When he discovers water it is not by logical thought but by accident. The scientific impulse of measurement and classification has nothing in common with the tao. The first principle of taoism is the relativity of all attributes, that Tokyo is no better than the pit-village. Nothing is in itself long or short. But the entomologist has made science his life, and he is proud of the impending recognition of his discoveries. He does not realize that fame is also relative. When he throws away his insect collection it is a great step forward.

The entomologist's male escorts lead him to the pit, "the dwelling place of the tao." It is inhabited by a woman. Her femininity is a count in her favor. She is already more in the tao than her guest, and she lives in a pit. However, the pit is dry. Water has to be imported by the villagers, until the guest discovers water by accident. Then the pit, indeed, becomes "the valley of the mysterious female," complete with water and a pregnant woman. Significantly, the guest's discovery of water comes at a time when he is indeed "in the tao," when he has abandoned his desire for fame and escape.

The guest first yields by descending into the pit. It does

not matter if he has been tricked; one can reach the tao only by complete acceptance of the unknown. On the way to the tao you can never know what you are getting into until you have reached it. When Okada reaches the bottom of the pit, the woman prepares his dinner, as is her function, then takes off her clothes and goes to sleep. She behaves with disarming naturalness. She later explains that sleeping nude is only yielding to the nature of things. Naked sleep is the path of least resistance—wearing clothes to bed is useless for it will result only in skin rash. However, she does not speak immediately, but lets the guest learn for himself. There is a taoist saying, "Those who speak do not know; those who know do not speak."

In the morning, the guest arises to find the ladder gone. Then he starts his rebellion, which will last through most of the film. He tries to climb the walls of the pit—a futile action. The sand only follows its nature and collapses on top of him. All escape is futile—only nonaction (wu-wei) brings salvation. After hours of futility, the entomologist goes to his hostess; she tells her guest that he is now a permanent fixture of her pit. It is only natural that he should live with her because she is a lonely woman who needs love, and the sand needs to be dug out of the pit. He should follow the path of the least resistance (tao) and accept his new position. She must dig in order to save the village. They need her and she needs them. It is a dynamic balance, the balance of the taoist yin/yang—the dual principle of the universe necessary to maintain the order of the village, which is also the order of the world. For nothing exists independently, but each part is dependent upon the whole made of other parts. Thus we have the taoist images of lions and insects. The lion with all his hairs is at the same time found within a single hair—unity within multiplicity. The lion would not exist without his hairs. The lion hairs would not exist without the lion. The many combine into one as in the unified motion of centipede's legs—a conspicuous image at the start of *Woman in the Dunes*. The widow points out that hers is not the only house in a pit. Everyone must work in order to keep the whole alive. The sand is not particular as to where it falls; neither is she particular, but accepts whatever man falls into her pit. They must shovel out the sand slowly. Hurry is disastrous for there is no goal to be conceived. She will dig out the sand, and it will fall back in. It is a senseless life with no goals, an aimless life. But the tao is aimless and illogical. Digging sand out of a sand pit is the perfect example of *wu-wei*—purposeless nonaction. The woman teaches the man to shovel sand, paraphrasing two more taoist sayings, "Be still while you walk and keep full control over all." "Much talk means much exhaustion."

The guest refuses to accept the path of the least resistance and ties up the woman, a futile action entirely contrary to the tao. "Violence leads nowhere." The entomologist is dehydrating himself, removing himself further and further from that essential moisture (tao) necessary for life. When no sand is dug, no rations arrive. The guest can either do what he is supposed to do, or die of thirst. Finally, the guest yields; he releases the woman and makes love to her, following nature. In the evening they dig sand. Water arrives. The tao has been followed and brings its rewards—more tao—both woman and water.

Still, Okada does not completely accept his new way of life, but clings to his "outside" life as surely as he clings to his flasks, his camera, his watch, his insect collection, and his Western clothing. He still longs to escape and finally does so through cleverness and deceit. Lao-Tzu condemned conventional cleverness as being alien to tao. The guest's escape is a false one. He has only deceived himself. Randomly running over the countryside, he is followed, but *not chased,* by the villagers with their lanterns. The villagers know that they do not need to catch Okada—that he will catch himself. The unlucky entomologist wanders into quicksand. When he is being sucked under, he rapidly reconciles himself to circumstances and calls upon the villagers for help. This is the second time that he has followed the path of the least resistance, but only because he will die if he does not. He has yet to willingly accept his position. Okada has made only the first step on the road to tao.

Once in the pit again, a sense of the futility of all action is realized by the entomologist as he follows the yielding path of nonaction (wu-wei) and reconciles himself to his position. He assumes a more comfortable dress compatible with his environment. He admits that his hope of rescue is a faint one. Finally he throws away his insect collection. His reward is his unintentional discovery of water. His scientific method of climbing out of the pit ended in failure. The tao only reveals itself slowly and cannot be forced; the water slowly and inscrutably rises in the crow pit. The sand itself is a "natural pump" and draws the water to it. The dryness of the sand attracts the moisture—the yin/yang principle at work.

But still the guest-husband is not content. He desires even more water, even more tao. He wants to see the ocean, which leads him to acquiesce to the male villagers' demand of the presentation of a sexual show. But the tao does not exist for anyone or anything outside of itself, but is self-sufficient in itself, much like autonomous art. Realizing that natural processes cannot be hurried, that good (taoist) relationships grow slowly out of their potential, the female rebels against the brutality and unnaturalness of that which is not tao. The tao operates in secret and should remain a mystery. The villagers leave unsatisfied.

Unhappily, Hiroshi Teshigahara himself distances the spectator and kills belief with his brutal presentation of the masked villagers' demand for public sexual intercourse between the woman and her husband-guest. The spectator is totally unprepared for this event and Teshigahara's shock technique does not succeed despite its purposeful exploitation of cinema's hypnotic possibilities. There is no motivation for the actions of the villagers and the whole sequence is extremely distasteful and serves no purpose whatsover, except to gain sympathy for the characters immediately concerned. Even in this it fails; because the entomologist himself becomes merely pathetic or even repulsive. Viewed in long shot, the insect collector is viewed as an insect. Why distance the main character in a movie where identification with this character is necessary for the success of the film? Due largely to this unhappy sequence, it is hard to understand Okada's reasons for his actions at the end of the film. It is not enough to say with Lao-Tzu that the tao has no why. The tao grows out of itself—action must be motivated—content must grow out of the preceding material. Even in the taoist context the treatment of the masked voyeurs has no justification.

As the tao grows out of itself, so the water forms in the hole, so the child forms in the womb of the woman. Yet for the first time, the widow rebels against her fate. When the guest-husband sends for the villagers to take her to the hospital, she does not want to go. The baby is clearly premature, but after the woman leaves, the guest sees a little boy at the top of the pit. The stare of this little boy seems to indicate a healthy birth. The villagers leave the rope ladder for the guest because they know he will not leave. Okada climbs the ladder and walks to the sea. After contemplating the calmness of this great expanse of tao, he willingly returns to the pit. He goes to look at the water-symbol in the hole he has dug. He sees the promise of fertility in the reflection of the child. The tao can only be "mirrored in a still pool." The guest-husband-father now rests content and happy in his private awareness of his oneness with all things, that he is a part of the whole, that the whole of the tao would not be what it is without him. He is finally "in the tao." The film ends.

The tao has no why. It just is. The tao has no self-knowledge like Western gods; it does not know how it creates the universe. This taoist principle would seem to be against the rules of dramatic art because it would seem to imply that characters need no motivation for their actions, that actions happen just because they exist. This is not necessarily true. Because the tao creates itself and grows out of itself, every piece of the taoist film is a growth of the potential of the preceding segment. Thus motivation must grow out of the content of the film itself. Above all, it must not be imposed on the film. All content must naturally develop out of the preceding content. The motivation of the entomologist-guest of *Woman in the Dunes* grows naturally out of this situation. Thus belief is maintained through most of the film. Belief is essential to the success of a film based upon such a peculiar situation; otherwise, the film becomes a parable, and we look at its characters much as the entomologist contemplates an insect. In order for the spectator to accept *Woman in the Dunes*, he must actually be in the pit with the guest—he must *be* the guest. There must be no distancing of the spectator or belief will be destroyed.

With the exception of the aforementioned voyeur sequence, *Woman in the Dunes* fits perfectly in content and form with the principles of taoist art. The film seems to be a taoist Bible explaining how salvation can be achieved.

A Selected Bibliography

A SOURCE FOR 16MM FILMS:

Limbacher, James L., *Feature Films on 16: A Directory of 16mm Sound Films Available for Rental from Major Distributors in the United States*, New York, Continental 16, Inc., 1966

HISTORICAL SURVEYS OF THE CONTEMPORARY PERIOD:

Armes, Roy, *French Cinema Since 1946*, A.S. Barnes, 1966, Vols. I and II

Houston, Penelope, *The Contemporary Cinema*, Penguin, 1963

Knight, Arthur, *The Liveliest Art: A Panoramic History of the Movies*, Macmillan, 1957

Rondi, Gian Luigi, *Italian Cinema Today*, Hill and Wang, 1966

Rotha, Paul, and Griffith, Richard, *The Film Till Now*, Spring Books, 1967

THEORETICAL AND APPLIED CRITICISM:

Agee, James, *Agee on Film*, Vol. I, Grosset and Dunlap, 1967

Arnheim, Rudolph, *The Art of Film*, U. of Calif. Press, 1966

Balazs Bela, *Theory of Film*, Roy, 1953

Bazin, André, *What Is Cinema?*, trans. by Hugh Gray, U. of Calif. Press, 1967

Eisenstein, Sergei, *The Film Sense and Film Form*, Meridian, 1957

Geduld, Harry M., ed., *Film Makers on Film Making*, U. of Indiana Press, 1967

Gessner, Robert, *The Moving Image: A Guide to Cinematic Literacy*, Dutton, 1968

Graham, Peter, ed., *The New Wave: Critical Landmarks*, Secker and Warburg, 1967

Kael, Pauline, *I Lost It at the Movies*, Bantam Books, 1966

———, *Kiss Kiss, Bang Bang*, Atlantic-Little, Brown, 1968

Kracauer, Siegfried, *Theory of Film*, Oxford University Press, 1965

MacCann, Richard, ed., *Film: A Montage of Theories*, Dutton, 1966

Sarris, Andrew, ed., *Interviews with Directors*, Bobbs-Merrill, 1967

Talbot, Daniel, ed., *Film: An Anthology*, U. of Calif. Press, 1966

FURTHER READINGS ABOUT THE DIRECTORS AND THEIR FILMS:

Anderson, Lindsay

Callenbach, Ernest, "*This Sporting Life*," *Film Quarterly*, Summer, 1964
Kauffmann, Stanley, *A World of Film*, Harper and Row, 1966
Milne, T., "*This Sporting Life*," *Sight and Sound*, Summer, 1962

Antonioni, Michelangelo

Aristarco, Guido, "*La Notte* and *L'Avventura*," *Film Culture*, No. 24, Spring, 1962
Cowie, Peter, *Antonioni, Bergman, Resnais*, A.S. Barnes, 1963
Harrison, C., "*Blow-Up*," *Sight and Sound*, Spring, 1967
Houston, Penelope, "*Red Desert*," *Sight and Sound*, Spring, 1965
Leprohon, Pierre, *Michelangelo Antonioni*, Simon and Schuster, 1963
Simon, John, *A View from the Sixties*, Macmillan, 1966
Strick, Philip, *Antonioni*, Motion Publications, 1965
Taylor, J. R., *Cinema Eye, Cinema Ear*, Hill and Wang, 1964

Bergman, Ingmar

Archer, Eugene, "The Rack of Life," *Film Quarterly*, Summer, 1959
Brightman, Carol, "The Word, the Image, and *The Silence*," *Film Quarterly*, Summer, 1964
Donner, Jorn, *The Personal Vision of Ingmar Bergman*, U. of Indiana Press, 1964
McGann, Eleanor, "The Rhetoric of *Wild Strawberries*," *Sight and Sound*, Winter, 1960–61
Sarris, Andrew, "*The Seventh Seal*," *Film Culture*, No. 19, 1959
Sterne, Brigitta, "Archetypal Patterns in Four Screenplays of Ingmar Bergman," *Scandinavian Studies*, XXXVII
———, *Ingmar Bergman*, Twayne, 1968
Wood, Robin, *Ingmar Bergman*, Praeger, 1969

Bresson, Robert

Bazin, André, "*Le Journal d'un Curé de Campagne* and the Stylistics of Robert Bresson," *What is Cinema?*, U. of Calif. Press, 1967
Petrie, Graham, "*Mouchette*," *Film Quarterly*, Fall, 1968
Roud, Richard, "The Early Work of Robert Bresson," *Film Culture*, No. 20, 1959
Sontag, Susan, "Spiritual Style in the Films of Robert Bresson," *Against Interpretation*, Farrar, Straus, and Giroux, 1966

Bunuel, Luis

Durgnat, Raymond, *Luis Bunuel*, U. of Calif. Press, 1968
Garcia-Abrines, Luis, "Rebirth of Bunuel," *Art of the Cinema*, Yale French Studies, No. 17, New Haven, 1956

Hammond, Robert M., "The Literary Style of Luis Bunuel," *Hispania XLVI*, 1963

Kyrou, Ado, *Luis Bunuel*, Simon and Schuster, 1963

Robinson, David, "Thank God I Am Still an Atheist: Luis Bunuel and *Viridiana*," *Sight and Sound*, Summer, 1962

Chaplin, Charles

Chaplin, Charles, *My Autobiography*, Simon and Schuster, 1964

Warshow, Robert, *The Immediate Experience*, Doubleday, 1962

Demy, Jacques

Armes, Roy, *French Cinema Since 1946*, Vol. II, A. S. Barnes, 1966

Film Heritage interviews: Spring, 1965 and Spring, 1967

De Sica, Vittorio

Reisz, Karel, "*Umberto D.*," *Sight and Sound*, Oct.–Dec., 1953

Hollywood Quarterly, Vol. IV, "*Shoeshine*" and "*Bicycle Thief*," 1949–1950

Rondi, Gian Luigi, *Italian Cinema Today*, Hill & Wang, 1966

Dreyer, Carl

Bowser, Eileen, *Carl Dreyer*, Museum of Modern Art, 1964

Neergaard, Ebbe, *Carl Dreyer: A Film Director's Work*, British Film Institute, 1950

Sémolué, Jean, *Dreyer*, Ed. Universitaires, Paris, 1962

Wright, Elsa Gress, "Danish Film: The Living Dreyer," *Kenyon Review*, XXVI, 1964

Fellini, Federico

Boyer, Deena, *The Two Hundred Days of 8½*, Macmillan, 1964

Budgen, Suzanne, *Fellini*, British Film Institute, 1966

Castello, Giulio Cesare, "*Juliet of the Spirits*," *Sight and Sound*, Winter, 1965–66

Fellini's 8½, Etudes Cinématographiques, Nos. 28 and 29

Peri, Enzo, "Federico Fellini: An Interview," *Film Quarterly*, Fall, 1961

Solmi, Angelo, *Fellini*, Humanities Press, 1968

Godard, Jean-Luc

Godard, Jean-Luc, film script of *Masculine-Feminine*, Grove Press, 1968

Macbean, James Roy, "Godard's *Week-end*, or The Self Critical Cinema of Cruelty," *Film Quarterly*, Winter, 1968–69

Mussman, Toby, ed., *Jean-Luc Godard: A Critical Anthology*, Dutton, 1968

Roud, Richard, *Godard*, Doubleday & Co., 1968

The Films of Jean-Luc Godard: a Symposium, Studio Vista, London, 1967

Hitchcock, Alfred

Rohmer, Eric and Chabrol, Claude, *Hitchcock*, Classiques du Cinéma, 1957
Perry, George, *The Films of Alfred Hitchcock*, Dutton, 1965
Truffaut, François, *Hitchcock*, Simon and Schuster, 1967
Wood, Robin, *Hitchcock's Films*, A. S. Barnes, 1965

Kubrick, Stanley

Austen, David, *The Cinema of Stanley Kubrick*, Zwemmers, London, 1969
Macdonald, Dwight, "*Dr. Strangelove*," *Esquire*, February, 1964
Macklin, F. A., "Sex and *Dr. Strangelove*," *Film Comment*, Summer, 1965
Manvell, Roger, *New Cinema in the USA: The Feature Film Since 1946*, Dutton, 1968

Kurosawa, Akira

Barbarow, George, "*Rashomon* and the Fifth Witness," *The Hudson Review*, V, 1952
Bernhardt, William, "*The Throne of Blood*," *Film*, Winter, 1962
Brook, Peter, "Finding Shakespeare on Film," *Tulane Drama Review*, Fall, 1966
Davidson, James F., "Memory of Defeat in Japan: A Reappraisal of *Rashomon*," *Antioch Review*, XIV, 1954
Richie, Donald, *The Films of Akira Kurosawa*, U. of Calif. Press, 1965

Losey, Joseph

Brunius, Jacques, "Joseph Losey and *The Servant*," *Film*, No. 38
Isis, Feb. 1, 1964, special no. on *The Servant* (Robert Maxwell Co. Limited)
Leahy, James, *The Cinema of Joseph Losey*, A. S. Barnes, 1967
Milne, T., "Accident," *Sight and Sound*, Spring, 1967
————, ed., *Losey on Losey*, Doubleday, 1968

Mizoguchi, Kenji

Anderson, Joseph L., and Richie, Donald, *The Japanese Film*, Rutland, Vt., 1959
Rhode, Eric, *Tower of Babel*, Chilton, 1967

Penn, Arthur

Film Heritage, *Bonnie and Clyde* issue, Vol. III, No. II
Arthur Penn, Studio Vista, London, 1968
Samuels, Charles, "The American Scene: *Bonnie and Clyde*," *The Hudson Review*, Vol. XXI 1968

Schickel, Richard and Simon, John, eds., *Film 17/78*, Simon and Schuster, 1968

Ray, Satyajit

Barnouw, Erik, and Krishnaswany, S., *Indian Film*, Columbia U. Press, 1963
Krupanidhi, Uma, ed., *Montage*, July, 1966, special issue on *Satyajit Ray* (Anandam Film Society, Bombay)

Resnais, Alain

Armes, Roy, *The Cinema of Alain Resnais*, A. S. Barnes, 1968
Duras, Marguerite, film script of *Hiroshima, Mon Amour*, Grove Press, 1961
Holland, Norman N., "Film, Metafilm, and Un-film," *The Hudson Review*, XV, 1962
Oxenhandler, Neal, "Marienbad Revisited," *Film Quarterly*, XVII, 1964
Robbe-Grillet, Alain, film script of *Last Year at Marienbad*, Grove Press, 1962

Sjoberg, Alf

Cowie, Peter, *Swedish Cinema*, A. S. Barnes, 1966
Young, Vernon, "The History of *Miss Julie*," *The Hudson Review*, VIII, 1955

Tesigahara, Hiroshi

Shatnoff, Judith, "*Woman in the Dunes*," *Film Quarterly*, Spring, 1963
Film Comment, Winter, 1965

Truffaut, François

Greenspun, "Elective Affinities: Aspects of *Jules and Jim*," *Sight and Sound*, Spring, 1963
Kael, Pauline, "*Shoot the Piano Player*," *Film Culture*, No. 27, 1963
Klein, Michael, "The Literary Sophistication of François Truffaut," *Film Comment*, Summer, 1965
Marcorelles, Louis, "Interview with Truffaut," *Sight and Sound*, Winter, 1961–62
Shatnoff, Judith, "François Truffaut: The Anarchist Imagination," *Film Quarterly*, Spring, 1963

Welles, Orson

Belfrage, Cedric, "Orson Welles' *Citizen Kane*," *Introduction to the Art of the Movies*, ed. by Lewis Jacobs, Noonday Press, 1960
Bogdanovich, Peter, *The Cinema of Orson Welles*, Museum of Modern Art, 1961
Cowie, Peter, *The Cinema of Orson Welles*, A. S. Barnes, 1965
McBride, Joseph, ed., *The Persistence of Vision*, University of Wisconsin Film Society, 1969

Index

Index

Page numbers in italic type indicate complete essays.

10-100

ST. JOHN FISHER COLLEGE LIBRARY
PN1993.5.A1 B45 1970
Bellone, Julius, com   010101 000
Renaissance of the film. Edite

0 1219 0064454 7